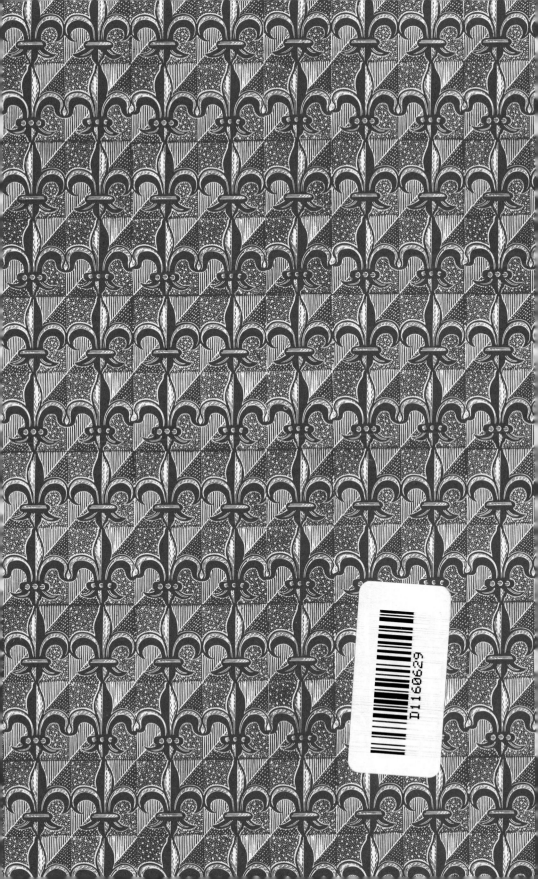

# A PECULIAR MAN
## A Life of George Moore

# A
# PECULIAR
# MAN

## A Life of George Moore

## TONY GRAY

SINCLAIR–STEVENSON

*For Pat,*
*for everything, yet again.*

First published in Great Britain 1996
by Sinclair–Stevenson
an imprint of Reed International Books Ltd
Michelin House, 81 Fulham Road, London sw3 6rb
and Auckland, Melbourne, Singapore and Toronto

Copyright © Tony Gray 1996
The author has asserted his moral rights

A CIP catalogue record for this title
is available from the British Library

isbn 1 85619 578 3

Typeset by Deltatype Ltd, Ellesmere Port, Cheshire
Printed and bound in Great Britain by Clays Ltd, St Ives plc

# Contents

# List of Illustrations

# A Peculiar Man

'I am a peculiar man,' George Moore told his mother in a letter accompanying a copy of his fifth novel *Mike Fletcher*, published in 1889, which he was sending to her at the family home, Moore Hall, in County Mayo in Ireland; not, I dare say, that this information came as any great shock to the lady. He went on: 'That it [the book] is peculiar, it goes without saying. I was born, I live, I shall die a peculiar man. I couldn't be commonplace, were I to try.'

He was not exaggerating. Let me set down, as far as possible in his own words, and in those of his contemporaries, a sample cross-section of some of the circumstances which made George Moore, Misunderstood Child, Absentee Landlord, Eccentric Author, Aspiring Lecher and Prose Stylist, such a very peculiar man.

But, even before I do that, it is necessary to establish who George Moore was. When, in 1994, in a spoof centennial Booker Prize contest organised as part of the Cheltenham Festival, his best-seller of a century ago, *Esther Waters*, was picked as the outright winner – by a panel of judges which included Melvyn Bragg and Victoria Glendinning, from a short list of books which included *The Jungle Book* by Rudyard Kipling, *The Prisoner of Zenda* by Anthony Hope, *The Memoirs of Sherlock Holmes*, by Sir Arthur Conan Doyle, and George and Weedon Grossmith's *Diary of a Nobody* – the general reaction was either 'George Who?' or 'Oh, the Moore's Melodies man?'

Yet, a century ago, Moore was more famous than any of the others. His *Esther Waters*, published in March 1894, was Britain's number one best-seller, and also sold well in the United States and on the Continent. It had received rave reviews everywhere; London's leading critic, Arthur Quiller-Couch, referred to it in the *Spectator* as 'the best book of its kind in the English language' and even the former Prime Minister, W. E. Gladstone, felt constrained to send Moore a postcard congratulating him on the high moral tone that the book had achieved, and had praised it in a letter in the *Westminster Gazette*.

Moore's first book of poems, *Flowers of Passion*, had earned him the nickname 'the bestial bard'; one reviewer gave it as his considered opinion that 'the author should be whipped at the cart's tail, while the book is publicly burned by the common hangman'. None of his critics claimed that he wrote badly, only that he wrote indecently, though the indecencies seem fairly harmless in these days. Moore did not have it in his nature to be nearly as wicked as he liked to believe himself to be.

His first novel, *A Modern Lover*, published in 1883, was banned by W. H. Smith and other circulating libraries as immoral and highly unsuitable for young ladies. It was about the adventures of an artist in London and Paris and what Smith's and Mudie's principally objected to were some scenes in which a young working girl poses naked for the artist. This was a theme that recurred frequently in Moore's stories and indeed the subject of naked women was seldom very far from his mind; on his own admission, he spent hours day-dreaming of undressing women and drooling over the wicked memories of the life that once he led, or would like to have led, or perhaps even believed that he had led, though his friends thought they knew better.

All of George Moore's subsequent books were similarly banned by W. H. Smith until the success of *Esther Waters*, when a partner in the firm warned his colleagues of the heavy losses they would probably incur by continuing to ban Mr Moore's books, particularly books that Gladstone had read and of which he had publicly approved.

Moore was also an influential journalist, a distinguished critic, a controversial polemicist, a man who could always be guaranteed to give an opinion on any topic which would make the headlines; with Lord Randolph Churchill and Cardinal Manning, he was among a selected few celebrities who were invited in 1896 to contribute to the first weeks' issues of Lord Northcliffe's new popular newspaper, the first of its kind in the world, the London *Daily Mail*. He was the eldest son of George Henry Moore, a nationalist Irish politician who was also a Westminster MP.

At this period Moore was living in London; previously he had lived for over seven years in Paris. Initially, he had set out to be a painter – and the principal attraction of that trade, from Moore's point of view, it goes without saying, consisted of the opportunities it seemed to offer him to contemplate naked female models – but when he discovered he had no talent for drawing and painting, he turned to writing. Like many art students in Paris around that period, he lived in the Latin Quarter; unlike most of the others, however, he lived in a fairly luxurious hotel, and had his own personal valet living with him, a man he calls Mullowney.

For Moore was then a rich man, a gentleman Bohemian, an absentee landlord with a big house, Moore Hall, and vast estates in County Mayo, in the West of Ireland, which he had inherited at the age of eighteen, from his politician father.

His *Confessions of a Young Man* predated and foreshadowed James Joyce's *Portrait of the Artist as a Young Man* by sixteen years and *Ulysses* by thirty-four years, and was, in Moore's opinion, far better than either of them; his three-part autobiography, *Hail and Farewell*, was widely recognised as a monumental achievement and the most comprehensive account of the Irish Literary Revival around the turn of the century; and only Moore would have had the sheer audacity to take the New Testament and rewrite it as a novel, giving it a different ending; Jesus of Nazareth does not die on the Cross in *The Brook Kerith*, but survives to be confronted in an Essene monastery, where he works in his old age as a shepherd, by a furious St Paul, who very understandably feels that, by having the temerity to survive crucifixion, Jesus has made a nonsense of his whole life's work.

Only Moore would have had the gall to class himself in the same street as Shakespeare and Milton; he once remarked to Charles Morgan that there had only been two English sagas written since Milton's *Paradise Lost*; and his own version of the old Daphnis and Chloe legend was one of them. When Morgan asked what the other one was, he replied, instantly and unblushingly: 'The Brook Kerith, of course.'

When he travelled out from Paris to Médan to call on Emile Zola, at Manet's suggestion, and was at last admitted into the great man's presence, he began with some small talk, wondering how soon he could bring the conversation around to reveal himself as the serious literary figure that he considered himself to be, wondering at the same time whether Shakespeare or Homer would have got through the preliminary pleasantries any more adroitly. Even more monstrous, many people would feel, is the fact that he saw distinct parallels between his own *Confessions* and those of St Augustine.

At the time of his death, Moore had become the Grand Old Man of English Letters, and was known in the tabloids as the Sage of Ebury Street. On his eightieth birthday, February 24, 1933, he received a telegram from the Prince of Wales, and a round-robin letter of congratulation signed by, among others, Ramsay MacDonald, Max Beerbohm, Sir Edward Elgar, André Gide, James Joyce, Harold Nicolson and Paul Valéry was published in *The Times*. It said, among other things, that he was 'an artist, who, since he came to London from Paris many years ago, has not ceased to labour with a single mind in the perfecting of his craft, who has written in *Daphnis and Chloe* a flawless translation, in *Esther Waters* a tale that marks a period in our literature, in *Hail and Farewell* an autobiography that has a rank with Rousseau's, in

*Héloise and Abélard* a philosophical romance of supreme beauty, and in *The Brook Kerith* a prose epic unique in the English language.'

I first heard of George Moore some time in the 1930s when I was staying, as a young boy of eight or nine, with my cousins in Rhyl, in North Wales. My Uncle Hugh caught me looking through his shelves for something to read, and recommended George Moore's novel *Esther Waters*. I read the book, found it extraordinarily vivid and realistic, but thought no more about either it or its author for several years.

I next became aware of George Moore's existence when, soon after I joined the *Irish Times*, I was sent out to meet the mail-boat and interview Dr Oliver St John Gogarty, who had been lecturing in America at the outbreak of the war, and was not able to return until after it ended. As it happened, I was the only reporter there, and we spent the evening together and he talked about life in Dublin as he remembered it, and a lot of the talk was about George Moore.

One of my friends when I first joined the *Irish Times* was Desmond Rushton, public relations officer for a number of Dublin theatres and cinemas; and he had a flat in Ely Place, overlooking, he told me proudly, George Moore's garden, where the famous apple-tree still flourished and a few blackbirds still sang in the evenings.

Like Moore, I had wanted to go to Paris as soon as I left school to study painting, but I left school during World War Two and it was not possible to travel to Europe – even if my parents would have allowed it, which they would not – so I did the next best thing and joined the *Irish Times*, at that time edited by the legendary R. M. Smyllie, doyen of Dublin's only Left Bank café, the Palace Bar. The Palace Bar crowd at this period included a very young Flann O'Brien, an equally young Patrick Kavanagh and the deputy-doyen of the group, Seamus O'Sullivan, the only man lampooned in Moore's *Hail and Farewell* who appealed successfully to Moore to have some references to him deleted, not for his own sake, of course, he couldn't care less personally, but for the sake of his family.

Moore's name frequently cropped up in the Palace Bar at that period, and I kept intending to read something else by him but for some reason never got around to it until relatively recently. His books may then have been out of print; certainly none of them was available in the Penguin series, at that time almost the only paperbacks available.

Nearly fifty years later, about 1989, when I started to do some research for a book about the *Irish Times* and its famous editor, which I called *Mr Smyllie, Sir*, I discovered that my own personal experience of Smyllie's total refusal even to glance at any letters addressed to him – like that of his predecessor, John Healy – was by no means unique. Lionel Fleming, one of my predecessors in the job of editorial assistant, recalled in a book called *Head or Harp* that, when he tried to thin out the Everest of unread and unanswered correspondence in the corner of Smyllie's office, he had come across a letter from George Moore, dated Paris, 1900, complaining that there had been no answer to his three previous letters to the editor of the *Irish Times*. And this at a period when any document bearing George Moore's signature would have fetched a fair amount at Sotheby's and a fortune in America.

Then, when I began to research another book, *Ireland This Century*, and started to go through the files of the Irish papers in the British Museum's newspaper library at Colindale, I soon came to the period when George Moore had his road-to-Damascus experience in Chelsea and returned to Ireland to contribute his celebrity and his expertise to the Irish theatrical and literary renaissance, and hardly a day passed by without some mention of him in the files.

The more I read about Moore, the more fascinated I became. I came across yet another curious coincidence when I recently read the one-volume paperback edition of Moore's *Hail and Farewell*, published in England in 1985 by Colin Smythe and in the United

States by the Catholic University of America, and edited by Richard Cave. During my last two years at school, when what used to be called *girls* suddenly became of far more urgent interest to me than anything else in the world, I became very friendly with two sisters, Sinéid and Maura Tanham, daughters of a former Free State army officer, who lived in Tymon Lodge, a small Georgian villa in the foothills of the Dublin mountains at Firhouse, near Tallaght.

And, from Cave's notes, I learned that Tymon Lodge was in fact what Moore had called the Moat House, a house a few miles above Rathfarnham which he found for his friend Stella, a painter who had come with him to Ireland, though they never lived together. I knew that house as well as I knew our own house in Sandymount. You could walk out of the back door and climb up through a few fields to the ruins of a great house Moore once thought of renting, Mount Venus, and on up past it, to the summit of Mont Pelier and the ruins of an old Georgian gambling den known as the Hell Fire Club, where Moore claims to have spent a night once, *en plein air*, so to speak, with Stella.

I found other, curious parallels. Like Moore, I think Ireland is a fatal disease from which both of us were lucky enough to escape for the greater part of our lives, though it undoubtedly left its unmistakable mark on us.

And, as soon as I began to read his books seriously, I very quickly came to the conclusion that for all his affectations, for all his infernal, audacious cheek, for all his tedious posturing, and above all for all his extraordinarily immature fantasies about almost every known aspect of sex, he was, nevertheless, a very considerable writer whose work deserves to be far more widely read than it is today. His descriptions of Paris, of Sussex, of the Riviera and of Provence, and above all of the West of Ireland, are magically evocative.

I also realised that a great many of his problems, real or imagined, stemmed from the way his parents had treated him as a child. It is impossible to read his own very few, very shy, descriptions of his childhood, without feeling sorry for him. They explain the black moods of despair and melancholia which used to descend upon him; and they explain a lack of self-confidence so abysmal that he often found himself obliged to put on an act to disguise it – and it probably was not his fault either that, in disguising it, he often behaved outrageously anti-socially, though people who knew him well obviously found him extremely charming, whenever he chose to be charming. Ultimately, the way he was treated as a child would also explain his confusion and timidity (abject terror, sometimes) when confronted by normal, healthy women, expecting to get something tangible out of their relationships with men whom they had accepted as partners, even on a short-term basis.

That he became unfashionable within a decade or so after his death – indeed this had started to happen well before his death – was partly his own fault. One reason why Moore's books probably ceased to be as widely read as they were when they were first published is that, during a decade or so in Dublin at the beginning of the twentieth century, he began to recreate himself – recreating himself was one of the principal pursuits of his life – in the role of an Irish *seanchie* or story-teller.

To avoid interrupting the flow of his prose, and to make it resemble more closely the rambling narrative of a *seanchie* telling the tale from memory, Moore removed most of the punctuation from his writings. Throughout his career, he rarely used inverted commas to indicate dialogue, but initially picked up several variations of the French style of using dashes at the start of each quote, and, in his final revisions, omitted anything that might indicate what was dialogue and what narrative. He also permitted his paragraphs to ramble on for five or six pages at a time, which could appear daunting to a generation of people brought up in the era of tabloid newspapers in which every sentence starts a fresh paragraph.

I found Moore a fascinating writer: always fresh and full of ideas, sometimes hauntingly evocative, often hilarious, usually incredibly modern, despite some curious lapses into Victorian prudery, and eminently readable if you could school yourself to overlook his wilder flights of fantasy, and once you had ironed out the problem of reinserting enough punctuation of one sort or another, mentally or physically, into his prose, to make it read smoothly.

I felt, too, that I should at least try to do something to reawaken the interest of ordinary readers in an extraordinary man and in his work, and this book is the result. What it sets out to do – and what I hope it has achieved – is to present the main events in Moore's life, both as a man and as an artist, along with a fairly representative selection of examples of his views and his opinions, his ideas and his style, above all his style, both in life and in literature. I have tried to reconstruct Moore's life and career, as far as possible by using or reworking his own words and phrases – as well as those of some of his contemporaries – taking material from his own autobiographical fiction: *Confessions of a Young Man* (1888); *Memoirs of My Dead Life* (1906); the three volumes of *Hail and Farewell*, *Ave*, *Salve* and *Vale*, published between 1911 and 1914; his *Conversations in Ebury Street* (1924); as well as from some of his newspaper and magazine articles which were published in book form as *Impressions and Opinions* in 1891 and from his vast output of letters, addressed mainly to the multitude of young women whom he fancied, after his peculiar fashion, throughout his long life; and from his *A Communication to My Friends*, upon which he was working when he died.

I have altered his punctuation as little as possible, and have tried to indicate which sections are direct quotes and which are paraphrases.

But I have not yet fully explained why I call Moore a peculiar man in the title of this book.

Moore never married – he once remarked to his brother Maurice that he was far too interested in other men's wives to think of having one of his own, though that was both a lot more and a lot less than the simple truth – but, for an extremely busy and prolific writer, he spent an inordinate amount of time in correspondence with women all over the world, and, at least according to his own account of things, had a scarifying succession of love affairs with women of all ages and from all walks of life. This, both on internal and external evidence, seems unlikely; indeed, it seems most likely that he died as he was born, a County Mayo virgin, and that all his extravagant romantic memoirs were pure fantasies.

And some of them were highly extravagant. For example, just before he finished *Esther Waters* in September 1893, when he was forty-one, he took a short holiday in France where he claimed to have had a 'love-adventure' with a golden-haired siren aged eighteen, though he did not indicate who she was, if indeed she ever existed; from his own account, in 'The Lovers of Orelay', she must, from internal evidence, have been aged thirty-three at least. In another fantasy which he seems himself to have at least half-believed, he was once approached in Ely Place in Dublin, when he was in his late forties or early fifties, by an attractive young woman who had come all the way from Houston, Texas, to make his acquaintance, so impressed had she been by his books, *Evelyn Innes* in particular. In response to Moore's inquiries, she told him that she had not married because she had never met a man in Texas distinguished enough to become the father of the sort of son she wanted to bear. Her son would be a poet, a writer, or perhaps a painter. Her fondest ambition was to provide Texas with a son who would make a mark on art or literature, so perhaps Moore would consent to oblige? According to his own account, he graciously did agree to oblige the lady, whom he calls Honor, and asserts that he heard from her only once again, when her son was born. In a baffling footnote to the affair, he concludes: 'And now I'll doze an hour in this comfortable armchair, and dream that I am on my way to Texas, to seek out Honor and her boy.'

He was fascinated, to the very end of his very long life, with every aspect of sex. And when the extremely outspoken Nancy

Cunard, daughter of his life-long friend Lady Cunard (Nancy had known him since she was four, and regarded him a sort of father figure), asked him how he felt about Lesbians, he replied, as told in her book GM: *Memories of George Moore*: ' "Oh, well, Lesbians . . ." And began to chuckle.

' "One says 'dearest' and the other replies 'darling', and then they gaze into each other's eyes, and they tickle each other a little. But what can they *do*?"

'And he chuckled: "Tyck, Tyck, Tyck." '

Whether he could do anything himself either remains a moot point. Nancy Cunard clearly believed that he could, but she was taking his word for it and she believed a lot more of what he told her about himself than most other people did. And, by the time she had grown up, Moore was clearly past it, even if he ever had been a dab at it, as he claimed, though she must have been puzzled by the fact that a man whom she had once said she would like to have had for a father was always pestering her to take off her clothes so that he could see her body in all its beautiful nudity. She eventually succumbed to his pleas when he was in his seventies, dropping all her clothes to the floor in a pool at her feet in his house in Ebury Street and standing in front of him naked. He observed, with apparent satisfaction, that she had a back 'as long as a weasel's'.

Both the poet, W. B. Yeats, and the writer and doctor, Oliver St John Gogarty, who knew Moore better than almost anyone else, seriously considered the possibility that he was impotent, and discussed the subject at length, after his death. According to Gogarty's *As I Was Going Down Sackville Street*, whose reported conversations are probably not much more reliable than Moore's own, though in both cases they had foundations in fact, Yeats once put the question to Gogarty directly: 'Do you think George Moore was impotent?'

Gogarty, always the cautious Dublin doctor, replied: 'I don't know. It is rare for a man to be impotent. He may be unable to propagate, but organic impotence is very rare.'

'Was he a man?'

'He had the pelvis of a woman, as artists are said to have. There is little to be deduced from that. The only arguments that come to my mind are based on deduction more than on facts, physical or otherwise.'

'Well, go on.'

'Take the evidence of women. Susan Mitchell [an Irish writer, who had known Moore well, and had written a book about him, *George Moore*, published in 1916] sensed something lacking. Women are like that. She wrote, "Some men kiss and do not tell, some kiss and tell; but George Moore tells and does not kiss." Kiss may mean . . . ? Well, she was hardly likely to say more.'

Gogarty was himself acutely aware of the nature of what might have been Moore's problem. Later, in a poem, Gogarty referred to the effects of advancing age: 'And all my limbs are growing stiffer; / Did I say all? Well, all but one.'

Even more revealing, perhaps, is the fact that in Moore's multitudinous letters to women, and particularly to young women, from whom he always demanded the most intimate details of their own love-making, he sometimes advocated what he called kissing – oral sex – as a totally satisfactory and far less dangerous form of intercourse than penetration.

It is perhaps typical of Moore that he received some time in the 1890s a letter from a John Oliver Hobbes asking him whether he would be interested in dramatising a story. Moore did not bother to reply until he learned that Hobbes was the nom-de-plume of Mrs Pearl Craigie, a very beautiful, clever, fashionable (and rich) young woman, whereupon he called on her at once and fell in love with her instantly. They spent a lot of time together and collaborated on several plays, including *The Fool's Hour*, which was published in the *Yellow Book* in April 1894. This relationship ended with Moore, according to his own account, planting a kick fair and square across her behind, leaving the clear imprint of his boot on the back of her dress, in Green Park, Piccadilly, in broad daylight, though many of Moore's friends considered this incident as being every bit as apocryphal as his accounts of his amorous adventures.

Of all the peculiar things about this peculiar man, nothing, perhaps, was more so than the way he elected to make his final exit from this stage. At the time of his mother's death, horrified at the thought that all the bodies that had already accumulated in the family vault near Moore Hall, in County Mayo, would have to be shuffled about in order to accommodate his, when his own time came, he wrote to his brother stipulating that he wished to be cremated, and the ashes scattered on Hampstead Heath.

He later amended these instructions in favour of a pagan pyre on Castle Island in Lough Carra, County Mayo. In the end, he had to settle for a compromise; when he died in London in 1933, in his eighty-first year, he had already been cremated before his brother Maurice was reminded of his wishes by their sister, Nina. The ashes were duly transported to Dublin in a crate, taken by train to County Mayo and placed in an urn. This was ceremoniously laid to rest on Castle Island by his friend, Dr Oliver St John Gogarty; his brother, Colonel Maurice Moore, his sister, Mrs Nina Kilkelly and Dr Richard Best of the National Library of Ireland. This ceremony took place without participation on the part of any of the clergy, Catholic or Protestant, who were afraid of upsetting the local people by taking part in a flagrantly non-Christian ritual, and with the police keeping a watchful eye on the proceedings in case there should be a protest at the impudence of anyone attempting to hold a pagan burial in holy, Catholic Ireland.

Reilly, a former steward from Moore Hall, put two new pennies under Moore's urn for good luck, or possibly because he felt instinctively that it might be wise to leave some contribution towards the price of the boat-ride across the Styx, or however his peasant mind conceived the final journey which all of us members of mankind will ultimately be obliged to make, and the sad little group of relations and friends went through the motions of a non-denominational, semi-pagan burial service.

They had all been extremely worried that there might have

been some serious trouble with the railway people over so unusual a cargo as a crate containing the remains of an extremely celebrated member of the human race, but, as Gogarty reported, they paid no more attention to it than if it had been a crate of eggs.

In an urn which was a careful copy of an old Celtic Bronze Age urn in the Irish National Museum, commissioned by Colonel Maurice, the mortal remains of George Moore were laid to rest in a hollow under a flat stone on Castle Island, almost exactly opposite the ruins of the house which had been the home of four generations of George Moores, a big house known as Moore Hall, in County Mayo.

# ONE

# The Moores
# of Moore Hall

Moore Hall was built on a hill called Muckloon on a little peninsula jutting southward into Lough Carra, County Mayo, almost exactly opposite Castle Island, so-called after the ruins of an old Norman fortification there.

As part of the eleventh-century invasion of Ireland by a force of Anglo-Normans, who initially came mainly from Wales under Strongbow, the Earl of Pembroke, some troops under the command of William Barret, or William Fionn (the fair), made their way into Connaught and built a stronghold on Castle Island. It had fallen into ruins centuries before George Moore's great-grandfather decided to build himself a house on Muckloon hill, which he would call Moore Hall, itself long since in ruins, burned down by the republicans during the Troubled Times, in 1923.

George Moore's great-grandfather was the first of a succession of four remarkable men: George Moore the Wine Merchant; George Moore the Historian; George Moore the Politician; and George Moore the Author. The wine merchant, the historian and the author are self-explanatory. George Moore the Politician did not enter the political arena until relatively late in life; he had previously been an extremely successful racehorse owner and trainer, as well as an intrepid Victorian explorer, but it is as a politician that he is remembered in Irish history.

A house called Ashbrook in Straid, County Mayo, had been

bought by an earlier George Moore, born in 1600, who had arrived in Mayo from Dublin and who, according to his headstone, had held the title of Vice-Admiral of Connaught in the time of William III, though no subsequent member of the normally inquisitive Moore family seems to have bothered to try to find out which admiral he was supposed to be representing, or indeed why a vice-admiral of any kind should be required for a peat-bog wilderness like Connemara.

Ashbrook was a small, rather insignificant two-storey house, and the Moores who lived there had come from the ranks of what were known as the 'new English' in Ireland. They had arrived in Ireland during the course of one of the many replacements of rebellious Irish by loyal English yeomen – always for some reason called 'plantations' – which followed every Irish attempt at a revolt against British rule. They were Protestants; they despised the peasants, and regarded all Catholics as dangerous savages. Many of them were poor, but as soon as they arrived in Ireland as settlers they became members of the landlord class and were expected to live off the land they had acquired.

The 'old English', on the other hand, were the descendants of families who had come over in the wake of the first Anglo-Norman invasions of Ireland; they had mixed easily with the Irish Celts, becoming in the process – and in the popular phrase – more Irish than the Irish themselves. Most of them resented the Reformation as bitterly as did the Celtic Irish and many of them had remained Catholics. There was a tradition in the Moore family that they were descendants of Sir Thomas More, Henry VIII's Chancellor, but the connection seems to have been a bit tenuous, though there was a portrait of Sir Thomas More at Ashbrook. There is also some doubt about the authenticity and the antiquity of the Moore motto, reproduced in Colonel Maurice Moore's book about his father, *An Irish Gentleman*, which could be very roughly translated from the Latin as: 'Scratch a Moore and your own blood will flow.'

Until a century or so ago, only the peasant tenants tilled the soil in Ireland; young members of the landed gentry normally idled their lives away, or became cattle ranchers. A rigid caste system discouraged them from raising sheep, which were always associated with the despised native Irish. They went into the army or the militia, entered the foreign service, or remained at home, hunting and shooting and playing cards, spending most of their time 'galloping around in the wake of a few famished hounds', as Maria Edgeworth put it, or tearing up and down the country in search of the few unfortunate females of their own class who were available, and whose parents could be persuaded to part with a dowry generous enough to keep them in the same sort of comfort, or discomfort, they had enjoyed, or endured, until then, by courtesy of their parents.

The Moores had established themselves firmly in the West of Ireland by the early part of the eighteenth century, when a George Moore of Straid married Sarah Price, the daughter of a local Protestant clergyman. Their son John broke with the family tradition of Protestantism but established important commercial connections in the process when he married a Catholic, Jane Athy of Renvyle, County Galway, a member of one of the illustrious twelve tribes of Galway who had trading concerns in Spain, and whose house eventually fell into the hands of George Moore the Author's friend, Dr Oliver St John Gogarty. Renvyle House is now a popular hotel.

In the early eighteenth century, Spain was still luxuriating under the weight of Inca and Aztec gold, stolen and shipped home in sagging caravels by the *conquistadores*, and represented roughly the same sort of Eldorado, in the eyes of the poor Irish of the period, as the United States of America represented to their descendants, the even poorer Irish of the mid-nineteenth century.

John Moore and his wife Jane were not particularly poor, but they were not very rich either, and their son George (the Wine Merchant) decided to emigrate to Spain in search of a fortune.

He prospered there; before long he was managing a wine business in Alicante and had a fleet of ships operating between

Spain and Galway; he was also doing a very considerable trade on the side in iodine, produced from kelp imported from Connemara.

In 1765, in Bilbao, he married Katherine de Kilkelly, a Catholic descendant of the O'Neills of Tyrone. Her family had left Ireland after an unsuccessful rebellion in Elizabethan times, at the time of the Flight of the Earls of Tyrone and Tyrconnell, who had taken with them into exile ninety-eight of the brightest and best of the old Ulster Celtic chieftains.

Having amassed a fairly considerable fortune in Spain, George Moore the Wine Merchant eventually returned to Ireland. He had inherited Ashbrook, but found it too small for his liking, and decided to build a big house for himself. During the course of a journey through Mayo, he came upon Lough Carra, fell in love with the place, and bought 800 acres of the foreshore there, as well as big estates at Ballintubber and Partry in the same neighbourhood, to supply staff and servants for the house, tenants to till his land, cut his wood and turf, and to provide the sort of infrastructure that the landed gentry required to pursue their highly civilised lifestyle in the wilds of Connaught in the eighteenth century.

And on the Muckloon Peninsula, in 1792, he started to erect a square Georgian mansion in a clearing in the woods. Moore Hall, which took four years to build, was a solid limestone house three storeys high, fronted by an immense circular gravel drive-way, wide enough for coach and four to wheel and turn with ease. Three flights of limestone steps led up to a high, pillared portico, where a massive oak door opened into a hall with a pretty Adam ceiling.

In common with most big houses of the period, Moore Hall was completely self-supporting, with a bakery, a brewery, a laundry, a blacksmith's shop, a vegetable garden, greenhouses for the cultivation of more exotic crops, and extensive quarters to house the army of servants that the maintenance of such an establishment required. It had to be self-supporting, because it was built at the back of nowhere.

At the rear of the house a huge stone wall enclosed a collection of sculleries and outbuildings; and from this courtyard double-doors opened into a long, dark tunnel which led to the stables, the coach-house, other farm buildings, and the kitchen garden.

By the time the house was built and occupied, the Moores of Moore Hall had established themselves as an important county family, and the returned exile, with an income from his property of about £4,000 a year (worth roughly £200,000 today) could spend his declining years in the improvement and management of his estates.

But, in other respects, the Moores were not so lucky. They had already suffered the loss of two children: a son and daughter had died as infants, from smallpox, in Alicante, and another of Moore's sons, Peter, had to be kept under constant medical care; he remained witless to the end of a very long life. But the most pressing problem with which they had to cope was their eldest son, John, who showed alarming signs of republican sentiments.

He went to Dublin to read for the Bar but, instead of studying, became attracted to the United Irishmen Republican Movement. Republican and democratic sentiments, though by now common enough among the mass of the Irish people, were not shared by the Catholic gentry, any more than they were by the Protestant Ascendancy.

In 1798, a force of Frenchmen, under General Humbert, landed at Killala on the northern coast of Mayo, to support an Irish rebellion which had already collapsed two months earlier, and George Moore's son and heir John, ignoring his parents' entreaties, rode off at the head of a body of Moore tenantry, to place his services at the disposal of the French Commander.

A rapid march by some nine hundred French troops and a few badly armed Irish rebels resulted in a clash with an English force of ten thousand redcoats, assembled at Castlebar, and the latter, inexplicably, broke ranks and fled. Citizen John Moore so distinguished himself in this engagement that he was made President of the Republic of Connaught, the first Irish republic in history.

The document conferring this distinction upon John Moore of Moore Hall found its way into the family archives and was preserved there until the house was burnt down in 1923. The Connaught Republic lasted exactly one week, until September 8, 1798, when Humbert and his troops were surrounded and forced to surrender at Ballinamuck.

The terms of surrender imposed by the English Commander, Lord Cornwallis, were not ungenerous to the French, but a terrible campaign of revenge was visited upon the Irish rebels; raiding troops marched all over County Mayo shooting and pillaging and harassing the unarmed peasants. The news of Humbert's defeat was brought to Moore Hall by a peasant tenant who warned the Moores that the troops were searching everywhere for the rebel leaders, including their son. By that time, President John Moore had already been arrested, and he died while still on trial, on December 13, 1798, of an 'obstinate disorder', as they quaintly phrased it in those days. There was no suggestion of foul play: he had enjoyed the best of medical attention and had had three physicians attending him while in prison.

One final disaster befell George Moore the Wine Merchant: he went blind in his sleep, shortly after his son's death, and died within a year, of a stroke. And it is interesting, in view of his great-grandson's subsequent religious proclivities, that despite a successful career in Spain as a Catholic he had made a specific request to be interred among his ancestors in the Protestant cemetery at Straid Abbey. His widow, however, ignored his wishes and had him buried in the graveyard of a little ruined Catholic chapel nearby.

His successor, John's younger brother, George Moore the Historian, was the Wine Merchant's second son. He had married Louisa Browne, a niece of the second Earl of Altamont, and a cousin of the first Marquess of Sligo. The Altamonts were among the first families of the Irish Protestant Ascendancy, but for some reason Louisa had been brought up as a Roman Catholic and remained a staunch one until her death.

George Moore the Historian was only too ready to let his wife take over the management of the house and the family finances; he retired quite happily to his study to pursue his career as a historian. His first book was a study of the British Revolution of 1688, published by Longmans of London in 1817, and he made it clear that he looked on the 1798 rebellion, in which his brother John had taken such a prominent part, as 'wicked and profligate', and regarded the Act of Union of 1800, which abolished the Irish Parliament and provided for Irish representation in the Parliament at Westminster, as an indispensable step towards the civilisation of Ireland. 'It will diffuse British customs and manners among the inhabitants [of Ireland] and gradually wear away those of their old primitive habits which still infest them', he wrote, adding that: 'if the entire bundle of Irish MSS, pedigrees, histories and traditions were finally to perish, abundant good would be done to the country. They only serve to nourish and foster vacuity, idleness and habits pernicious to industry.'

His other books included biographies of Cardinal Alberoni and the Duke of Riperda and he was working on a history of the French revolution when he died in 1840; it was never published despite the fact that he left £500 (worth £25,000 today) towards its publication in his will.

His son and heir, George Henry, later known as George Moore the Politician, and father of George Moore the Author, was born in 1810. He was something of a child prodigy and used to read *The Times* leading articles aloud to his father before he was three.

After a brilliant career at St Mary's, a Catholic preparatory school at Oscott near Birmingham – which contrasted sharply with that of his sons, George Moore the Author, and Colonel Maurice Moore the Soldier – George Henry the Politician idled his way through university, learning nothing, according to his family, apart from billiards; and, when his parents recalled him to the West of Ireland, he spent his time gambling, racing, hunting and quarrelling with the neighbours. But not drinking; curiously, for a horse-owning family in the West of Ireland, none of the

Moores ever became a serious drinker and, even at the height of his fame, George Moore the Author always had hot water served at dinner-time to enable his guests, if they so wished, to water down their wine, as he normally did.

George Henry loved his mother, but they quarrelled fiercely. There were faults on both sides; she kept a bust of his brother John – who had been killed in a riding accident at the age of seventeen – in the drawing room at Moore Hall and never wanted to see a horse near the place again.

But horses were the absorbing passion of County Mayo, and, if he had paid the slightest attention to his mother's wishes, George Henry would have had to cut himself off from all social contacts. Instead, he rode madly, passionately and violently, and his mother was always terrified that he, too, would some day be carried home dead on the back of a plank.

There exists a description of an Irish steeplechase in 1830, over loose stone walls about five feet high and two feet broad, quoted by Joseph Hone in his book *The Moores of Moore Hall*; during the encounter, a rider falls from his horse with a fractured skull and breast-bone, but the remainder of the field carries on regardless.

'After the poor man had been repeatedly bled, so that he lay on the turf weltering in his own blood, he was taken away and the last heat began at the appointed time as if nothing had happened; the winner [perhaps he was George Henry Moore] arriving so exhausted at the post that he could hardly speak. In a space of less than an hour, he had run twelve English miles at full speed, and leaped the wall [the scene of the accident] twelve times.'

After he had spent three or four years hanging around Moore Hall, mixing with various undesirable companions, George Henry's mother decided to send him to London to study law. He was soon heavily in debt to, among others, a horse dealer, a tailor, a bookmaker and a banker, and was brought home in disgrace but soon escaped again to London, Bath and Dublin. In Bath, he became heavily involved with a married lady and, when his mother ordered him to stop seeing 'that woman' or forfeit for ever the affection of his parents, he escaped to the continent, talking airily of 'wintering in Vienna'. When he returned to Britain in the spring, it was to stay with an aunt in Bath, not very far from Cheltenham, where 'that woman' lived, and he continued to see her.

While in Bath, he looked up his surviving fifteen-year-old brother, Augustus, another child prodigy who had challenged the whole University of Cambridge to solve a mathematical problem which he had concocted; furthermore he had couched the problem in Latin. Augustus was so advanced that his father felt justified in consulting the most eminent mathematician of his day, Sir William Rowan Hamilton, who had been Astronomer Royal of Ireland at the age of twenty-two; Sir William opined that, with perseverance, the boy could scarcely fail to become an eminent mathematician. In this prediction he turned out to be quite wrong.

But the mother of the mathematical genius was far more concerned about his elder brother, George Henry. When next his family heard from him, in 1835, he had set off on a journey to Russia and the Near East with a friend and neighbour, Charles Kirwan. Such accounts of the voyage as exist are fragmentary since the only source of information was a series of letters George Moore wrote to his mother; and because of his extremely complex relations with her, and his feelings of guilt about 'that woman', the letters broke off abruptly, at one point, when the lady in question arrived, with her apparently complaisant husband, to join him, and did not resume for the best part of two years, when, for some unknown reason, his relationship with the lady ceased. Furthermore, most of the earlier and later letters – before the arrival of the lady, and after her departure – were destroyed.

Apparently Moore and companion went first to Russia; there still exists a description of the Countess Orloff's stud farm at Krinavaia in November 1834, where there were boxes for 1,500 horses – Arab, English, Russian and Dutch. There are also accounts of a Russian wedding, a visit to Tiflis, the capital of

Georgia, and one to Teheran, where they remained until March 1835.

The diary resumes on December 5, 1836: 'We threaded our way through the thousand gardens, that, in the springtime of their youth and beauty, are considered by Asiatics to be no unworthy type of the glories of a world of hope, but which now, black and desolate, were to me a fitting emblem of vanished happiness, of withered memories and days that are no more . . .'

These sentiments must have afforded his mother a great deal of sinister satisfaction, in the light of the very curious relationship which seems to have existed between them.

In a later letter to his mother he wrote: 'I seem to be forgotten by the world; and yet not so. There is still one heart that loves me, though every chaplet that Fate or fancy wreathes, wither upon my brow. He whose heart and sword is mine today may desert me tomorrow, if his interest beckon him away; and the love of a woman, that but yesterday seemed passionate and eternal, may today have passed, like a shadow on the waters, for her false and reckless heart, but a mother's love lives on alike through storm and sunshine, follows to the grave and the throne alike with unchanged and unchangeable devotion; and yet for how vile a thing would I have betrayed my mother's heart.'

Even allowing for a fair measure of extravagant Victorian sentimentality, that still remains a bizarre letter for a man of twenty-six to write to his mother.

With various companions, impossible to identify because of the missing letters, George Henry travelled around the Damascus area, sketching camels, ancient monuments and, preferably, and whenever he could possibly arrange it, young girls. He greatly admired 'the dark-eyed rosy girls of Jerusalem, their young bosoms glancing bare' and did a drawing of the daughter of a sheik, whose shift, as he put it, 'revealed at every motion the voluptuous outline of her faultless form'.

At one stage, George Henry with one or other of his companions bought a boat and carried it on mules from Jaffa as far as the Dead Sea. During the course of their explorations, they were nearly drowned in a sudden storm but survived to report the curious nature of that inland waterway. At this period nothing was known in Britain about the Dead Sea other than what had appeared in the Bible, and Moore and his companion were the first to report – to the Royal Geographical Society in London – that the Dead Sea was well below sea level and so buoyant that their lead sounding-weight floated on the surface of the water.

The expedition came to an end when an insurrection among some of the tribes in the area meant that their safety could no longer be guaranteed; in those days the British, which then included the Irish, rarely ventured anywhere where their safety could not be guaranteed by the local British Ambassador.

On his return to Ireland in 1839, George Henry's mother continued to dominate him, and to look for 'suitable' wives, to such an extent that he even threatened to leave again for the Near East.

In 1840, his father, George Moore the Historian, died. George Henry the Politician and his brother Augustus Moore the Mathematician were now concentrating their energies and their resources entirely on a life of hunting, riding, horse-racing and gambling, and George Henry's bird's-eye blue racing colours were soon to be seen at all the principal race meetings in the British Isles. He was now known as 'Wolfdog Moore', after one of his horses, and the Moore brothers were famous for jumping iron-spiked walls more than six feet tall. If the horses balked, George Henry and Augustus would simply blindfold them and try again.

They had a number of spectacular successes; for example, one of George Henry's horses, Corunna, won the Chester Cup worth £10,000 in 1845 (£500,000 today); he later lodged £1,000 of the cash in his mother's account in Westport for the relief of any of his tenants suffering from the effects of the Great Famine, and used the remaining £9,000 to pay off some of his debts.

In the 1845 Grand National at Aintree, Augustus Moore had a bad fall while riding a horse called Mickey Free. George Henry went immediately to Liverpool to be with his brother, who died on March 22 and was buried at Moore Hall.

It was a widely held belief at the Moore household that George Henry's character changed completely after his brother Augustus's death; that he then immediately turned against all his former pursuits and became preoccupied with his country's problems. It is true that, on his brother's death, he returned to Mayo, sold his horses and began to devote all his time and attention to his tenants, and to politics, but he had in fact first conceived the idea of entering public life as early as 1840, when Daniel O'Connell founded an association to work for the Repeal of the Act of Union, later to be known under the far more effective slogan of Home Rule. George Henry was then twenty-nine; and the country was in a bad way.

Failures of the potato crop were increasingly frequent, a serious matter in a country in which there had been what is now called a population explosion. Between 1801 and 1840, the population of Ireland had increased from between four and five millions to over eight millions of people who had no source of livelihood other than the land, which naturally could not bear the ever increasing pressure on it, a circumstance in which the failure of the staple crop, potatoes, was bound to cause a disaster.

This is George Henry's own description of the state of the native Irish at the time of the Famine: 'The dense population subsisted entirely on the fruits of the soil, or rather, it should be said, upon one particular crop. The people were thickest on the worst land, in the bogs and mountains; they lived in mud cabins of one room, for the most part often without chimneys and with a feeble light struggling through windows one foot square. Reserves of money they had none; their whole fortune was the pile of potatoes in the pits or under the beds. Thus they lived from day to day, rearing great families of children, who, as they grew up, married and multiplied without a thought for the future: an immense swarm of half-naked and ignorant creatures, scraping a bare existence from swamps and bogs and rocks. Such a country was ripe for famine.'

George Henry Moore's first opportunity to contest a seat came in 1846 in Mayo, when Mark Blake, a country gentleman of Ballinafad, resigned from Parliament. As an Independent, he had the support of all the great landlords in the area, who promised to march their tenants under guard to the court house, to vote for him, but he was defeated by Joe MacDonnell, a twenty-tumbler man (of Irish whiskey, that is, and per day), standing as Repeal candidate, and backed by all the priests. Moore was in favour of the Repeal of the Union but didn't think that the time was right to press for it; in the wake of a disastrous famine, the country could not possibly raise enough revenue to support itself as a devolved independent state under the Crown. Such views were not popular with the electorate and at an election meeting at Ballyglass he was attacked by the mob. He immediately jumped on his horse, set it at a six-foot fence and cleared it cleanly, to a rousing round of applause from the very men who a few seconds earlier had been trying to kill him. The Irish respect for good horsemanship had won him the day, though it did not win him the election.

Not that such incidents were all that unusual for the period. Voting was not then the private pursuit it has since become. In Castlebar in 1846, according to Colonel Maurice Moore's book about his father (An Irish Gentleman), 'the polling was open and lasted a week. Lord Sligo, Lord Dillon, Lord Lucan, Sir Roger Palmer and Lord Oranmore and all the great lords of the soil marched their tenants under guards of soldiers to the polling booths. They kept them locked up in barns and coach-houses the night before, for fear they might escape or be carried away to the mountains by the popular party. The scenes on the roads were terrific, and some people were killed . . .

'With the exception of about a dozen, all the freeholders on both sides were caged up in houses, like cattle in the penfolds at Ballinasloe fair, with herds over them lest they should stray away. The streets seemed living masses of irritated, noisy people, tossing their shillelaghs aloft and groaning and hooting at all who seemed obnoxious to them. The Military, horse and foot, went through the town on duty, bugles sounding, infantry forming squares, hussars galloping, guarding into the town what appeared to be convicts [the electors], who were pulled off the cars by drivers and pitched into stables without beds or bedding . . .'

Bernal Osborne, he goes on, once greatly amused the House of Commons with an account of his adventures at a Waterford election. After telling the house how he had to flee down the street and take refuge from the angry mob in his hotel, he added: 'And remember, Mr Speaker, I was the popular candidate.'

George Moore the Politician now became the chairman of two relief committees set up in Ballintubber and Partry when at last the British Government realised the extent of the Great Famine. Until then, corn grown in Ireland was being exported to feed Manchester and Liverpool, because the Irish had no money to pay for it, and in the market economy of that period, not greatly different from today's, the Government refused to interfere with the free trade principle. Most of the rest of Europe was affected by the same potato blight, but elsewhere the governments had taken precautions to stop the export of corn. In Ireland, men too weak to turn up to claim relief were simply struck off the list and their families starved. Moore not only allowed his tenants to live rent free during the Famine, but also – with the Marquess of Sligo, and other landlord neighbours – chartered a ship and brought 1,000 tons of flour from New Orleans which they distributed at half-price, among their tenants. Not a single Moore tenant, out of more than 5,000 men, women and children, died of want during the Famine. To finance this benevolence, George Henry was obliged to sell 6,000 acres of his lands at Ballintubber.

With Lord Sligo, George Moore the Politician joined Dan O'Connell, thirty Irish MPs, twenty peers and even a few Orangemen on a platform in Dublin in January 1847, dedicated to a united demand for the restoration of an independent Irish Parliament under the Crown.

He stood for Mayo again in 1847, as a Repealer, stressing in his speeches the necessity for independence from British political parties on the part of the Irish MPs, and openly criticising British policy in Ireland, and he won the seat.

George Moore the Politician was now approaching his fortieth birthday and still remained unmarried. In 1851, he married a neighbour, a Miss Mary Blake, a daughter of one of the Blakes of Ballinafad, good Catholic landlords with properties in Mayo and Galway. Because he was now spending so much time at Westminster, Mrs Louisa Moore, his mother, remained on at Moore Hall as company for his wife.

During the parliamentary recesses, he cleared part of the demesne of the scrub which covered it, and with oak cut in his woods, and carved by local craftsmen, he supervised the construction of an oak-panelled dining room, and redecorated the drawing room in a style which he fancied to be a reproduction of what he had seen of Greek classical décor in his travels as a young man. Pictures of his racehorses now competed for wall-space with ancestral portraits, and the floor was covered in French parquet. These alterations augmented previous ones – made after earlier racing successes – in which he had had the roof lifted, the old-fashioned small slates replaced with large modern ones, and the small, bottle-glass window panes replaced with plate glass. The old glass, missing for years, was eventually found stored in a cellar at Moore Hall.

Although his wife naturally welcomed Moore's presence at Moore Hall during the recesses, she was slightly nervous that he might find life in the country boring after all the excitement of Parliament. One wet day, according to Colonel Maurice Moore's biography of his father, George Henry was sitting gloomily by the fire, when his wife and his widowed mother brought down from the attic a collection of neat little bundles of the letters he had written to his mother from the Near East, over fifteen years earlier, all tied up with white tape, and they suggested that he turn them into a book.

Whether his father's reaction to this suggestion was prompted by the disturbing memories stirred up by the sight of the letters, or whether it was the thought of the long and lonely labour of turning those letters into a book that upset him, Maurice Moore cannot say, but his father took the letters and slowly and deliberately threw them, packet by packet, into the fire, swearing that he never wanted to see them again. The ladies, however, had left behind them in the attic a few packets of letters which were discovered years later by Colonel Maurice Moore; and from these letters he was able to reconstruct the scrappy account of George Henry's travels which appears in his book about his father.

In any event, George Henry Moore now had a new interest in life. On February 24, 1852, his first son, George Augustus Moore, was born. This was George Moore the Author.

# TWO

# Young Master George

George Moore's first recollections were of the great hall of the house on Lake Carra. When he returned to his home in 1895, at the time of his mother's death – he was then aged forty-three – it was as if he had never left it.

If ever there was a time to live in the present, he thought, this was it; but never was the present further from his mind, nor the past clearer, than when he opened the hall door and stood once more in that hall, paved with grey stones, and painted grey and blue. Three generations had played in it; in that corner, over there, he had first tried to spin a top, and kept on trying, showing a determination that amazed his father, who had remarked: 'If George shows as much perseverance in other things as he does in the spinning of a top, he will not fail.'

He remembered that his father used to catch him trying, over and over again, to spin that top, whenever he came downstairs on his way out to the stables. And there is the very chair, he thought, on which his father used to put his hat and gloves, remembering that in those days tall hats were always worn in the country, and that it was the valet's job to keep them well brushed, remembering too how the little old valet used to watch him trying to spin his top, fearful lest he might overturn the chair on which his father's tall hat stood.

In 1852, the year when young Master George was born, his

father had stood as a Repealer for the Mayo constituency in the general election. He had by now lost the backing of the landlords, who had been alienated by his increasingly vocal support for the various tenants' rights' movements, but he still easily topped the poll; throughout his political career George Henry Moore fought against the three factors that in his view were plaguing any prospect of real progress in Ireland: political corruption, ecclesiastical interference and landlord domination. Above all, he was convinced that the time had come for the landlords to surrender their feudal claims.

Just how feudal a society young Master George was born into is reflected in his recollections in *Ave*, the first book of his semi-autobiographical trilogy, *Hail and Farewell*, of going to Mass as a small child at Carnacun Church. There was a painting there of the Crucifixion commissioned by his father and carried out by his cousin, Jim Browne, who happened to be staying at Moore Hall at the time; Tom Kelly, the lodge-keeper, had posed for the figure of Christ, the first nude model that ever stood in Mayo, Moore reckons.

Along this road, he remembered, the tenants used to come from the villages, the women walking on one side, the married women in dark blue cloaks, the girls hiding their faces behind their shawls, and carrying their boots in their hands (they felt more comfortable in bare feet – they would put the boots on in the chapel yard), the men walking on the other side, the elderly men in traditional swallow-tailed coats, knee-breeches, and worsted stockings, the young men in corduroy trousers and frieze coats. As the Moores passed, the women curtsied in their red petticoats; the young men lifted their round bowler hats; but the old men stood by, their hats in their hands . . . The Moore tenantry met the tenantry of Clogher and Tower Hill, and they all collected around the gateway of the chapel to admire the carriages of their landlords.

He recalls that they were received like royalty as they turned through the gates, and went up the wooden staircase leading to the gallery, frequented by the privileged people of the parish – by them, and by their servants, by the postmaster and postmistress from Ballyglass, and a few graziers. In the last pew were the police, and, after the landlords, these were the most respected.

The sermon was always in Irish, in those days the language of the country among the peasantry, and while he listened without understanding anything Moore found himself wondering whether any of the peasantry might be saved, and if so, what it would be like when they all met in heaven. Would the peasants look the other way and pass by without lifting their hats and crying, 'Long life to yer honour!'

Parliament was again dissolved in 1857, when young George was five, and at the general election Moore was opposed by Colonel Ouseley Higgins, who enjoyed Government patronage over the whole county of Mayo, and was a prime example of the type of corrupt politician that Moore detested. His other opponent was a Tory candidate, Captain Palmer, fresh from the Crimean War and the Charge of the Light Brigade, and a landlord celebrated for the savagery of his evictions. Moore had the support both of the hierarchy and of the local parish priests – despite his frequent outspoken attacks on ecclesiastical interference – and it is ironic that, when he won the seat, a parliamentary inquiry, instigated by a furious Colonel Higgins, found that Moore was ineligible because his agents had used 'undue priestly influence' during the election, and he had to relinquish his seat.

At this period George Henry seemed content enough to watch his two sons – Maurice, the future colonel, had been born in 1854 – grow into boys and learn to ride two ponies, Spark and Twinkle, which he bought for them. He also spent hours telling them tales of his adventures exploring the Near East.

George Moore the Author remembered those stories when he returned to Moore Hall for his mother's funeral and found himself once again in the summer room, 'a pretty room opening onto the balcony that the four great pillars support, and in an instant that room returned to what it had been forty years before, my father sitting at the rosewood table in the evening, drinking a large cup of tea, telling me stories of Egypt and the Dead Sea, Baghdad, the Euphrates and the Ganges, stories of monkeys and alligators and hippopotami, stories that a boy loves.'

In 1859, George Henry's thoughts began to turn again to horse-racing. In the stables at Moore Hall there was an old mare called The Cook, which had been quite successful on the race-course but had been put between shafts because she was believed to be barren. When it was discovered that she was still able to bear foals George Henry reared a colt from her, just for the fun of it. As a two-year-old, this colt, called Croaghpatrick after the nearby mountain, ran its first race at Howth in 1860 and in the same year won a race at Chester, in a record field of forty-five horses, and went on to win a number of other major races.

Moore Hall was soon reopened as a racing stables and its owner's bird's-eye blue racing colours once again became a common sight on English race-courses. Other racing successes followed – Moore, with his brother-in-law, Joe Blake, and his wife's brother-in-law, William Murphy, cleaned up £20,000 when Croaghpatrick won the Goodwood Stakes – and George Henry was able to pay off his election debts, re-roof Moore Hall, carry out a number of other improvements and send Master George to his own old school, St Mary's at Oscott. Run by priests, it was one of several Catholic schools in England where it was possible for the sons of Catholic Irish gentlemen to get a decent Catholic education without also picking up a brogue, as an Irish accent was then called by the Anglo-Irish landed gentry, who, though they might have had grander accents than the peasants, were neverthe-less instantly recognisable as Irish as soon as they crossed the water to Britain. For all his cosmopolitan airs and graces George Moore the Author seems to have had a thick Mayo accent to the end of his days; Nancy Cunard even tried to reproduce it phonetically in her book GM: Memories of George Moore.

Moore has left us a picture of himself at this period in his preface to Memoirs of My Dead Life. The publishers wanted a photograph of the author, he says, so he dug up an old portrait of himself, in a short jacket and trousers, and wearing a belt, taken about the time he was sent to Oscott, and suggested that they should use this as a frontispiece, assuring them it would be invaluable to them, 'for it will persuade the prudes into reading the book in the hope of discovering, in the stories, traces of the dear little boy in the frontispiece; he will be, I do assure you . . . a great asset . . . of a certainty the winning features will bring belief that the boy must have fallen into evil company or been neglected in his youth, for if he had been brought up properly he would be quite different from this book . . . and fortified by the memory of the dear fellow (who followed the photographer into the dark room in which the plate was developed in baths filled with various evil-smelling acids, and hung over him while he tinted, passing blue over the necktie and a touch of flesh colour over the face), they will return to the book and in a different mood.

'That little boy, whose thumb is in his belt (put there by the excellent photographer) was on his way in the 'sixties to a Catholic school, where he might have been made into a little Catholic if he had not lost his health from the bad food and the piercing draughts that ranged up and down the corridors and whirled in the classrooms.'

He goes into his arrival at Oscott in more detail in *Salve*, the second volume of his three-volume autobiography *Hail and Farewell*, during the course of a reported conversation between himself and his brother, Colonel Maurice: 'I left father and mother talking with the President in the pompous room reserved for visitors, and raced through the empty playgrounds (it was class-time) delirious; and it was with difficulty that I was found when the time came for mother and father to bid me goodbye. They were a little shocked, I think, at my seeming heartlessness, but I could only think of the boys waiting to make my acquaintance.

'A few hours later, they came trooping out of the class-rooms, formed a procession, and marched into the refectory, I bringing up the rear. Father Martin came down to the refectory and, to my great surprise, told me that I must hold my tongue. As soon as he had turned his back I asked my neighbour in a loud voice why the priest had told me that I wasn't to talk. The question caused a loud titter, and before the meal had ended I had become a little character in the school . . .

'. . . at Oscott, there was no one to help me. Imagine a child of nine getting up at half-past six, dressing himself, and beaten if he was not down in time for Mass. There was no matron, no kindness, no pity, nor, as well as I can remember, the faintest recognition of the fact that I was but a baby. When my parents returned they found that the high-spirited child they had left at Oscott had been changed into a frightened, blubbering little coward that begged to be taken home. In those days children were not treated mercifully, and I remained at Oscott till my health yielded to cold and hunger and floggings.'

There is another glimpse of his childhood, around this same period. In her book *George Moore*, Susan Mitchell says that Moore's attitude to verse could be summed up by a story she heard about his childhood: Moore himself mentions it in *Vale*, the final volume of his trilogy *Hail and Farewell*. On his tenth birthday, she writes, he was asked to select a special treat, and he chose to be dressed up as 'a Greek of Syria', a notion he could only have got from his father's tales of his travels in the Near East.

'With an ornamental sword and mounted on a grey pony with Eastern trappings he was led around his father's demesne, to the wonder of the peasants,' she writes, and adds that she believes it was his love of 'dressing up' that made him write verse and study painting.

Moore's own recollection of the affair is more colourful: 'Many swords, scimitars and daggers were brought back [by his father, from his expedition to the Near East] and Arab bridles looking like instruments of torture; and these were kept in a great press in the nursery, which I was forbidden to open. But a child cannot be gainsaid on his birthday, and my dearest wish was gratified when I was dressed as a Turk, and rode about the estate flourishing a Khorassan blade above the head of my pony.'

Yet another glimpse of his childhood is supplied by Moore himself, in *Ave*; he is in the Shelbourne Hotel, in Dublin, shaving, and from the bathroom window he sees Stephen's Green 'and it took me back to the beginnings of my childhood, to one day when I stole away, and inspired by an uncontrollable desire to break the monotony of infancy, stripped myself of my clothes, and ran naked in front of my nurse or governess, screaming with delight at the embarrassment I was causing her. She could not take me . . . along the streets naked, and I had thrown my clothes out of reach in a hawthorn . . .'

In 1863, after a second winter spent in draughty classrooms, corridors with broken windows and overcrowded dormitories, washing at dawn in ice-cold water, often frozen solid in winter, frequently beaten with a stick with a piece of waxed leather on the end of it, by a priest who clearly took great delight in the task, and subsisting on uneatable food (Moore and the Colonel recalled slop called tea; slop called coffee; grease called butter; stale bread for breakfast with never even an egg; irridescent beef, purple with blue lines running through it; and, one morning, lumps of minced meat from the night before, discovered among the tea-leaves), Master George went down with bronchitis, and had to be taken home to Moore Hall, where he nearly died at the age of eleven. But a diet of good country food and cod liver oil brought him back to health, and he remembers those two years spent recuperating as the best part of his childhood: long days on the lake, two boatmen rowing the children from island to island, showing them how to fish for trout and eels, how to look for bird's nests in the woods and in the bogs.

And when he went back to Oscott, in September 1865, aged thirteen, his brother Maurice went with him. Master George found that things had not improved greatly while he had been away and both boys were constantly in trouble for 'general uselessness' as Moore put it, and their father was forever receiving letters from the principal, complaining about them. It was almost certainly during the Christmas holidays, at the end of his first term back at Oscott after his illness, that Moore discovered literature. He describes it in a passage in his *Confessions of a Young Man*, which reads like a modern film script:

> Scene: A great family coach, drawn by two powerful country horses, lumbering along a narrow Irish road. The ever-recurrent signs – long ranges of blue mountains, the streak of bog, the rotting cabin, the flock of plover rising from the desolate water. Inside the coach there are two children. They wear new jackets and neckties, their faces are pale with sleep, and the rolling of the coach makes them feel a little sick. Opposite them are their parents, and they are talking of a novel the world is reading. Did Lady Audley murder her husband? Lady Audley! What a beautiful name! . . .
>
> . . . When he returned home I took the first opportunity of stealing the novel in question . . . I read its successor and its successor. I read until I came to a book called *The Doctor's Wife*, a lady who loved Shelley and Bryon. There was magic, there was revelation in the news, and Shelley became my soul's divinity . . . the book – a small pocket edition in red boards – opened at *The Sensitive Plant*, and henceforth the little volume never left my pocket and I read the dazzling stanzas by the shores of a pale green Irish lake, comprehending little, and loving a great deal.

He took Shelley back to school with him as a bulwark against Oscott and the general unpleasantness of a Catholic education, but was never out of trouble. George Moore had already learned a good deal of French from various governesses they had had at Moore Hall before he went to Oscott – and presumably while he was convalescing – but he forgot it all at Oscott, and forgot any English he had ever learned. One priest in particular seemed to pick on him, often keeping him in after class, learning lines he knew very well, while the other boys were out playing cricket, sometimes letting an arm droop casually on to his shoulder, and once, while he was checking through one of Master George's corrective exercises, trying to slip his hand into the boy's trouser pocket.

Without quite knowing why, he felt instinctively that this was wrong, but, instead of reporting it to the headmaster, just mentioned it casually the next time he went to confession. A few days later, they heard that the priest in question was leaving Oscott, an outcome which young Master George found extremely gratifying on two counts; it rid him of a schoolmaster who had been bothering him and it confirmed his doubts about the sacred secrecy of the confessional.

Always sexually precocious, at any rate in his own mind, young Master George, as he grew up, began to show an increasing interest in the school housemaids who, at mass, worshipped in a corner of the chapel, as far out of sight of the boys as possible.

One evening he skipped confession and was discovered dallying with one of them – a pretty girl whom he remembers as Agnes – under the stairs. When he heard that the headmaster was writing to his father to complain about his behaviour, Moore immediately assumed that it was the matter of the maidservant that was uppermost in the headmaster's mind, and wrote to his father himself to say that, if the housemaid in question should happen to be dismissed as a result of this incident, he would run away from school and marry her, a dire threat which brought his father packing post-haste to Oscott.

Being a Catholic school, the matter of missing confession took precedence over the affair of the maidservant. When questioned as to why he had failed to attend confession, young Master George said that he wasn't sure that he even believed in confession, so why should he feel obliged to go? And, when the headmaster registered surprise and shock at this admission, Moore gently reminded him that at one time he himself hadn't believed in confession either. Which was true; the headmaster, Northcote – who had a son attending the school – had been a Protestant until his wife's sudden death, when he decided to embrace her religion and enter the priesthood. George Henry – an extremely intelligent and liberal man – had some difficulty in hiding from Northcote his amusement at this exchange.

Whether Oscott ever contributed anything towards George Moore's success as an author is extremely doubtful but his brother Maurice remained convinced that, if his father had not been lucky with his horses at this period and therefore in a position to send George Moore to Oscott to get a decent education, English literature would have been the loser. 'Literature in the twentieth century,' he pontificated, in *An Irish Gentleman*, 'depended on the struggle of a horse and on the efforts of a jockey half a century before.'

Moore claims that he was expelled; he was certainly removed from the school in 1867, when he was about fifteen, and spent a year or so hanging around the stables, shooting and hunting and going to race meetings while Maurice went back to Oscott with the third brother, Augustus; the other two children, Nina and Julian, were too small to be of any interest to a precocious young man of fifteen.

Augustus was to prove every bit as resistant to education as his two elder brothers; when he was sent to Beaumont, after a short period at Oscott – possibly because the latter institution had had all it could take of this particular generation of the Moores of Moore Hall – he tried to set the place on fire, as a general protest against the English educational system.

Looking back on his 'learning difficulties', in his mature middle age, Moore was inclined to blame his parents, not only for the folly of sending him to a useless school like Oscott, but also for giving him an inferiority complex which dogged him throughout his long life.

In *Ave*, Moore confessed that it was difficult for him to believe any good of himself . . . 'And the question has always interested me, whether I brought this lack of belief in myself into the world with me, or whether it was a gift from Nature, or whether I was trained into it by my parents at so early an age that it became part of myself. I lean to the theory of acquisition rather than to that of inheritance, for it seems to me that I can trace my inveterate distrust of myself back to the years when my father and mother used to tell me that I would certainly marry an old woman, Honor King, who used to come to the door begging. This joke did not wear out; it lasted through my childhood; and I remember still how I used to dread her appearance, or her name, for either was sufficient to incite somebody to remind me of the nuptials that awaited me in a few years. I understood very well that the joke rested on the assumption that I was such an ugly little boy that nobody else would marry me.

'I do not doubt that my parents loved their little boy, but that love did not prevent them laughing at him, and persuading him that he was inherently absurd; and it is not wise to do this, for as soon as the child ceases to take himself seriously he begins to suspect that he is inferior, and I began to doubt if I would ever come to much, even before I failed to read at the age of seven, without hesitating, a page of English written with the long *ff*'s, whereas my father could remember reading *The Times* aloud at breakfast when he was three.' The thought occurs here that Moore might have been dyslexic.

He went on: 'I could see that he [my father] thought me a stupid little boy, and was ashamed of me, and as the years went by many things happened to confirm him in his opinion.'

Later, in the same book, referring to his first successes, he says: 'The slight success that has attended my writings did not surprise my relations as much as it surprised me, and what seems curious is that, if the success had been twice what it was, it would not have restored the confidence in myself that I lost in childhood. I am always a novice, publishing my first book, wondering if it is the worst thing ever written; and I am as timid in life as in literature. It is always difficult for me to believe that my friends are glad to see me . . . If an editor were to return an article to me tomorrow, it would never occur to me to suppose he returned it for any other reason than its worthlessness' . . . and even at the height of his success, when he published *Memoirs of My Dead Life* (and it went into edition after edition) he wrote in 'Bring in the Lamp':

'Whosoever he may be, proof is not wanting that the world can do well without his work.'

Spelling remained a problem for him all his life, and when he was finally taken away from school, his father, as he puts it, 'shut Master George up in a bedroom from morn to eve to learn spelling-books by heart'. After some months of spelling-books and dictations, George's father gave up the job of his son's education, saying to his wife, 'George is but a chrysalis, and we do not know if he will develop into a moth or a butterfly.'

'But the memory of his own glorious schooldays compelled George's father [George continuing to write of himself in the third person] to intermittent efforts to cultivate George's mind outside of the spelling-book, for when all hope was dead in him that his son would ever realise in his mind the shape of a word with such clearness as would allow him to find it in the dictionary, he bethought himself of the artifice of an occasional disparagement of Shelley's poetry – "It is strange that you should admire mediocre verses," he once remarked – and he put Pope's *Homer* into George's hands; but George's ears were deaf to rhymed couplets, and when he was not reading *The Revolt of Islam* he was in the billiard-room, practising the "jenny", a stroke in which his father excelled. In the middle of a break of five or six, the door would open and his father would enter with a large volume in his hand.'

'Lay aside your cue,' he would say, 'and read Burke's speeches.' But George's amiability could not overcome his instinctive dislike of Burke; Burke was the proverbial straw, and he undertook instead to teach his sister Nina's governess how to ride. His father acquiesced, but despite the sly pleasures young Master George derived from helping the shapely governess into the saddle and placing her dainty feet in the stirrup, the boy was conscious of being overshadowed by his father, and he sought his own individual life unconsciously, as he says, like a sapling under the parent tree.

But there is no doubt that the return of the racing days at Moore Hall provided George Moore with a lot of the colour and some of the characters for *Esther Waters*, and he was extremely proud, as a boy of nine or ten, when one of his father's horses, Master George, was named after him. Master George, he recalls in *Vale*, was 'a terrible buck-humper that would have dislodged any cowboy. The little ponies that these horsemen ride have not sufficient strength to throw them out of the high Mexican saddles, but Master George was sixteen hands and a half and when his head disappeared between his legs, it was no easy thing to keep on a six-pound saddle, and the tightest might have been flung out of it, as I was three times one morning before breakfast, these falls irritating my father scarcely less than the long f's had done eight years before, compelling him to declare that no horse could unseat him. Joseph Appleby [a former jockey, at this period employed as a butler at Moore Hall] smiled and went out of the room, and the next morning my father was thrown in front of the house, by the holly trees, breaking his collar-bone and the doctor had to be sent for.'

'I returned [from Oscott] to a wild country home,' he writes in *Confessions*, 'where I found my father engaged in training racehorses. For a nature of such intense vitality as mine, an ambition, an aspiration of some sort was necessary; and I now, as I have often done since, accepted the first ideal to hand. In this instance, it was the stable. I was given a hunter, I rode to hounds every week, I rode gallops every morning, I read the racing calendar, stud-book, latest betting, and looked forward to the day when I should be known as a successful steeplechase rider. To ride the winner of the Liverpool seemed to me a final achievement and glory . . .'

In 1867, George Henry Moore was made High Sheriff of County Mayo. It was the year of the aborted Fenian insurrection, planned by a new revolutionary movement founded by Irish emigrants in New York in the wake of the Great Famine. A number of Fenian suspects were rounded up and incarcerated, without trial, in British jails, and it occurred to George Henry that he might once more be of service to his country as a politician; a general election was imminent, and he decided to offer his services to the Mayo electorate.

In 1868 the horses again suddenly disappeared from Moore Hall: the stables were closed, this time for good; and George Henry went back into politics, very soon becoming the effective leader of the Irish Parliamentary Party. He shut up Moore Hall and moved with his family to a house in London, to be near Parliament at Westminster.

'My dream of doing on Slievecarn what my father had hoped to do on Anonymous [two of the Moore racehorses] died in South Kensington, where we had taken a small house at the corner of Alfred Place, opposite South Kensington Station, a pleasant suburb then thinly populated,' he wrote in *Vale*.

'The Exhibition Road was building, and it was at the corner of Prince's Gardens that we met Jim Browne, a cousin and the painter of the *Crucifixion* that hangs in Carnacun Chapel, in the roof high above the altar . . . Jim told my father that he and his sisters were now living in Prince's Gardens; he invited us to come and see his pictures on the following Sunday, and during the intervening days, I could neither speak nor think of anything but Jim Browne . . .'

A few days afterwards, he begged money from his father to buy drawing materials, and from then on a pencil was rarely out of his right hand. He was in bed with a bad cold when Jim Browne was invited over to Alfred Place for dinner, to give a professional opinion on Moore's first sketches which, unsurprisingly, consisted of 'girls riding bicycles showing a great deal of stocking'. Browne was not impressed, but by now young George was totally determined to become an artist and began to plague his father to buy plaster casts so that he could sketch the Venus de Milo, the Discobulus and some other antique busts in his bedroom.

'He did not refuse to send me to the Kensington School of Art, but he sent my brother with me, and this jarred a little, for I looked upon my wish to learn drawing as a thing peculiar to myself, and my brother was so subaltern to me that I looked pitying over his shoulder until one day the thought glided into my mind that his drawing was as good as mine, if not better.'

George Moore the Politician now decided that there was nothing for it but to try to get both of his older sons into the army. As an Irish Nationalist MP, he was bitterly opposed to everything the British army stood for, but what else could you do with a pair of sons who were good for nothing more demanding than the army? And what other army was there?

But, as Moore puts it, 'so that our soldiers may not be altogether too booby, the War Office had decreed a certain amount of ordinary spelling and arithmetic and history to be essential, and to get such as I through examinations, there are specialists'.

Among these specialists was Dick Jurles's military academy, a cramming establishment on the Marylebone Road in which George Henry the Politician now enrolled his two sons – and it seemed to Moore that his father felt that, if there were some miracles that even Jurles's academy could not achieve, his decision would at least have the useful effect of redeeming Alfred Place from the annoyance of being obliged to watch young Master George trick-riding on a bicycle up and down the street. He adds: 'And Jurles's would save me also from the Egertons, the daughters of a small tradesman living in Hammersmith, whither some other wastrels and myself were wont to go to sup on Sundays. Alma and Kate were on the stage, and photographs of Alma in tights and Kate in short skirts were left about the house, and disgraceful letters turned up . . . in the drawing-room.'

Moore agreed to attend Jurles's Academy for the sake of peace; he had no intention whatever of becoming a soldier and dying in some distant corner of a foreign field, but could not think of any acceptable career that he did want to pursue, and so could not argue sensibly with his father; Maurice, on the other hand, seemed cut out for a military career, and in fact had a very successful one.

Master George was still seeing Jim Browne, the great blond man who talked incessantly about art and loose women and naked models, and managed to convince Moore that what he really wanted to do was to go to Paris and study art as soon as possible.

In the meantime, Master George was content enough to attend evening classes at the School of Art in South Kensington Museum, where he spent his time flirting with the girls copying the paintings in the museum; by now, he had made the pleasant discovery that he appeared to possess a very considerable talent for cultivating the company of young women. As he put it himself, he was becoming a dab with the ladies.

At Westminster, his father was pressing for a parliamentary inquiry into the treatment of political prisoners in England. Many of the Fenian suspects were languishing in British jails, some in solitary confinement, with their hands manacled behind their backs, and only released at meal times. Many of these men had been arrested on suspicion and never been tried. The English, he told Parliament, considered every man innocent until he was proved guilty, 'but that principle had never ruled their conduct in dealing with the Irish'. His initial motion for a public inquiry into the treatment of these prisoners was defeated.

He next called a mass meeting in Dublin to demand an amnesty for the Fenians, which was attended by 250,000 people. It was held in Cabra, on the outskirts of Dublin, because the police had refused to allow it to take place anywhere in the city centre, and it was chaired by Isaac Butt, a Dublin lawyer who invented the far more telling title of 'Home Rule' for the Repeal movement. Moore said: 'When I say God save Ireland – as I do with all my heart – I say God save the English people; God save them from every evil and every wrong, and God save them – above all other things – from the wrongs and evils of foreign rule. May God deliver the Irish people from the same, and God send that Englishmen and Irishmen may one day live together really united, each people self-governed in its native land.'

At a subsequent political meeting in Castlebar, referring to English rule in Ireland, Moore said: 'Her sceptre has been the sword, her diadem the black cap, and her throne the gallows during the seven hundred years of her fatal rule.' This statement was widely reported and caused an uproar in the British Press. *The Times* dared Moore to repeat it on English soil, and Moore immediately went to London and made the same speech in Trafalgar Square. He followed this up with a letter to *The Times* in which he said: 'If my countrymen are to pass the next winter in chains, I shall occupy the time in delivering a series of discourses in which the Government of England, and its mode of repressing resistance – in Canada as long as it governed that country, in the Ionian islands as long as it possessed them, in India, in Jamaica, in Ireland – will be fully and specifically stated. To France and to America I will carry the appeal of my countrymen and my country.'

By this time, George Henry had joined the Fenian movement and taken the oath, probably hoping to divert its thoughts to the sort of force of Irish Volunteers, under an international directorate, that he had been advocating a decade earlier.

By this time, too, the Manchester Martyrs, Allen, Larkin and O'Brien, had been hanged for their part in the murder of a police sergeant killed during the escape of two Fenian leaders from a Manchester jail on September 18, 1867, and Gladstone had agreed to Moore's proposal for a public inquiry into the treatment of the political prisoners and promised that, as soon as the agrarian outrages which were currently disturbing Ireland had ceased, he would release all political prisoners who were not directly connected with crimes of violence.

The agrarian disturbances to which Gladstone referred had had highly personal repercussions for George Henry Moore the Politician. After the collapse of the Fenian movement, the ribbon societies,* which had always had an agrarian rather than a

---

* The Ribbonmen were members of agrarian secret societies known as the 'Ribbon Societies' because they wore ribbons of different colours for identification. The societies were formed to protect the tenant-farmers from exploitation and to protest against the payment of tithes to the established (Protestant) Church. The methods by which they achieved their aims included intimidation, the maiming of cattle, the destruction of crops and, on occasion, murder.

political objective, had begun to spring up again, and, as early as January 1868, George Henry Moore heard that one of these societies, based in Ballintubber, had been urging his tenants to demand very considerable reductions in the rents on his Ballintubber Estate.

He at once decided to refer the whole matter to arbitration by a committee of four locals including two priests, Father O'Shea and Father Lavelle. The arbitrators examined the farms, heard the tenants' case and fixed what appeared to them to be a fair rent in each case. The adjusted rents were paid in full that year, but in 1870 word reached Moore that the tenants were agitating for another cut in the rents. He immediately wrote to Father Lavelle, his own parish priest: 'If it is supposed that, because I advocate the rights of the tenants, I am to surrender my own rights as a landlord; if it is suspected that I am so enamoured of a seat in Parliament that I am ready to abandon my own self-respect rather than imperil its possession; if it is hoped that because I alone of all the landlords of the parish of Ballintubber have not cleared my estate of the people, the people are to send me to jail – those who count on taking this base advantage of my political position will find that they have mistaken their man. I did not seek a seat in Parliament for my own personal advantage, and I do not wish to retain it a day longer than I can do so with advantage to the people and honour to myself. I am determined to vindicate my rights without fear or flinching, and if it be necessary to evict every tenant who refuses to pay his rent in full – whatever the consequences – I will take that course.'

This was the urgent private business which brought George Henry Moore in such a hurry to Moore Hall on Good Friday 1870, in the middle of a number of public engagements and at a time when he was fighting Parliament almost single-handedly for the cause of his country. He had written to his agent to meet him at Moore Hall immediately after Easter, so that they could go over to Ballintubber together to see his tenants.

But on Easter Monday he retired to bed around midday, and, despite the attention of two doctors, died of a stroke around two o'clock on the afternoon of Tuesday, April 19. Father Lavelle wrote: 'Our poor country! How badly you could spare your son at this juncture! . . . He died of cerus apoplexy – heartbreak I call it. My presence in his last hour was providential.'

All the Irish papers the next day came out with reversed (black) column rules, and even the English papers were full of tributes to his talents and to his integrity.

THREE

# Man about Town

Moore has left for us a number of accounts of his father's death, and its effects upon him, just as he has left us a bewildering variety of accounts of most of the other events – and the even more numerous non-events – in his subsequent and most peculiar life. If the proper study of mankind is man, Moore refined this notion still further, and decided, at the outset of his literary career, that the particular, single specimen of the human race which would most richly repay his observations, examinations, dissections and descriptions, was himself – a very early manifestation of what the *New Yorker* magazine was later to christen 'Infatuation with Sound of Own Voice Department'.

For example: 'So my youth ran into manhood, finding its way from rock to rock, like a rivulet, gathering strength at each leap. One day my father was suddenly called to Ireland. A few days after that, a telegram came, and my mother read that we were required at his bedside. [His recollection is wrong here; the whole point, as he makes perfectly clear later, was that George Henry had told his wife to go to Ireland if she did not receive a telegram from him by a certain date.]

'We journeyed over land and sea; and on a bleak country road, one winter's evening, a man approached us, and I heard him say that all was over, that my father was dead. I loved my father, and yet my soul said, I am glad. The thought came unbidden, undesired, and I turned aside, shocked at the sight it afforded of my soul.'

Whatever else one may feel about George Moore, or GM as he came to be known in London early this century, one has to admit that he was scarifyingly honest, to use an Irish expression that would undoubtedly have greatly appealed to him, about his innermost feelings. He was, to use one of his favourite expressions, a dab at self-analysis, just as he was, in his own view at least, a dab at all sorts of other things, like seducing women, dancing the Boston Cake-Walk and playing croquet.

And nobody could ever have put his life's aim more forcibly, if not exactly succinctly: 'My father's death freed me, and I sprang like a loosened bough up to the light. His death gave me power to create myself – that is to say, to create a complete and absolute self out of the partial self which was all that the restraint of home had permitted; this future self, this ideal George Moore, beckoned me, lured [me] like a ghost; and, as I followed the funeral, the question – Would I sacrifice this ghostly self, if by so doing I could bring my father back? – presented itself without intermission, and I shrank horrified at the answer which I could not crush out of my mind.

'Now my life was like a garden in the emotive torpor of spring; now my life was like a flower conscious of the light. Money was placed in my hands, and I divined all it represented. Before me the crystal lake, the distant mountains, the swaying woods, said but one word, and that word was – self; not the self that was then mine, but the self on whose creation I was enthusiastically determined. But I felt like a murderer when I turned to leave the place [that I had] so suddenly, and I could not but think unjustly, become possessed of. As I probe this poignant, psychological moment, I find that, although I perfectly realised that all pleasures were then in my reach – women, elegant dress, theatres, supper-rooms – I hardly thought at all of them, but much more of certain drawings from the plaster cast. I would be an artist. More than ever, I was determined to be an artist, and my brain was made of this desire as I journeyed as fast as railway and steamboat could take me to

London. No further trammels, no further need of being a soldier, of being anything but eighteen, with life and France before me! I would feel the pulse of life at home before I felt it abroad, and a studio arose in my imagination – tapestries, models, and preparations for France.'

In a second account of the affair, he goes about it a different way. He talks about the sudden tension he became aware of, between his mother and father, one evening in London, and, characteristically, attributed this tension to the possibility that his father was about to complain yet again about yet another bad report from school, in this case the Jurles Academy. Of course he was wrong, as he had been so often before: what had happened was that his father had just received the letter from his land agent, telling him that his tenants were demanding further reductions in rent. Just before he left London for Ireland for the last time, George Henry the Politician called young Master George back to the front door to say goodbye to him and to slip a sovereign into his hand.

A couple of days later, young Master George and his mother set out for Ireland. 'Something dreadful must have happened!' she kept saying to herself, and she informed him that his father had told her that, if she did not get a wire from him by a certain day, she was to come to Ireland at once; and from this information he made up his mind that his father had decided to die a Roman death, by his own hand, rather than become involved in some financial wrangle with his peasant tenants. Moore persisted in this notion for years, until eventually it led to a rift between him and his brother, Colonel Maurice, which had the result that, before the end of their lives, they would pass each other on a staircase without a hint of recognition.

In the midst of his grief, he says, he could not help remembering that his father's death had redeemed him from the army, from Jurles's, and meant that he would now be able to live as he pleased. That he should think of himself at such a moment shocked him deeply, and he remembers how frightened he was at his own selfish wickedness, yet a voice that he could not restrain – it was the voice of his soul, he believed – had been demanding, all the way to Moore Hall, whether, if he could bring his father back, he would have done so, if it meant giving up painting, and returning to Jurles's.

It was a sacrifice he was not prepared to make, he concludes, and goes on: 'I tried to grieve like my mother, but I could not . . . the dead man lay on the very bed in which I had been born . . . until the seventies, Ireland was feudal, and we looked on our tenants as animals that lived in hovels round the bogs, whence they came twice a year, with their rents; and I can remember that once when my father was his own agent, a great concourse of strange fellows came to Moore Hall in tall hats and knee-breeches, jabbering to each other in Irish. An old man here and there could speak a little English, and I remember one of them saying: "Sure, they're only mountainey men, yer honour, and have no English; but they have the goicks", he added with unction.

'And out of the tall hats came rolls of bank-notes, so dirty that my father grumbled, telling the tenant that he must bring cleaner notes; and, afraid that lest he should be sent off on a long trudge to the bank, the old fellow thrust the notes into my father's hand and began jabbering again . . . and if they failed to pay their rents, the cabins that they had built with their own hands were thrown down, for there was no pity for a man who failed to pay his rent. And if we thought that bullocks would pay us better, we ridded our lands of them; cleaned our lands of tenants is an expression I once heard, and I remember how they used to go away by train from Claremorris in great batches, bawling like animals. There is no denying that we looked upon our tenants like animals, and they looked on us as kings; in all the old stories, the landlord is the king.

'Everything was beginning for me, and everything was declining for my mother. She would like to have lingered by her husband's grave a little while, but I gave her no peace, urging the fact that sooner or later we would have to go back to London.'

His honesty becomes at times almost distressing, until you

consider that it was both an effective and profitable way of off-loading his feeling of guilt: 'Why delay, mother? We cannot spend our lives here going to Kiltoome, with flowers. An atrocious boy, as I relate him, but an engaging manner transforms reality as a mist or a ray of light transforms a landscape, and my mother died, believing me to have been the best of sons, though I never [once] sacrificed my convenience to hers.'

To return to reality: when George Henry the Politician died, young Master George, then aged eighteen, was the chief mourner at the funeral. The poor tenants came from all over County Mayo and the coffin was borne on the shoulders of sixteen of them to the Chapel of Carnacun, a townland in County Mayo not far from Moore Hall.

The property to which George Henry's son and heir, George Moore the Author, had now succeeded, consisted of 12,371 acres in County Mayo and 110 acres in County Roscommon, with a valuation of over £3,568 a year. The rents, when they were paid, provided over £4,000 a year, though after the deduction of interest on mortgages taken out over the years on the property this sum dwindled to around £500 a year (£25,000 in today's money); not a fortune, exactly, but by no means a bad income for a young man of eighteen. All Moore could think about were Jim Browne's words: 'Think of the life. Think of the models. If you want to learn painting, go to Paris.'

But his mother and his guardian, his uncle, the Earl of Sligo, were united against the idea of him going to Paris, and decided that he would have to remain in London, as a young man about town, with his own income, until he had reached his majority. Young George continued to study art in a half-hearted sort of way, admitting that he regarded it as little more than an amusement, a means of access to nude models, among other things: 'It was painting that interested me, and a studio was sought as soon as I arrived in London. My aspiration did not reach as high as a private studio; the naked was my desire and a drawing class would provide me with that.'

Around this period, he went down to Sussex with his friend from Jurles's Academy, and got to know the Bridgers. He always refers to Harry Colvill Bridger as Colville with a final 'e' in *Hail and Farewell*, but this is probably merely a lapse of memory; Moore rarely checked any facts but relied on his memory and his own impressions. Now, suddenly and unexpectedly, he meets Harry's mother: 'It was in the vastness of Westminster Hall that I saw her for the first time,' he writes. 'The next time I met her was in her own home [in Southwick, near Brighton in Sussex] in a garden planted with variegated firs [where] she tended her flowers all day; in the parlour, we assembled in the evening. Her husband smoked his pipe in silence; the young ladies, their blonde hair hanging down their backs, played waltzes; she alone talked, and her conversation was effusive, her laughter abundant and bright. I had only just turned eighteen, and was deeply interested in religious problems, and one day I told her [that] the book I carried in my pocket and sometimes pretended to study was Kant's *Critique of Pure Reason*, and with a burst of laughter she declared that she would always call me Kant.' And she always did so, though the rest of the family found other nicknames for him.

There was no reason, he says, why he should have become a friend of these people. He was opposed in character and temperament to them, but somehow they seemed to hit it off. There was little reflection on either side, certainly none on Moore's; at that time he reckons he was incapable of any deep thought, his youth was a vague dream, and his companions shadows in that dream.

In such a mood, visit to the Bridgers in Sussex succeeded visit, 'and before I was aware, the old squire, who walked about the Downs in a tall hat [had] died, and my friend [had] moved into the family place, distant about a hundred yards – an Italian house sheltered among the elms that grew along the seashore. And in their new house, they became more real than shadows . . .'

Through Harry Colvill Bridger, he met again another young man he had earlier known at Jurles's, who had a horse running at

Croydon, but was without a jockey. It was another of those non-events that punctuated Moore's long life.

What had apparently happened was that Moore had volunteered to send to Moore Hall for his father's racing breeches and boots, and had offered to ride the horse as a steeplechase jockey.

'No doubt with some luck I should have got the horse round the course as well as another, but the owner having scratched the horse, and the day being wet and the Ring a couple of inches deep in mud, the result of the Croydon meeting was for me a severe cold that prevented me from taking my driving-lesson from Ward, one of the great coachmen of that time, a lesson that I sorely needed, for I had engaged to drive a horse down to Epsom.

'These excursions passed the summer away . . . hours were spent at the tailors considering different patterns; at the hosiers turning over scarves, neckties and shirts of many descriptions, frilled and plain . . . to be ridiculous has always been *ma petite luxe*, but can anyone be said to be ridiculous if he knows that he is ridiculous? Not very well. It is the pompous that are truly ridiculous.'

He was also reading a lot; the study of Shelley's poetry had led him to devour very nearly all the English lyric poets, and what he calls 'Shelley's atheism' had led him to Spinoza, Godwin and Darwin, as well as Kant. Was there or was there not a God? he asked himself. At this stage his agnosticism had progressed no further than this very basic stage, though he felt obliged to confide to his mother that he no longer believed in a God. She was leaning against the chimney-piece in the drawing room when she was entrusted with this shattering piece of news, and, to Moore's amazement, she did not seem in the least disturbed, but merely remarked: 'I am very sorry, George, that it is so,' as if he had just said to her that he thought it was going to rain.

But life, he recalls, he loved far better than books, 'and very curiously my studies and my pleasures kept pace, stepping together like a pair of well-trained carriage horses: while waiting for my coach to take a party of *tarts* and *mashers* [his italics] to the Derby, I would read a chapter of Kant and put the book in my pocket in the hope of finding a few spare moments to devote to it on the racecourse.'

Interestingly enough, this is the only time he uses the term 'tarts'; thereafter he talks about prostitutes as 'lights o' love', a phrase that may have been in the coinage of the period, but strikes an oddly coy note today. One cannot help feeling that he was looking for a casual, non-committal way of referring to them and probably could not find a better one, though the terms 'ladies of the town' and 'ladies of the night' were both in common use at that period. Maybe Moore, with his curiously Victorian sense of gallantry, felt that his phrase presented them in a more favourable light. He more or less admits it, later.

He also admits that he liked to spend 'on scent and toilette knick-knacks as much as would keep a poor man's family in affluence for ten months . . . I liked the fashionable sunlight in the Park, the dusty cavalcades – and to shock my friends by bowing to those to whom I should not bow . . . Bouquets, stalls, rings delighted me; and of all, the life of the theatre – that life of raw gas-light, whitewashed walls, of doggerel verse, slangy polkas and waltzes – interested me beyond legitimate measure, so curious and unreal did it seem.'

He lived with his family in Thurloe Square, but dined out every lunch-time at fashionable restaurants: and, by half-past eight most evenings, he was at the theatre. After the theatre, it was usually supper in the Cremorne or the Argyle Rooms, and home in the small hours.

'My mother suffered, and expected ruin, for I took no trouble to conceal anything; I boasted of dissipations. But there was no need to fear, for I was naturally endowed with a very clear sense of self-preservation; I neither betted nor drank, nor contracted debts, nor a secret marriage; from a worldly point of view, I was a model young man indeed; and when I returned home about four in the morning, I watched the pale moon setting, and, repeating some verses of Shelley, I thought how I should go to Paris when I was of age and study painting.'

# FOUR

# Paris at Last

The day came, and, with a great many trunks and cases and boxes filled with clothes, books and pictures, George Moore set out for Paris accompanied by his valet, to whom he refers in the books as Mullowney. He was in fact a Mayo peasant called William Maloney, formerly second man at Moore Hall; his father had been George Henry the Politician's steward and butler in the 1840s. That Master George should embark on his new career as an art student in Paris with a valet in attendance was partly, at least, his mother's idea; as soon as Mrs Moore became convinced that her son was indeed determined to go to Paris as soon as he was twenty-one, she made it her main concern to see that he should take his 'man' along with him, on the principle that a young man with a valet to look after his needs would be that much less likely to go to the bad straight away than one left to his own devices in that wicked city. Moore arrived in Paris on March 13, 1873, less than one month after his twenty-first birthday.

The whole matter of Maloney the valet is a very early example of Moore's baffling habit of changing names and dates and events, and spelling names differently and giving the same people different names in various accounts of the same event; for a man who was always extraordinarily fussy about the precise variety of paper upon which his books were to be printed, and the exact type faces in which they were to be set, he seems unprepared even to cross a room, to look up a reference book and check the spelling of a word. He writes about Berthe Morisot, the Impressionist painter, in *Confessions* and spells her name Morizot and Morisot within a few pages, and can never make up his mind whether the art classes he attended in Paris in the '70s were run by a man called Julien or Julian. Did he not have a copy-editor or proof-reader? Or did he override the copy-editor and take the whole thing over himself, and make a mess of it? Or was it a deliberate perversity? It's hard to say; in this, as in almost every other respect, he was a most peculiar man.

In the matter of Mullowney (or Maloney), he gives us a bewildering variety of accounts of how he and his valet parted. In one version, in *Vale*, he says that he let him go after six or eight months, when Maloney went back to England 'sighing after beef, beer and a wife', and full of complaints about 'beds he couldn't sleep in and wine he couldn't drink'; this version does not at all concur with another of Moore's accounts of Maloney in Paris – where, as Moore has the valet himself putting it, 'women could be had for the asking, and claret for half nothing' – and this account of the affair is corroborated to some extent by the fact that, when he did leave Moore, Maloney did not go back to his wife and children in County Mayo but went instead to London where he persuaded Jim Browne to find him a lucrative position as a butler in London.

In yet another version, in his *Confessions*, Moore claims that when he wrote his first play, *Worldliness*, his valet 'liked the play, seeing in it a means whereby he might get back to London . . . thinking of the happy evenings that awaited him in the Sun Music Hall at Knightsbridge'. And again, in the same book he claims that he did not get rid of Maloney until he decided to leave the Hôtel de Russie and live with his friend, Marshall, in an apartment in the Passage des Panoramas. What seems most likely is that he decided to send Maloney back within six or eight months of his arrival in Paris, and for two reasons: he could not really afford to keep a valet, once he had started to buy his way into the expensive night life of the French capital; and, also, he wanted to be part and parcel of the Paris art student scene, and he could not very well do that with a valet in train. As he himself put it – and he was always almost embarrassingly honest – he wished above all other things to be himself, to enter into the inner as well as the outer life of the *quartier* in which he was living.

He recorded his first impressions of the city in *Confessions*, and he was clearly disappointed with the place: 'We all know the great grey and melancholy Gare du Nord at half-past six in the morning; and the miserable carriages, and the tall, haggard city. Pale, sloppy, yellow houses; an oppressive absence of colour; a peculiar bleakness in the streets. The *ménagère* hurries down the asphalt to the market; a dreadful *garçon de café*, with a napkin tied round his throat, moves about some chairs, so decrepit and so solitary that it seems impossible to imagine a human being sitting there. Where are the Boulevards? Where are the Champs-Elysées? I asked myself; and feeling bound to apologise for the appearance of the city, I explained to my valet that we were passing through some by-streets, and returned to the study of a French vocabulary.'

Nevertheless, as he freely admits, when the time came to formulate a demand for rooms, hot water and a fire, his French deserted him and the proprietress of the hotel, who spoke English, had to be summoned. The hotel was the Hôtel Voltaire, on the Quai Voltaire, on the Left Bank of the Seine, almost opposite the Louvre, and Moore took a suite of rooms which included bedrooms for himself and Maloney and one spare room, as he was intending to invite Jim Browne to come over from London to join him. The choice of this hotel was probably dictated by the fact that he had read somewhere that it was here that Wagner had lived while he was composing *Meistersinger*, and Moore had recently discovered music and, more especially, the music of Wagner. It was a big, old-fashioned family hotel, and fairly expensive, as he was soon to discover.

He spent the first three weeks in France trying to learn French, or at any rate trying to learn by heart enough French to be able to explain what he wanted; and to organise private tuition in painting from a French artist called Alexandre Cabanel, whom he had chosen because Cabanel's nudes greatly appealed to him, and he assumed that private tuition would include instant access to Cabanel's models.

Cabanel was unable to take him on, but suggested that he should instead attend classes at the Ecole des Beaux Arts, where Cabanel was employed as a professor. He looked at some sample drawings Moore had brought and suggested that the best thing Moore could do would be to apply to the British Embassy; no doubt the Ambassador would be able to obtain, from the Ministry of Fine Arts, permission for him to enter the school without taking the standard formal entrance examination.

Moore hailed a *fiacre* and dashed off to call on the Ambassador, Lord Lyons, 'an elegant old gentleman, who promised to intercede on my behalf . . . A few days later an official letter was handed to me, and the morning after I introduced myself to many turbulent fellows whose aspects and manners soon convinced me that I would not be able to endure the life of the Beaux Arts . . . and the facilities the schools afforded were not those I sought for.'

The facilities he was referring to were the models, and his principal complaint was that the life class nude models sat only three times a week; the rest of the time the students were obliged to work from plaster casts. Also, he had to be there at the unheard-of hour of eight o'clock in the morning, which took a far greater effort of will than Moore was then capable of summoning up on any sort of long-term basis.

After about a week, he abandoned the project altogether and began to spend his days wandering up and down the boulevards, studying photographs of the salon pictures, and trying to find a painter, as he phrased it, to whom he might address himself with confidence; in other words, he was looking for another painter whose models appealed to him as much as Cabanel's had.

Suddenly he remembered an odd little domestic scene from the past; his father showing him, one day while the latter was shaving, three photographs of paintings of nudes by Sèvres which they apparently proceeded to discuss in some detail: 'My father liked the slenderer figure, but I liked the corpulent . . . the beauty of this woman, and what her beauty must be in the life of the painter, had inspired many a reverie and I had concluded . . . that she was his very beautiful mistress, that they lived in a picturesque happiness in the midst of a shady garden full of birds and tall flowers . . . and these dreams of her had accompanied me in my rides over the plains of Mayo . . . I conceived a project of becoming Sèvres's pupil and being loved by her!' And he adds, somewhat unnecessarily, 'For I was a childish boy of one and twenty who knew nothing, and to whom the world was astonishingly new.' He was naive, certainly, but not entirely innocent of the facts of life; he had, after all, spent many childhood hours hanging around the racing stables, and had watched stallions covering the mares.

At the Exposition aux Champs-Elysées, he persuades the concierge to copy down M. Sèvres's address for him, and we next find him in Enghien, a suburb not very far from Paris, walking up a gravelled path hoping to catch a glimpse of the painter's lovely mistress among the young oak trees, feeding the pigeons perhaps, from a silver plate, and asking himself whethert M. Sèvres will invite him to breakfast.

At this point, you pause and begin to wonder at what unearthly hour did Moore set out upon this odyssey, if it is still only breakfast time. Then you remember further unlikely references to breakfast, in other pieces by Moore, and you suddenly realise that you are up against yet another of his many peculiarities: he frequently refers to luncheon as breakfast. It could be that initially he confused the French terms *petit déjeuner* and *déjeuner*, but he persisted in referring to lunch as breakfast for so long after he must have become well aware of the difference, that one can only assume it became an affectation with him, the sort of mistake a man who liked to think that he still thought in French might well make from time to time.

However, to return to Enghien. A maidservant opens the door, shows him into the studio, and before he has time to examine the sketches on the walls Sèvres marches in, a tall, reedy-looking man, who did not, Moore thought, carry the mark of genius, as Cabanel did. He tells Moore, as Cabanel had done, that he has no room for a private pupil in his house, and conducts Moore down the green garden towards the gate. Moore remarked that he thought he had seen those trees before, in Sèvres's paintings, in the meantime scanning every nook and cranny, hoping that he might catch a glimpse of the model mistress reading, and that she might even raise her eyes to meet his, as he passed.

He fancies he did catch a glimpse of a white dress behind the trellis, but that could have been the painter's wife, or his daughter perhaps, and in the train on the way back to Paris he consoles himself with the thought that the painting his father had shown him might have been painted a long time ago and the model could well be an old woman by now.

At this period, both Moore and his valet Maloney seem to have been very lonely. Moore says he allowed his valet to 'smoke his clay' in his room in the evenings, and Maloney frequently urged him, in his rich Mayo brogue, to go back home to his mother.

But Moore persevered in his search for a painter with models that appealed to him, and one day was stricken with the art of Jules Lefèbvre: '. . . my nature was too young and mobile to resist the conventional attractiveness of [his] nude figures, [their] indolent attitudes, long hair, slender hips and hands, and I accepted Jules Lefèbvre wholly and unconditionally.'

Lefèbvre did not, however, accept Moore unconditionally; but instead wrote out the address of Julien's Academy, a studio where he gave instruction every Tuesday morning. As nobody seemed anxious to take him on as a private pupil, Moore decided that perhaps, after all, a public studio might suit him better since he would meet there all sorts and conditions of Frenchmen, and in their company would have a far better chance of learning the language and assimilating the spirit of France.

In the studio to which he had been recommended, perched high up in the Passage des Panoramas, he found M. Julien, or Julian, as the case may be, whom he describes as a typical *méridional*: dark eyes, crafty and watchful, a seductively mendacious manner, and a sensual mind. They became friends at once and unashamedly used each other. For Julien, Moore's forty francs a month were a godsend and his frequent invitations to dinner and the theatre an added bonus; for Moore, Julien was a passport which secured for him entry at one level into the social life of Paris, and he was never lonely again.

In the class at Julien's, Moore found some eighteen or twenty young men and some eight or nine young English girls, 'young and interesting . . . one of the charms of the place, giving, as they did, that sense of sex which is so subtle a pleasure'. However, instead of falling in love with any of the girls, he quickly came under the sway of a young male student, a distant relative whom he had once met with Jim Browne in London.

Here again we come across yet another example of Moore's perversity. He calls his new friend Lewis Ponsonby Marshall in *Confessions*, and refers to him normally as Marshall; he calls him Lewis Hawkins in *Hail and Farewell* and Lewis Seymour in his first novel, *A Modern Lover*, subsequently rewritten as *Lewis Seymour and Some Women*, and sometimes, whether perversely or forgetfully it is impossible to say, refers to him simply as Hawkins. In real life, the young man in question was Lewis Weldon Hawkins, a cosmopolitan, born in Stuttgart of British parents, brought up in Belgium, a naturalised Frenchman who spoke French fluently. He was a sponger by profession, though he clearly had some talent as an artist, and he dominated the early part of Moore's stay in Paris; he had enough charm to survive as a pimp and to sponge for years on Moore and others of his friends.*

Moore took Lewis Marshall out to dinner on the evening of the

---

* Since Moore refers to him as Lewis Marshall more often than using any of the other variations, I shall refer to the real character as Lewis Marshall, for the sake of consistency, as I shall refer to Moore's painter friend Clara Christian as Stella, which was the name he always called her in his writings.

day he renewed his acquaintance with him at Julien's and before dinner met what he calls 'a beautiful young English girl called Alice', who was in love with Lewis. When he encountered Lewis first, in London, in Jim Browne's company, he recalled that Lewis 'had come over to London with a young Frenchwoman whom he called Louise'. It was the same girl; she was, in fact, a Belgian prostitute, and Marshall was at this period her *mec* or, as Moore puts it, her *amant de coeur*.

Moore had by now moved from the Hôtel Voltaire to a much cheaper apartment in the Hôtel de Russie, near the Boulevard des Italiens, not far from the Opéra, and he had been obliged to let Maloney go, because he could not afford to pay him. Moore was discovering that Paris was not nearly as cheap as he had first expected it to be – certainly not if one was obliged, as Moore appeared to be, to buy popularity at the price of lavish entertainment – and also that his income was not nearly as vast as it had seemed to be in London, when he was living at home with his mother.

A long truancy from the art classes now begins; Lewis takes him to a succession of Paris night spots where they meet various ladies of the town, known only by their Christian names, and it seems to Moore that at this period they lived mainly in *fiacres* and restaurants: 'Marshall took me to strange student *cafés*, where dinners were paid for in pictures; to a mysterious place, where a *table d'hôte* was held under a tent in the back garden, frequented by the lights of love of Montmartre, with whom we went to walk in the gardens of *Bullier*, the *Château Rouge*, or the *Elysées Montmare*.'

Julien was quick to see how Moore's dependence on Lewis could be exploited and soon began to arrange all sorts of expeditions, including painting trips out to Meudon, picnics on the Seine, and visits to open-air restaurants, most of them very largely financed by Moore: 'We found the others waiting for us at the doors of the restaurant, very impatient, and to my delight our table was laid under a trellis, and the green leaves and the white table appealed to my imagination and the cutlets and the omelettes linger in my memory ... The night gathered about the green banks of the Seine, and the dim poplars struck through the last bar of light which seemed as if it could not die; the month being June, it lingered between grey clouds ... and then, bridge after bridge, the landings, the separations, each one returning to his bed, his mind filled with remembrances of blue air, and flowing water, and swaying trees? Did Alice return with Lewis? I think so.' Was Moore really so innocent at this stage that he even wondered whether Alice had gone home with Lewis, who was living with her, on her earnings, and had nowhere else to go?

On another occasion they return to Meudon, so that Lewis can paint a landscape, but instead Lewis decides to go for a swim, and a boat is hired, and, predictably enough, while Lewis is disporting himself in midstream, Moore is in the shallows, flopping about with Alice, pretending to teach her how to swim, although he admits that he himself 'could swim but a little'.

On another, similar trip, Lewis goes off to paint one morning, leaving Alice in bed and Moore skulking around her hotel room, trying to persuade her to get up. When he fails, she invites him, after some hesitation, Moore has to admit, to join her in her room, and they spend the time gossiping. Only Moore, finding himself alone in her bedroom with a woman of patently loose morals, would not only have spent the entire day merely gossiping with her, but would have thought this achievement worth placing on record.

This became a daily pattern, until Lewis finally objected, not because he felt for a second that Moore was up to anything, but because people were talking and this might have affected his image. 'Of course I know she wouldn't have anything to do with you,' Lewis said. 'All the same, I don't wish to pass for a cuckold.'

Subsequently, Moore has a long and unbelievably childish debate with Alice about eating what he calls 'something incredibly nasty', and because the whole episode is so bizarre, I shall quote

Moore verbatim:* 'And the depth of her passion may be judged from the discussion . . . Alice's point was that it mattered a great deal from whence the nastiness came; if it came from Lewis she would sooner eat a pound than a pinch if it came from me, and she woke Lewis up to ask him if he would not return her compliment and was very angry when he said that a crap was the same the whole world over, and he would prefer to swallow a pinch rather than a pound, no matter who owned it.'

At this period, Moore was very heavily under Lewis Marshall's influence though he realised at the time – or did, at any rate, by the time he wrote *Confessions* at the age of thirty – how shallow Marshall was. 'To anyone observing us at this time, it would have seemed that I was but a hanger-on, and a feeble imitator of Marshall. I took him to my tailor's, and he advised me on the cut of my coats; he showed me how to arrange my rooms, and I strived to copy his manner of speech and his general bearing; and yet I think I always suspected that Marshall's brilliancy was owing to the superficiality of his talent, and that my nature was a deeper one than his, and would become deeper as the years went by . . . and I used him without shame or stint.'

Moore admits here that, even as early as this, he had begun to use everybody with whom he had come in close contact, in one way or another, as he was to do throughout his life, either as role models for his own life or as characters for his novels and stories.

It was at this period at the *table d'hôte* at the Hôtel de Russie, that he met M. Duval, author of 160 plays, a man who kept flashing names like Dumas, *père* et *fils*, Gautier, and Balzac at him, and put the idea into Moore's head that he might himself contemplate writing a play, based on Lewis Marshall and Alice. Moore went to a library and for a month studied Congreve, Wycherley, Vanbrugh and Farquhar and came up with a comedy which he called *Worldliness*. When Duval reappears in *Vale* – and all Moore's dramatis personae keep reappearing in different guises

* The passage appears on page 501 in the 1985 one-volume edition of *Hail and Farewell*.

in different books – it is as Bernard de Lopez, but the role he plays is exactly the same. The man was in fact Bernard de Lopez, a French writer of Spanish origin, who had a big success with one play, *Le Tribut des Cent Vierges*, in 1839, and thereafter wrote mainly in collaboration with other authors, including Théophile Gautier and Gérard de Nerval, as well as Moore.

Moore, homesick for English food and the English language, went back to London for a time in 1874, took a studio in Cromwell Mews and attended art classes run by a Frenchman called Barthe in Limerston Street, though the main object of his visit was to try to get his play performed on the London stage. He appears to have spent several months at least in London in the spring and summer of 1874, and arranged for the publication of the play, probably paying the cost himself.

It was during this visit that he first met Whistler, who used to drop into Barthe's art classes. James McNeill Whistler, the American artist who had made his fame in London with impressionistic cityscapes, long before the word 'Impressionism' was invented, was then in his late thirties and approaching the apex of his fame. Whenever he turned up at the studio, a crowd would collect around him and hang on his every word. Moore clearly resented Whistler's success as a celebrity; even as early as this he liked to be the centre of attention. Years later, when Moore was every bit as famous as Whistler, Whistler challenged him to a duel, and Moore accepted the challenge with alacrity, secure in the knowledge that duelling was forbidden in England, and that both of them would have been far too sea-sick after the channel crossing even to consider the possibility of meeting at dawn, with or without seconds. It came to nothing, like so many other of Moore's – and indeed Whistler's – gestures.

At this period, Moore – later a great champion of Whistler's painting – had no time for what he then considered to be Whistler's offhand approach to art: 'his drawings on brown-paper slips seemed to me very empty and casual, altogether lacking in that attitude of mind which interested me so much in Rossetti. His jokes were very disagreeable to me; he did not seem to take art seriously, but I must have disguised my feelings very well, for he asked me to come to see him.' This is an early example of Moore's own power to attract attention; you would not think that a celebrity like Whistler would be very easily impressed by a gauche young man of twenty-two from County Mayo, who had just spent rather less than a year in Paris, and so far had not made any reputation as anything.

The very next Sunday, Moore visited Whistler in his studio at 96, Cheyne Walk – and the address is, in itself, an indication of how successful Whistler then was – and there he saw 'a melancholy portrait of his [Whistler's] mother which he had just completed', and another picture of 'a girl in a white dress dreaming by the chimney-piece, her almost Rossetti-like face reflected in the mirror', two of the most famous pictures that Whistler ever painted, but clearly Moore was not impressed.

And, as Whistler rushed around the studio, 'laughing boisterously and rattling iced drinks from glass to glass', Moore stood back silent and abashed: 'I think that I despised and hated him when he capped my somewhat foolish enthusiasm for the pre-Raphaelite painters with a comic anecdote.'

And it could have been what Moore himself calls his 'somewhat foolish enthusiasm for the pre-Raphaelite painters' that drew him to another pupil at Barthe's drawing classes in Limerston Street, Oliver Madox Brown, son of the pre-Raphaelite painter Ford Madox Brown – 'a strange boy, even stranger than I . . . I could not keep him out of my thoughts, for he seemed to me even more unfortunate than myself, less likely to win a woman's love'.

Oliver Madox Brown was both a painter and a writer; he painted in the mornings and wrote in the evenings, when he was not at class. And, when he was at class, he would read aloud what he had written the previous evening, and was every bit as much an attraction there as Whistler; even the model Mary Lewis ('a shapely little girl she was', Moore cannot help recalling) joined the crowd around Oliver, and sometimes became so entranced by what Oliver was reading that she allowed her shawl to slip from her shoulders, and Moore adds (it goes without saying) that on one occasion he noticed that she became so fascinated by what Oliver was reading that she let the shawl slip down to the floor, and stood there, listening to him, quite naked . . .

He goes on: '. . . a few months later we crowded together, forgetful of the model [all that is, except Moore, who remains so conscious of the model that he has to make a point of the fact that the others were forgetful of her presence at that moment], telling how typhoid had robbed England of a great genius; and after Oliver's death my interest in the class declined.'

During this visit to London, Moore also met again, at his mother's house, Edward Martyn of Tullyra Castle in County Mayo (it is now spelled, probably more correctly, Tullira), not very far from Moore Hall; they had known each other as children, and Martyn was to become 'dear Edward', Moore's closest friend when Moore returned to London finally, at the end of his Paris period.

Moore had his play copied out professionally, 'with the stage directions inscribed in red ink', and had high hopes of having it produced at the St James's Theatre, 'when the backers refused to supply any more money and the theatre had to be closed'. All copies of the printed version of it seem to have disappeared, possibly because they were bought up by Moore himself. When he became successful, Moore began to buy up copies of some of his early books and plays and destroy them, in order that his posthumous reputation would not be tarnished in any way by what he openly acknowledged was extremely immature, amateurish work.

On his return to Paris, he learns from 'the fat Provençal' (M. Julien or Julian) that Alice has now become one of the most fashionable courtesans of Paris, and he finds Lewis living luxuriously off her earnings 'in a vast apartment, cumbered with sofas, armchairs, mirrors, and great gilt cornices, wallowing in the finest of fine linen – in a great Louis XV bed, and there were cupids above him'.

Moore and Lewis would have been perfectly happy to spend the evenings lounging around Alice's luxurious apartment in the Rue Duphot – the *Monsieur* who was paying for all this splendour, an international financier who owned an island in the Mediterranean, only visited her once a week, and then only in the afternoon – but, as Moore reports, Alice was now very nearly in the front rank (of the Paris courtesans) and, to keep her there, they had to take her out every evening to be seen.

If they did not go to a theatre, they went to a music hall; the Folies Bergère was coming into fashion around that time, and they often went there until it was time to go to the Mabile. Dinner cost over eighty francs, and the box at the Folies Bergère 'broke into a second hundred-franc note', but Moore did not resent any of that as much as the five francs that it cost him to walk in the Mabile Gardens for half an hour. Ladies entered the Mabile free, and Alice usually paid for Lewis Marshall, though sometimes he had to borrow the money from Moore and it annoyed Moore to see Lewis fling the borrowed coin down with the air of *un grand seigneur*.

If he himself had been Alice's *amant de coeur* at that time, Moore reflects, he would have behaved, and would have been prepared to be treated, quite openly, as a ponce; to be an *amant de coeur*, as Lewis was, *en cachette*, would have filled him with shame, his instinct being, as he never ceases to remind us, always to be ashamed of nothing but to be ashamed, 'and it was from the day that Lewis confessed himself ashamed of the role he was playing that he lost caste in my eyes . . . and it was with some unwillingness that I followed them one night to a masked ball dressed in the fantastic costume of Valentine in *Le Petit Faust*'.

If Moore ever lost his virginity in any sort of conventional sense, which is extremely doubtful, it could well have happened that night, after that masked ball. Moore tries to give the impression that he had lovers like everybody else – he even refers to various ladies he knew as his lovers – but he remains curiously unconvincing. Most of the people who knew him really well in Ireland, including his brother Maurice, the poet W. B. Yeats, and

his friend Oliver St John Gogarty, believed that all his sex
adventures were pure fantasy and that he left the world – in 1933,
at the age of eighty – as pure and as innocent as he was when had
entered it, in February 1852.

He calls the lady in question *la belle Hollandaise* and, in view of
the general peculiarity of his sexual proclivities, it is perhaps worth
examining this episode in some detail. It is related in *Vale*:

> . . . she was sitting by Cora Pearl [Eliza Emma Crouch, one of the
> most famous courtesans of the Second Empire, whose *Memoirs*
> were a best-seller] watching me, attracted no doubt at first by the
> red and yellow tights that I wore, and recognising in her eyes a quiet
> look of invitation, I summoned up all my courage and crossed the
> ballroom to inquire if she would dance with me; which she did,
> passing into my arms with a delightful motion, making me feel her
> presence without any vulgar thrusting of her body upon me. The
> music ceased, and she said: 'You're with friends?' Then my heart
> misgave me, and I answered: 'Would you like to be introduced?'
> She said she would and it was plain that Alice was jealous of my
> new friend; like myself [poor Moore, still hearing, still believing,
> those shrill voices from his childhood, reminding him that he is so
> ugly, so unattractive to women, so dull that he will be forced to
> marry the smelly old beggar woman, because nobody else would
> ever have him] . . . like myself, she believed that it could not be me,
> but Lewis, that she sought; but as soon as she was assured that this
> was not so, her attitude toward *la belle Hollandaise* became
> friendlier, and we four at the close of the *bal* drove to a fashionable
> restaurant, and afterwards to the Rue Duphot, Alice proposing a
> grand bivouac, for she did not care to sleep in her bed while her
> guests slept upon the floor. But she [*la belle Hollandaise*] would not
> accept her [Alice's] bed; and my heart again misgave me, thinking
> that the evening, like many an evening before, would prove
> platonic . . . for me. As if reading my thoughts, *la belle Hollandaise*
> asked me at what moment in the evening I had begun to love her.
> 'When you kissed me.'
> 'But I haven't kissed you at all yet,' she said. 'Wait a little while.'
> And leaning her cheek against mine, she whispered strange,
> incomprehensible things in a low, quiet voice that drove me mad,
> her eyes, curious and enigmatic, fixed on me, her pointed face lifted
> to mine, her chin enticing, and her soft brown hair brushing my
> cheek. I can recall the sweet moment when she drew her bracelets
> from her wrists. But cannot call to mind any part of her undressing,

only that she was always beside me, curled serpent-like, a serpent of
old Nile, for a woman can coil like one, and during the night I often
cried out in terror, awakening Lewis and Alice, who lay asleep in
the rich imperial bed . . . and if I relate the incident of our meeting
it is because we never forget her who reveals sensuality to us.

And that's it. He has not really committed himself to anything
on paper, any more than he did, perhaps, on the floor of that
bedroom in the Rue Duphot, if there ever was a *belle Hollandaise*, if
it is not all pure fantasy. And, as to the sensuality he talks about, it
seems possible that even at this early period of his life, such
sensuality as he experienced was very readily assuaged, and
perhaps even more easily, and from his viewpoint, much more
conveniently sublimated, into verse, or his own peculiar form of
what in these days is known as faction.

# FIVE

# Impressions
# and Impressionists

Shortly after the evening that they spent with Moore and the beautiful *Hollandaise* at the fancy dress ball, Alice and Marshall started to split up. Moore gave the impression – probably because Lewis Marshall gave him, Moore, the impression – that it was he who had instigated the break-up. He would; he was that kind of man, and Moore would have believed him, because he always had an exaggerated view of Marshall's charm and sex appeal.

'A few evenings later, he offered Alice to me,' Moore remarked laconically, 'for they had outlived their love for each other, and were now seeking to maintain it in excess and orgy.

'Her face wore an odd smile when he proposed her to me, so the thought may have come to her rather than to him, the instinct of every woman being to turn to him who has witnessed her love as soon as she wearies of her lover.' Heaven knows where Moore picked up this fragment of homespun human behaviourism but the facts, as related by Moore himself, do not support his thesis, and the odd smile on Alice's face, when Lewis suggested that Moore should now take Alice over, could have been either horror at the very thought of the idea, or amazement at Marshall's audacity, since quite clearly it was she who had decided to end it.

A few evenings later, Alice agreed to dine with Moore, and when he arrived before she had even had time to take her bath, she suggested that he might like to wait for her in the drawing room, unless he would prefer to accompany her into her *cabinet de toilette*, which, of course, being Moore, he did, admiring 'a more beautiful model than any that had ever appeared in Julien's studio, even if her breasts were too large for a nymph's'; and, when she stepped out of her bath and began to dry herself, 'in many picturesque attitudes', they talked: 'of her perfections, the length of her leg from the ankle to the knee, and the spring of her hips. But of love, not a word was spoken . . .'

'She would not believe me at first,' Lewis Marshall said to Moore three months later, after telling him that he had now finally left Alice for good, 'she would not believe me at first, and all she could find to say to persuade me to remain was: "You couldn't leave such a pretty pair of breasts!"' But Marshall assured Moore that the total break-down in their relationship had now been accepted and confirmed by Alice herself, who had passed him in her carriage in the Champs-Elysées, and had turned her head the other way. It does not seem to have occurred to Moore that Marshall, who had been living in great luxury on Alice's earnings, would never have ended this state of affairs himself.

Alice, once she had thrown out her *amant de coeur*, went from strength to strength, in her role as a *demi-mondaine* of Paris; Lewis Marshall, on the other hand, found himself forced to earn his own living, and took a job painting china in a small factory at Belleville, near the Porte d'Italie. Moore used to visit him occasionally on a Sunday, and Marshall showed him the secrets of manufacturing china *au petit* and *au grand feu*.

Around this time, too, probably in the spring or summer of 1875, Moore's family from County Mayo visited him in the Hôtel de Russie in Paris. Moore had less time than he would otherwise have had to spend with them, because he was once again becoming deeply involved with Marshall.

Moore had been discussing Marshall's plight with Julien one evening in the Café Véron, when Julien advanced the idea that the cause of art had suffered a great blow as a result of Marshall's being forced to earn his living painting china. Furthermore, he suggested, if some arrangement could be arrived at, by which Marshall could return to his art classes, this might also encourage Moore to return to his studies and achieve his aim of becoming a painter. Casual loans were no longer of any use; what Julien was now suggesting was that Moore should leave the Hôtel de Russie, rent an *appartement*, give Marshall a room and at least guarantee him a couple of square meals a day, and pay for his laundry. Marshall's mother, Julien assured Moore, would send him a little pocket money, and he himself would waive all tuition fees. Moore and Marshall could thus both then return to Julien's Academy and resume their study of art.

Moore wrote to Marshall, telling him of Julien's proposal, and Marshall called the next day to say that he was starting to look for a suitable apartment. He soon found one that appealed to him in the Passage des Panoramas in the Galerie Feydeau – a narrow walk-way between the Boulevard Montmartre and the Bourse, not far from the Musée Grévin and right beside Julien's studio – and, although Moore did not like it one bit, he agreed to move in, on a temporary basis, and together they returned to Julien's art classes.

Around this time Moore went with Marshall and a crowd of other art students to an exhibition by a group of Impressionists at the Hôtel Drouot. They had acquired the name Impressionists from an exhibition the previous year in the salon of the photographer Nadar; they had advertised this exhibition under the title of 'The Limited Company of Painters, Sculptors and Engravers', and the word Impressionists had been coined as a derisory term by the critic Louis Leroy, and it had stuck. At this stage, Moore was happy to join his companions in their jeers and taunts, knowing in his heart – he says – that he was lying, that he really felt very differently about the paintings. Or perhaps, with hindsight, Moore thought that he thought differently when he came to write about the exhibition in *Confessions*: 'We could but utter coarse gibes and exclaim, "What could have induced him to paint such things? Surely he must have seen that it was absurd? I wonder if the Impressionists are in earnest or if it is only *une blague qu'on nous fait?*"

'Then we stood and screamed at Monet, that most exquisite painter of blond light. We stood before the "Turkeys" and fell to wondering seriously if it were serious work – that *chef d'oeuvre!* The high grass that the turkeys are gobbling is flooded with sunlight so swift and intense that for a moment the illusion is complete. "Just look at the house! Why the turkeys couldn't walk in at the door. The perspective is all wrong."

'Then followed other remarks of an educational kind; and when we came to those piercingly personal visions of railway-stations by the same painter – those rapid sensations of steel and vapour – our laughter knew no bounds. "I say, Marshall, just look at this wheel; he dipped his brush in cadmium yellow and whisked it round, that's all." Nor had we any more understanding for Renoir's rich sensualities of tone . . . There was a half-length nude figure of a girl. How the round fresh breasts palpitate in the light! Such a glorious glow of whiteness was attained never before. But we saw nothing except that the eyes were out of drawing.'

And of a Pissarro painting of a group of young girls gathering apples in a garden he wrote: 'Sad greys and violets, beautifully harmonised. The figures seem to move as if in a dream; we are on the thither side of life, in a world of quiet colour and happy aspiration. Those apples will never fall from the branches, those baskets that the stooping girls are filling will never be filled, that garden is the garden that life has not for giving, but which the painter has set in an eternal dream of violet and grey.'

During this period – from the autumn of 1885 until the summer of 1886 – Moore tried very hard to learn painting, often working solidly for eight hours at a stretch: 'I remember the first day of my martyrdom. The clocks were striking eight; we chose our places, got into position. After the first hour, I compared my drawing with Marshall's. He had, it is true, caught the movement of the figure better than I, but the character and quality of his work was miserable. That of mine was not. I have said I possessed no artistic facility, but I did not say faculty; my drawing was never common; it was individual in feeling, it was refined. I possessed all the rarer qualities, but not that primary power without which all is valueless – I mean the talent of the boy who can knock off a clever caricature of his schoolmaster or make a lifelike sketch of his favourite horse on the barn-door with a piece of chalk.' Moore is probably telling us here that he could not draw.

At the end of the first month, Marshall's work was steadily improving, and Moore was left helplessly toiling in his wake. Moore stuck at it doggedly for nine months: 'I was in the studio at eight in the morning, I measured my drawing, I plumbed it throughout, I sketched in, having regard to *la jambe qui porte*, I modelled *pour les masses*. During breakfast [lunch] I considered how I should work in the afternoon, at night I lay awake thinking of what I might do to obtain a better result.'

One day he suddenly decided that he had made a ghastly mistake: '. . . horrified at the black thing in front of me, I laid down my pencil: saying to myself, I will never take up pencil or brush again, and slunk out of the studio home to the Galerie Feydeau to the room above the umbrella shop, to my bed, to my *armoire à glace*, my half-dozen chairs; and on that bed, under its green curtains I lay all night weeping, saying to himself: My life is ended and done. There is no hope for me . . .' Moore kept the vow he made at that time; he never again attempted to draw or paint, for the remainder of his life.

He goes on: 'The Galerie Feydeau had never seemed a cheerful place to live in; it was now as hateful to me as a prison, and Lewis was my gaoler . . . I think I was as unhappy in the Galerie Feydeau as I had been in Oscott College. I seemed to have lost everybody in the world except the one person I wished to lose, Lewis . . . At last the thought came to me of my sister's school friend, and at her home I met people who knew nothing of Julian and L'Ecole des Beaux-Arts, and at a public dinner I was introduced to John O'Leary and his Parisian society and these people interested me, because of my father.'

John O'Leary was the man to whom the poet W. B. Yeats had
referred when he wrote: 'Romantic Ireland's dead and gone, it's
with O'Leary in the grave . . .' O'Leary had been President of the
Supreme Council of the Irish Republican Brotherhood, and had
taken part in the abortive Fenian Rising of 1848; he had been
imprisoned for nine years in England and then released on
condition that he would agree to remain in exile until his full
sentence of twenty years had expired. He spent most of this period
in Paris, where he had meetings with Parnell and Devoy. From a
subsequent account of their first meeting, it seems probable that
John O'Leary was as bored as Moore clearly was: he wanted to talk
about Ireland but all Moore wanted to talk about was painting.

Moore goes on, with the confidence of an accepted member of
the landed gentry: 'One can always pick one's way into society,
and three months later I was moving in American and English
society, about the Place Wagram and the Boulevard Malesherbes,
returning home in the early morning, awakening Lewis frequently
to describe the party to him, awakening him one morning to tell
him that a lady whose boots I was buttoning in the vestibule had
leaned over me and whispered that I could go to the very top
button . . . if I liked.' The three dots are Moore's, presumably
inserted to indicate the hesitation and confusion he felt about
proceeding.

His first big row with Marshall occurred in the summer of 1876.
Moore told Marshall that he was leaving the Galerie Feydeau and
going off to spend some time with fashionable acquaintances in
Boulogne – by now his circle of grand friends included the
Duchesse de la Trémoïlle, of the first ducal family in France;
Madame Howland, the widow of a rich American in whose house
he met Fromentin, Gustave Moreau and the painter Degas; and
Madame de Ratazzi, a grand-daughter of Lucien Bonaparte – and
he added that he expected Marshall to be out of the place by the
time he returned.

However, so far from getting out, he found on his return, three
months later, that Marshall had merely taken over most of the

apartment and was now using the sitting room as a workshop. He made a few more half-hearted attempts to give Marshall notice, which Marshall simply ignored. 'He came and went as he pleased, passing me on the staircase and in the rooms, his splendid indifference compelling the conclusion that however lacking in character a reconciliation would prove to be, I could no longer forgo one.'

The plain truth seems to be that although Moore greatly resented the fact that Marshall had shown no sympathy or understanding whatever when he made the – to him – shattering discovery that he was never going to be able to succeed as a painter, he was really totally dependent upon Marshall as the one permanent relationship in his very unfocused life at this period. In *Confessions* he admits it: '. . . he was as necessary to me as I to him, and after some demur on his part, a reconciliation was effected.'

Marshall found and furnished a new apartment for them, and they moved in, early in 1877, Moore once again paying the rent; it was in one of the old houses on the Rue de la Tour des Dames, a narrow street that runs from the Trinité church, between the Rue de Clichy and the Rue Blanche, to the Musée Gustave Moreau, with a window overlooking a tangled garden containing a dilapidated statue. Moore liked it as much as he had hated the apartment in the Galerie Feydeau, with its grimy glass roof.

And Marshall had certainly gone to town on the décor. As Moore wrote, he lavished on the rooms the fancies of imagination that suggested the collaboration of a courtesan of high degree and a fifth-rate artist. 'Nevertheless our salon was a pretty resort – English cretonne of a very happy design – vine leaves, dark green and golden, broken up by many fluttering jays. The walls were stretched with this colourful cloth, and the armchairs and couches were to match. The drawing room was in cardinal red, hung from the middle of the ceiling and looped up to give the appearance of a tent; a faun, in terra-cotta, laughed in the red gloom, and there were Turkish couches and lamps. In another room, you faced an altar, a Buddhist temple, a statue of Apollo, and a bust of Shelley.

The bedrooms were made unconventional with cushioned seats and rich canopies; and in picturesque corners there were censers, great church candlesticks and palms; then think of the smell of burning incense and wax and you will have imagined the sentiment of our apartment in the Rue de la Tour des Dames. I bought a Persian cat, a python that made a monthly meal off guinea pigs; Marshall, who did not care for pets, filled his rooms with flowers – he used to sleep beneath a tree of gardenias in full bloom. We were so, Henry Marshall [this is the only time he calls him Henry] and George Moore, when we went to live in 76 Rue de la Tour des Dames, we hoped for the rest of our lives. He to paint, I to write.'

Moore had by now renewed his acquaintance with Bernard de Lopez, whom he had met when he was living in the Hôtel de Russie; he is the man he calls M. Duval in *Confessions*, the dramatist of 160 plays, the collaborator of Balzac, Dumas *père et fils* and Gautier, the man who had encouraged Moore to try his hand at the play *Worldliness*. De Lopez would have been about fifty-seven or fifty-eight when Moore met him first; under de Lopez's influence, Moore now began to write poetry as well as collaborating with him on a play about Martin Luther.

Plays in those days were published as often as not before they were performed and this work was indeed published three years later, in 1879, with a series of 'letters' between Moore and de Lopez as a Preface, in fact written reconstructions of conversations that had taken place during the collaboration in de Lopez's apartment in the Place Pigalle, a technique which Moore was to continue to exploit throughout his life, and one which enabled him to unburden himself of his already very strong views on other writers. His choice of a subject, and his insistence to de Lopez that the play must be written from a Lutheran point of view, were equally prophetic.

Having made the decision to become a writer, Moore now embarked on an intensive course of reading – Musset, Hugo and above all Gautier's *Mademoiselle de Maupin*: 'now I saw suddenly, with delightful clearness and intoxicating conviction, that by looking without shame and accepting with love the flesh, I might raise it to as high a place within as divine a light as ever the soul had been set in ... I stood as if enchanted before the noble nakedness of the elder gods ... I cried out with my master: the bold fearless gaze of Venus is lovelier than the lowered glance of the Virgin.' And he also came to share Gautier's scorn 'of a world exemplified by lacerated saints and a crucified Redeemer'.

He had already shaken off all belief in Christianity under Shelley's influence: I am what they made me, he says, referring to the authors who influenced him at this time, Baudelaire and *Les Fleurs de Mal*, Leconte de Lisle, Villiers de l'Isle Adam, Mallarmé, Verlaine, Flaubert, Goncourt, above all Zola and Balzac.

He also spent a good deal of time in Bernard de Lopez's apartment in Pigalle, working on the play about Luther, and sometimes, after they had finished work for the evening, they would go on to a night club called *Le Rat Mort*. It was there that de Lopez introduced him to Villiers de l'Isle Adam, who in turn scribbled an introduction to Mallarmé, who at that period had few friends and was happy to welcome Moore in his apartment in the Rue de Rome. Villiers de l'Isle Adam was a writer much better known then than he is now; he had been born in Brittany to an ancient but impoverished noble family, and he had enthusiastically embraced all of the 'isms' of the day, including Symbolism and Wagnerism, and had had one success with a play *La Révolte* in 1870, which had a similar theme to Ibsen's *A Doll's House*. At the time Moore met him, he had cut all ties with his family and was living in Paris as an impoverished vagabond.

Moore went sailing on the Seine with Mallarmé, in a small boat which the poet had bought with the 500 francs he had received from the publishers for his poem, *L'Après-Midi d'un Faune*, and only Moore's innate seamanship, acquired as a boy on Lough Carra, with the Irish-speaking boatmen, saved the day when they were struck by a squall. Moore appears to have thrown himself up on to the weather gunwale and shouted to Mallarmé to let the main-sheet go, and subsequently bailed the boat out, using his elegant straw hat.

In the summer of 1877, while he was still working with de Lopez on *Luther*, Moore went to London to try to find a publisher for a book of verses he had written during intervals in the collaboration. His mother was at Moore Hall, so he stayed at a hotel in Trafalgar Square, found a publisher for his poems – Provost & Co, who had offices in Henrietta Street, in Covent Garden – and, through an introduction which Mallarmé had arranged, met the poet William O'Shaughnessy. At this period he dressed like a Frenchman and wore a pointed beard.

On his return to Paris, Moore made a conscious decision to look for a suitable café in which to spend the evenings: '. . . today the café is the quest of a young man in search of artistic education. But the cafés about the Odéon and the Luxembourg Gardens did not correspond to my need. I wearied of noisy students, the Latin Quarter seemed to me a little out of fashion; eventually I immigrated to Montmartre and continued my search along the Boulevard Extérieur. One evening I discovered the ideal café on the Place Pigalle . . .'

# SIX

# The Nouvelles Athènes

Moore always boasted that he never went to Oxford or Cambridge, and claimed that his university was the café known as the Nouvelles Athènes, on the corner of the Place Pigalle and the Rue Lepic: 'He who would know anything of my life must know something of the academy of the fine arts. Not the official stupidity you read of in the daily newspapers, but the real French academy, the café. The Nouvelles Athènes is a café on the Place Pigalle . . . With what strange, almost unnatural clearness do I see and hear – the white face of that café, the white nose of that block of houses stretching up to the Place, between two streets. I can see the incline of those two streets, and I know what shops are there; I can hear the glass door of the café grate on the sand as I open it. I recall the smell of every hour. In the morning that of eggs frizzling in butter, the pungent cigarettes, coffee and bad cognac; at five o'clock the fragrant odour of absinthe; and soon after the steaming soup ascends from the kitchen; and, as the evening advances, the mingled smells of cigarettes, coffee and weak beer. A partition, rising a few feet or more over the hats, separates the glass front from the main body of the café. The usual marble tables are there, and it is there we sat . . . until two o'clock in the morning.'

Even then they were reluctant to go: '. . . the grey moonlight on the Place, where we used to stand on the pavement, the shutters clanging up behind us, loath to separate, thinking of what we had left unsaid, and how much better we might have enforced our arguments.'

Moore claims he cannot remember whether it was instinct that guided him there, or whether he had met someone who told him that Manet spent his evenings in the café. It was popular with both writers and painters; at the period when Moore first found it, probably around the end of 1877 or the early part of 1878, Zola had just stopped using the café, though some of his disciples still went there, and it was used by Villiers de l'Isle Adam, Catulle Mendès, Duranty and Cabaner among the writers, and by almost all of the well-known painters of the period, Manet, Monet, Degas, Pissarro, Renoir and Sisley.

'One generation of *littérateurs* associates itself with painting, the next clings to music. The aim and triumph of the Realist [school of writing] were to force the pen to compete with the painter's brush and the engraver's needle in the description, let us say, of a mean street, just as the desire of a symbolist writer was to describe the vague but intense sensations of music so accurately that the reader would guess the piece he had selected for description, though it were not named in the text. We all entertained doubts regarding the validity of the art we practised, and envied the art of the painter, deeming it superior to literature . . . and I think there was a feeling of relief among us all when the painters came in. We raised ourselves up to welcome them – Manet, Degas, Renoir, Pissarro, Monet and Sisley; they were our masters . . . two tables in the right-hand corner were reserved for Manet and Degas and their circle of admirers.'

Moore admits his longing to be received into that circle, his longing to speak with Manet, whom he now recognised as a great new force in painting. He remembers the first time he saw him: '. . . though by birth and education essentially Parisian, there was something in his appearance and manner of speaking that often suggested an Englishman.'

He goes into more detail about Manet's appearance: 'Perhaps it was his dress – his clean-cut clothes and figure. Those square shoulders that swaggered as he went across the room, with the thin waist; the face, the beard, and the nose, satyr-like, shall I say?'

Happily, we also have a record of how Moore appeared to Manet. They became quite close friends, it seems, and Manet made several portrait sketches of Moore, including a portrait in pastels, about which Moore complained a lot. Manet did three portraits of him, one in full colour in pastels, which gave it a fresh and spontaneous appearance, an effect Manet was rarely able to achieve. The use of pastels also enabled Manet to complete the portrait in one sitting, which was unusual. Manet referred to George Moore's 'somewhat eccentric appearance' and reported that Moore was dissatisfied with his portrait and wanted 'a change here and an alteration there, but I wouldn't change a thing. Is it my fault that Moore has the look of a broken egg-yolk, or that the sides of his face are not aligned?'

Maybe we need another opinion. Here is Susan Mitchell, describing Moore as he looked when she first met him around the turn of the century: '. . . a man of middle height with an egg-shaped face and head, light yellow hair in perpetual revolt against the brush, a stout nose with thick nostrils, grey-green eyes, remarkable eyes, a mouth inclined to pettishness, lips thick in the middle as if a bee had stung them. He had champagne shoulders, and a somewhat thick, ungainly figure, but he moved about a room with a grace which is not of Dublin drawing-rooms . . . he was the only man in Dublin that walked fashionably. That strange word suits him; perhaps he is the last man of fashion in these islands. He wore an opera hat. Nobody in Dublin wears an opera hat, and when Moore put it like a crown on his yellow head, or crushed it fashionably under his arm, it acted on Dublin like an incantation. I remember my own instant homage.

'This description I feel to be inadequate, and I have summoned to my aid the folklore of Dublin. Dublin is a crater of epithet, and whenever George Moore is mentioned out of the crater boil up such expressions as an over-ripe gooseberry, a great big intoxicated baby, a satyr, a boiled ghost, a gosling . . .

'George Moore's is a face dear to the caricaturist and in itself at times a caricature; the yellow hair, the fat features, the sly smile, the malice, the vanity. But . . . let someone begin to discuss an idea and in a moment the contours change, the fat shapelessness falls away, the jaw lengthens, the brows straighten, a hawk-like keenness is in the look. One does not caricature this Moore; it is the face of the thinker, the man who handles ideas like a master.'

Manet's first portrait of Moore was described by the critics as like that of a drowned man, taken out of the water. Another portrait of Moore by Jacques-Emile Blanche was described by Moore himself as making him look like a drunken cabby, while Sickert's portrait of Moore was called 'an intoxicated mummy, a boorish goat . . .' Moore must have preferred Manet's pastel portrait of him, for he chose it as a frontispiece for his collected essays (1893) which he called *Modern Art*.

Duret, the historian of the French Impressionists, remembered Moore as a golden-haired fop, an aesthete long before Wilde became infamous: 'He came to Paris to study painting, but soon fell under the influence of the Naturalists and turned to writing. None of us thought anything of him as a writer, but he was welcome wherever he went, for his manners were amusing and his French very funny. He tried to shock and astonish people; but he was always the gentleman, and would never associate with those whom he thought to be below his rank as an Irish landlord.'

At the time he first met Manet, Moore was pretending to be correcting some proofs – they would have been the proofs of his first book of poems, *Flowers of Passion*, due to be published in the spring of 1878 – when Manet went over to him and asked whether the conversation in the café was not distracting his attention.

Moore replied, 'Not at all. I was thinking of your painting,' and he adds: 'It seems to me that we became friends at once; he invited me to his studio in the Rue d'Amsterdam, where his greatest works were painted.'

Manet, Moore claims, was born in what is known as refined society; he was a rich man. In dress and appearance, he was an aristocrat but, to be aristocratic in art, one had to avoid polite society. Manet was obliged for the sake of his genius, Moore believed, to separate himself from his class, obliged to spend his evenings in the Nouvelles Athènes, and his friends were all artists; however poor or miserable, if they were artists, they were welcome in Manet's studio.

During all the years that Moore knew Manet, the artist never sold a single picture. And, after Manet's death, the prices sank again, sank almost to nothing, and it seemed as if the world would never appreciate Manet. There was a time when Manet's paintings could be bought for twenty, thirty or forty pounds apiece . . .

'The glass door of the café grates upon the sand again. It is Degas, a round-shouldered man in a suit of pepper and salt. There is nothing very trenchantly French about him either, except the large necktie. His eyes are small, his words sharp, ironical, cynical . . . it was Degas who introduced the acrobat into art, and the *répasseuse*. Anyone, Degas said, can have talent when he is twenty-five; the thing is to have talent when you are fifty.'

Monet, being a landscape painter, only appeared in the Nouvelles Athènes after long absences; he would return suddenly from the country, bringing with him twenty or thirty canvasses, all equally perfect: 'He seemed to be doing always what he set out to do, whether it was a row of poplars seen in perspective against a grey sky, a view of the Seine with a bridge cutting the picture in equal halves, or a cottage shrouded in snow, with some low hill over yonder . . .'

Renoir, too, was always in the Nouvelle Athènes, and Moore remembered well the hatred with which he used to denounce the nineteenth century – the century in which, he used to say, there was no one who could make a piece of furniture or a clock that was beautiful and that was not a copy of an old one.

The evenings that Pissarro did not come to take his coffee in the Nouvelles Athènes were very rare indeed, Moore reports. He was there more frequently than Manet or Degas, and when they were there he just sat listening, approving of their ideas, joining in the conversation quietly.

And as for Moore himself? He had been mentioned to Manet as a young English poet – in those days, no distinction was made between England and Ireland, certainly not in Paris – and his first book of poems, *Flowers of Passion*, had been published in the spring of 1878. When he was discussing this project with de Lopez, as they climbed up the Rue Notre Dame de Lorette and along the Rue des Martyrs, de Lopez suggested that Moore should choose subjects that would astonish the British public by their originality, and Moore came up with the idea that he should write about a young man's love for a beautiful corpse.

No one could take Moore's first publication very seriously. Clearly, he is setting out to shock; not only by writing a love poem to a beautiful corpse, but by expanding on a theme he borrowed from Shelley: the incestuous love of a brother for his sister.

It would be tiresome to go into any great detail about this book, but it would be a pity not to glance, in passing, at his first efforts as a writer. And it is only fair and realistic to add that later in life, when he had taught himself how to write, Moore had no higher opinion than anybody else of his early poems. He dismissed the two early books of poems as 'sterile eccentricities, dead flowers that could not be galvanised into any semblance of life, passionless in all their passion'.

Some extracts from his 'Ode to a Dead body': 'Ay verily, thou art a piteous thing,/So awful is death's sting./Poor shameful lips! That never knew a kiss/Of innocence, I wis.' 'Wis' is in the dictionary; it means 'know', or 'believe', partly, according to Chambers, 'from a misunderstanding of the adv. iwis (q.v.) as I wis, partly a new present from the past tense wist.' It is still a very odd word to use. There is worse to follow.

He goes on: 'Poor breasts! Whose nipples sins alone have fed./Poor desecrated head!/Thou hast no lover now, Why have they gone/And left thee here alone?'

In 'Ginevra', he talks about the fact that 'custom's bitter mouth has cursed the love that might, between brother and sister, grow,' and continues: 'Our father first encouraged our sweet love,/But when at length the whole truth dawned on him,/He tried by threats and prayers to wean us from/What he did blindly term unholy passion.'

His use and abuse of the English language is extremely odd even for a man who claims that he never learnt to speak English properly at school, and who had begun to speak in French as soon as he started to think about things. Here are a few words plucked at random from his first book of verse: dernful (spirit of my dream); fluctuant (of the tide); interlying (of space); mewards or meward (meaning towards me); and tedded (the tedded grass). They all exist but what other writer would use such awkwardly unfamiliar words?

He attempts internal rhymes with disastrous effect: 'The breath from her mouth is like air from the south/it kisses my face and eyes,/And the touch of her hair, which falls everywhere/in restless harmonies.'

Or this, in a poem called 'Annie': 'I dare not raise my face to look at ye [thee, surely?]/Ye [your?] years still dreaming in futurity/ Ye [the?] barren days and fruitless nights unborn.'

Some of it is pure doggerel: 'Believe me, Annie,/'Tis want of money/That forces us apart;/It is not any/Capriciousness of heart./ Pity me, Annie.'

This particular poem gets worse and worse as it goes on, and it ends: 'We shall wake to laugh or weep,/We shall know if death be deep,/Or we shall sleep perhaps a calm and dreamless sleep,/And men will shed their tears,/Aye, for a million years,/Till each in turn his burden lays at this goal of fears.'

The book ends with a poem which is translated from the French of Catulle Mendès, whom he met in the Nouvelle Athènes: 'My soul e'er dreams, in such a dream as this is,/Visions of perfume, moonlight and the blisses/of sexless love, and strange unreachéd kisses.'

He may be on home ground here, talking of sexless love and strange unreachéd kisses.

When the book appeared in print in England, it was greeted by an article by Edmund Yates in *The World*, entitled 'The Bestial Bard'. It began: 'The author of these poems should be whipped at the cart's tail, while the book is being burnt in the market-place by the common hangman.' It is hard to think that anybody could have taken it seriously enough to waste valuable space attacking it, and to call him 'the bestial bard' on the head of such flimsy stuff seems grossly unjustified. Nevertheless, during his next visit to London, Mrs William Rossetti, a sister of Oliver Madox Brown, his friend from Barthe's art classes in Limerston Street, advised him to withdraw the book – not on the grounds that it was bad poetry but because she considered it grossly immoral – which, surprisingly, Moore agreed to do.

During the early part of his Nouvelles Athènes period, Moore was still sharing the apartment in the Rue de la Tour des Dames with Marshall, who wanted to accompany Moore and meet the Impressionist painters they had ridiculed together a year or so earlier with the other art students. Once again, Lewis Marshall was getting on Moore's nerves: 'I should have done better to have left him in the Mont Rouge to get his living as a workman . . . and my spirits rose mountains high against him. An old man of the sea, I said, whom I cannot shake off . . . He was well enough in Julien's studio or in the Beaux-Arts or in English or American society, but he would seem shallow and superficial in the Nouvelles Athènes, and I always avoided taking him there.'

Nevertheless, he finally allowed Marshall to persuade him to take him along one evening, and to his surprise and chagrin Marshall made quite a hit with Degas, 'who very graciously invited us to sit at his table, and talked to us of his art, addressing himself as often to Lewis as he did to me. He opened his whole mind to us, beguiled by Lewis's excellent listening, until the waiter brought him a dish of almonds and raisins. Then a lull came, and Lewis said, leaning across the table: "I think, Monsieur Degas, you will agree with me that, more than any other artist, Jules Lefèbvre sums up all the qualities that an artist should possess."

'My heart misgave me,' Moore reports, 'and Degas's laughter did not console me, nor his words whispered in my ear, as he left: *"Votre ami est très fort . . . Il m'a fait monter l'echelle comme personne."* And a few days afterwards in the Rue Pigalle, he said: *"Comment va votre ami? Ah! Celui-là est d'une force."* '

This was the last straw: 'He must go, and at once, and as soon as I returned home I begged him to leave me . . . and a few days afterwards the concierge mentioned to my great surprise that Monsieur had left and had paid her the few francs that he owed her. Which he may well have done, because Moore later discovered that, before he finally left, Lewis had borrowed a hundred francs from one of Moore's lady friends, whom he describes, fairly typically, as 'his lover'. Lewis continued to paint and enjoyed some fashionable success.

Meanwhile, back in Ireland, a new leader had emerged. Charles Stewart Parnell was a wealthy landowner with radical ideas, who had arrived at the same conclusion as Moore's father, George Moore the Politician, had reluctantly reached just before his death: that the power of the landlords in Ireland would have to be broken. Parnell's father, Sir John Parnell, had refused a peerage he had been offered in 1800, in return for a vote for the Union, and his mother was American.

Parnell succeeded in getting the Liberal Party to adopt Home Rule for Ireland officially, as part of their election platform; but his principal accomplishment was the destruction of the power of the landlords. He achieved this by two means. By continually obstructing the business of the British Parliament at Westminster, he succeeded in drawing a good deal of attention – not all of it favourable by any means – to the Irish Question, and with Michael Davitt organised the Land League, a sort of trades union of Irish tenants. It was founded in Westport, County Mayo, just seventeen miles from Moore Hall, in August 1879, grew into a national movement, and marked the outbreak of open warfare between landlords and tenants, which spread throughout the whole country though nowhere was it waged so violently as in County Mayo, where George Moore had his estates.

League members would offer a greatly reduced rent to their landlords; and, if the landlord refused to accept the reduced rent, all League members would withhold all rent payments. The landlords normally replied by using their favourite weapon, eviction; the Land League would then turn to their second weapon, the boycott. This got its name from the first man against whom it was successfully employed: Captain Charles Cunningham Boycott, who was land agent for Lord Erne's estates at Lough Mask, County Mayo, a neighbour and close friend of both Moore and his father.

The boycott was very simple and very effective. When a landlord was boycotted, the entire neighbourhood would refuse to have anything whatever to do with him or his agent, or his family, or his servants or his staff; and any tenant who took land from which another had been evicted was himself boycotted. Nobody would work for a man who was boycotted, or serve him in any way, or farm his land, or feed his animals, or even bury his dead.

It was crude, but it worked. A series of Land Acts was passed, which transferred the power to fix rents from the landlords to the courts and gave tenants total security of tenure so long as they paid the rent fixed by the court. Rents in Ireland went down by an average of four shillings in the pound.

When the Land War broke out in Mayo, Moore's agent, who happened also to be his uncle – his name was Joseph Blake – wrote to Moore in Paris to say that he was afraid Moore was in deep financial trouble, because of the refusal of his tenants to pay their rents; Blake had already given Moore an advance on rents which it would now be impossible to collect, and it would be risking his own life to serve eviction orders on tenants who refused to pay their rents in the existing climate in County Mayo.

Moore's first reaction to the news from Mayo, recollected in *Confessions*, was violent and unreasonable: 'That some wretched farmers . . . should refuse to starve, that I may not be deprived of my *demi-tasse* at Tortoni's, that I may be forced to leave this beautiful retreat, my cat and my python – monstrous.'

Moore left Paris without saying goodbye to anybody, apart from Marshall; he left the apartment in the Rue de la Tour des Dames owing his concierge 100 francs – and presumably leaving it to the concierge to dispose of the Persian cat and the python – and hurried to London to meet Joe Blake. It was the autumn of 1879 and it was the end of Moore's Paris Period.

As a sort of coda to this episode, Moore includes in his *Confessions* a letter from a woman who had clearly been an intimate of his in Paris (from internal evidence, if the letter is genuine and not composed by Moore himself, as it probably was, she was married, and rich); and who attended the auction of all the belongings he had left behind him in the apartment: 'I was there the night before the sale. I looked through the books, taking notes of those I intended to buy – those which we used to read together when the snow lay high about the legs of that poor faun in *terre cuit*, that laughed among the frosty *boulingrins* which I instantly destroyed. You should not be so careless; I wonder how it is that men are always careless about their letters . . .

'So now that pretty little retreat in the Rue de la Tour des Dames is ended forever for you and me. We shall not see the faun in *terre cuit* again; I was going to see him the other day, but the street is so steep; my coachman advised me to spare the horse's hind legs. I believe it is the steepest street in Paris. [It is not, by any means, but Moore was writing for a public that did not know Paris and would take his, or his lover's, word for it.] And your luncheon parties, how I did enjoy them, and how Fay did enjoy them, too; and what I risked, short-sighted as I am, picking my way from the tramcar down to that little out-of-the-way street! Men never appreciate the risks women run for them. But to leave my letters lying about – I cannot forgive that.'

And in case one might be tempted to suspect that Moore made it all up to support the fantasy that he really was a dab with the ladies (and you would indeed suspect that, even if only because it seems strange that the lady, whoever she was, should write in a style so similar to Moore's own, even down to the endless successions of semi-colons), he then includes – or inserts – a thought intended perhaps to give the whole thing a ring of authenticity: 'I wish you would not make foolish remarks about men that *tout-Paris* considers the cleverest. It does not matter so much with me, but people laugh at you behind your back, and that is not nice for me.'

A natural first reaction to this is that Moore would never let himself down to his reading public, not to mention the much greater and more important public which posterity represented to him, by making himself look ridiculous in this way; but a second reaction is that this is exactly what Moore would have done: make himself look a little bit ridiculous, if he can, in the process, forestall someone else from making him look extremely ridiculous.

# SEVEN

# George Moore,
# Absentee Landlord

George Moore's first reaction to the news from Ballinafad seems to have been dictated by pure panic. He began by cursing his peasant tenants for causing him so much inconvenience, and hurried back to London to meet his land agent, Blake. They met in the smoking room of Morley's Hotel, where Moore was staying. Blake explained that Moore owed him several thousand pounds: this was money he had already advanced to Moore, and which he had expected to be able to collect from the tenants, but because of the Land League agitations the tenants were refusing to pay any rent at all unless the landlords agreed to an immediate reduction of thirty per cent. With the tenants in their present angry mood, it would be dangerous to attempt to collect any rent from them.

It now was obviously necessary for Moore to go to Ireland and negotiate with the tenants himself. Although his first reaction to their demands for a reduction in the rents had been anger, as soon as he had slowed down enough to think about the situation, he discovered that he had already absorbed a good deal of his father's conviction that the day of the landlord was over in Ireland, and all his own thoughts on the subject tended to lead him to the conclusion that it was unfair from a human point of view, and unsound from an economic one, that rich families with land should live entirely off the rents – and in effect off the labours – of their starving peasants, contributing nothing themselves to the wealth or prosperity of the community.

A few days later, he crossed over to Dublin, where his mother had taken a house for the Royal Dublin Society's Horse Show, and in his mother's house he again met his uncle and agent, Joe Blake, who was demanding an immediate payment of £3,000. Moore disputed the amount and accused Blake of fiddling the accounts.

Moore spent the autumn and winter off and on at Moore Hall with his sister Nina, and picked Tom Ruttledge of Cornfield to be Blake's successor as his land agent. To pay off the debt to Blake, he raised a further mortgage of £3,000 on his property, and, to support himself until he had sorted things out with the tenants and had started to make some money from his writing, he sold some timber from the woods around Moore Hall. He then went on a protracted tour of his estates, visiting the tenants upon whom the whole family until then had been dependent for their rather grandiose lifestyle. Unlike many other absentee landlords in the area, Moore was not in any personal danger from his tenants, because of his father's extremely good relations with them, and because he had continued his father's practice of avoiding evictions. He must, however, have presented a bizarre sight to them in what he calls an 'exuberant' necktie, a small top-hat, high-heeled shoes and wide trousers which he wore even when he went shooting, though he won the grudging admiration both of the peasants and of his peers by shooting more accurately than anyone else.

In a series of articles which he wrote first in French, and which were initially published in a French magazine – the essays were later collected together and published in book form as *Parnell and His Island* in 1887 – he describes his reactions during the course of this tour.

The book begins with him in Dublin, glorying in the magnificent view of Dublin Bay from somewhere in the hills above Dalkey: 'This is Dalkey, a suburb of Dublin. From where I stand, I look down on a cup of blue water; it lies two hundred feet below me, like a great, smooth mirror; it lies beneath the blue sky as calm, as mysteriously still, as an enchanted glass in which we may read the secrets of the future . . . No town in the world has more beautiful surroundings than Dublin. Seeing Dalkey, one dreams of Monte Carlo, or, better still, of the hanging gardens of Babylon, of marble balustrades, of white fountains, of innumerable yachts, of courts of love, and of sumptuous pleasure palaces; but alas, what meets the eye are broken-down villas. The white walls shine in the sun and deceive you, but if you approach, you will find a front-door where the paint is peeling, and a ruined garden.

'And in such ruins, life languishes here. The inhabitants of the villas are, for the most part, landlords whose circumstances have forced them to shut up their houses, and come here to economise; or, they may belong to a second class of landlords, widows living on jointures paid by the eldest son, or mortgages upon money placed by them or by their ancestors upon the land.'

Moore had now reached the shattering conclusion that the easy life that he and his family had led had been based solely and entirely on the incomes they derived from the land, and that in fact all the wealth in Ireland came from the land, and from the unending, grinding labour of the miserable peasants.

'For in Ireland there is nothing but land; with the exception of a few distillers and brewers in Dublin, who live upon the drunkenness of the people, there is no way in Ireland of getting money, except through the peasant.

'In Ireland, the passage, direct and brutal, from the horny hands of the peasant, to the delicate hands of the proprietor, is terribly suggestive of serfdom. In England the landlord lays out the farm and builds the farm buildings; in Ireland, he does absolutely nothing. He gives the bare land to the peasant and sends his agent in to collect the half-yearly rent; in a word, he allows the peasant to keep him in ease and luxury.

'In Ireland, every chicken eaten, every glass of champagne drunk, every silk dress trailed in the street, every rose worn at a ball, comes straight out of the peasant's cabin.'

Other things had started to worry Moore about life in Ireland, among them Dublin Castle, the seat and symbol of British power: 'To describe the Castle it is only necessary to compare it with an immense police barracks. It is devoid of all architecture, the brick walls are as bald as a police document; everybody, even to the red coats of the sentinels, reminds you of the red tape with which these documents are tied. The Castle rises like a upas tree amid ruins and death; the filth of the surrounding streets is extreme. The Castle dominates the Liffey – a horrible canal or river flowing between two embankments. Curious characteristic details; between the bridges great sea-gulls fly back and forwards with a mechanical regularity, diving from time to time after the rubbish which the current bears away to the sea.'

Moore is appalled at the system by which girls are presented at the Castle; he was to work his disgust at this marriage mart out of his sytem later in a novel called *Drama in Muslin*, and, later, simply *Muslin*, though he himself always thought of it and referred to it as *The Galway Girls*.

'They cannot kiss the hand of the Viceroy,' he remarked, 'as they kiss the hand of the Queen at Buckingham Palace, and so instead, the Viceroy kisses them, and that is it.' They were then on the market. Their mothers organised balls for them, usually at the Shelbourne Hotel, where the better-off families stayed for the duration of the season which lasted from shortly before Christmas until around Easter and was based on the first 'court' held in Ireland, in Dublin Castle, then a wooden pallisade, by King Henry II in 1171. There was a second, shorter season, based on the Royal Dublin Society's Horse Show in August and all the hunt balls held in association with it. In the period Moore was writing about, it cost, he says, about £3 [£150 today] per person per week to stay at the Shelbourne; today you would be lucky to get away with £175 for dinner, bed and breakfast.

And the real problem was that there were not nearly enough men, ghastly as most of them were, to go round. 'And ah,' said a girl with a terrible brogue to Moore, 'the worst of it is that the stock is for iver increasing; ivery year we are growing more and more numerous, and the men seem to be getting fewer.'

Towards the turn of the century, Moore reckoned that the girls outnumbered the men by a proportion of about three to one; and the competition for husbands was extremely severe. 'I know lots of girls, and very nice girls, too, who have been going up [for the season] for six or seven years, and have not been able to pull it off,' and he quotes one girl as saying, 'Nowadays a man won't look at you unless you have at least £2,000 [£100,000 today] behind you.'

Moore then left Dublin for a tour of County Mayo. At one stage he seems to have picked up with a party of bright young things who went out for a picnic which included a visit to his own house, Moore Hall, on Carra Lake. He inquired of one of his companions to whom the house belonged and was told: 'Oh, some mad fellow who lives in Paris, and writes French poetry. He never comes near the place.' Another girl was even more confidently reassuring: 'Pa is his agent and we can do what we like in his house.'

'As we drove to the picnic,' Moore writes in *Parnell and His Island*, 'we caught glimpses of the lake, the grey light of the beautiful mere-like lake flashing between the broken lines of the rocky coast and the sloping ridges of the moorland.'

A little later, he escapes from his smart friends, and, perhaps for the first time in his life, examines very closely and dispassionately the hovels and cabins in which his tenants and their children are obliged to live out their dismal lifespan.

'Down in the wet, below the edge of the bog, lies the village. The cabins are built out of rough stones, without mortar. Each is divided into two, rarely three compartments, and the windows are not so large as those of a railway carriage. And in these dens, a whole family, a family consisting of husband and wife and grandfather and grandmother, and from eight to ten children, herd as best they can.

'The cabins are roofed with green sods cut from the nearest field . . . the floor is broken in places and the rain collects in the hollows and has to be swept out every morning. A large pig, covered with lice, feeds out of a trough placed in the middle of the floor and the beast from time to time approaches and sniffs at a child sleeping in a cot by the fireside . . . Of cookery, they have no idea whatever; there is not a single plate or kitchen utensil of any kind in the hovel except the black iron pot that hangs over the fire. The mother, a great, strong creature fit for work in the fields, dressed in a red petticoat that scarcely falls below her knees – you see the thick, shapeless red legs – lifts the black pot off the fire and carries it to the threshold, where one of the children holds the sieve, and the water is strained off. Then the pig is hunted under the bed, and the family eat their dinner out of the sieve – cold water from the well washed down this repast.'

But that is by no means the worst. He passes on then to north Mayo, where some of his other estates were situated: 'So we enter on a new country, a country bleaker even than the one we left. No landlords live here, they only come to collect the rent.

'We pass a dwelling place that strikes me as being the farthest possible limit to which human degradation may be extended. Into the bank formed by the cutting of the peat, a few poles have been thrust, and on these poles sods of earth have been laid. The front and the sides are partly built up with soft, black mud. And in this foul den, a woman has brought up five children, and in the swamp a few potatoes are cultivated, but the potato crop has failed this year, and the family are living on the yellow meal the parish authorities allow them. They are boiling it now in the black iron pot and will probably eat it out of the pot, for the hut contains nothing but the pot and the straw on which the family will sleep.'

And, while he is there, he watches an eviction overseen by a Miss Barrett. 'Dressed as a man [and living] in a dilapidated house surrounded by thousands of acres from which the peasants have been driven and which are now stocked with herds of cattle – she looks forward to an eviction as men did to a cock-fight in the old days.'

'Hundreds of people have assembled, there is some blowing of horns on the hillsides and at first it seems as if the police will have to charge the people. But, having been fired on lately, they are frightened and allow themselves to be driven back with the butt-ends of rifles and the little army is posted about the wretched hut from which a human family is to be driven. So horrible is the place that it seems a mockery, a piece of ferocious cynicism to suggest that the possession of it is about to be contested, and that, to restore it to its rightful owner, an army has to be gathered together. It lies under the potato field, and the space between bank and wall is a stream of mud and excrement. The incessant rain has rotted the straw in the roof, and at one end it droops, ready to slip at every moment. The weak walls lean this way and that, and their foundations are clearly sinking away into the wet bog. Hard by the dung heap, in front of the door, where the pig strives to find a place dry enough to lie in, the mud and filth have lapsed into a green liquid where some ducks are padding . . . only the voice of a child crying is heard.

'The police try to gain entrance – they throw stones at the door, and to keens from within the house, and the bawling of the children and the jeers of the peasants on the dung-heap and on the road, the police force their way in – the father, covered only in a pair of trousers, rushes out to defend his house and is seized by the policemen: the iron pot, a few plates and three logs of wood that serve as seats, a chair, a cradle, some straw on which the whole family sleep are seized and carried away, watched by the wife in her red petticoat and her six half-naked children . . . meanwhile the police are making a large hole in the roof, the rafters are being torn up and a padlock is put on the door.'

These people, he says, are called small farmers; they possess (that is to say, they rent) from three to ten acres of land for which they pay twenty shillings to twenty-five shillings an acre. In these fields, not divided by hedges as in England, but by miserable, loose stone walls, they cultivate oats and potatoes. Never is a pot of flowers seen in the cottage window of an Irish Celt. 'You want to know what Ireland is like?' he bursts out. 'Ireland is the smell of paraffin oil! The country exhales the damp, flaccid, evil smell of poverty that is of the earth, earthy. And this smell hangs about every cabin, it rises out of the chimneys with the smoke of peat, it broods upon the dung-heap and creeps along the deep black bogholes that line the roadway, and the thin meagre aspect of the marshy fields and hungry hills reminds you of this smell of poverty – the smell of something sick to death of poverty.'

The Irish peasants, he muses, are the most moral people in the world: 'Their morality only fails them when the landlord covets one of their daughters, and that custom, being a survival of the past, is rapidly dying out . . . If you bear this in mind and if you take into account that the Irish peasant has lived for centuries in a damp, miserable hole from which he was expelled if he did not give up his daughter, or if he did not vote as the agent told him to, you will begin to understand why he is so grossly superstitious and stupidly improvident, and why he breeds like a newt in the slime. The Irish race is one that has been forgotten and left behind in a boghole; it smells of wet earth, its face seems as if made of it, and its ideas are moist and dull, and as sterile as peat.

'If an Irish girl gets pregnant and the young man continues to deny the seduction, and when at last it becomes clear that he cannot be forced into marrying, the fallen woman is driven from the hearth she disgraced and told to make her way to the workhouse, the proper place for her to bring her bastard brat into the world . . .

'The sheep generally dies, and the calf often dies, and if the milk does not fail, the family lives upon the yellow meal which is bought with the money the daughter sends home from America, where she works as a kitchen maid, and the money the son sends home from Manchester where he works as a barman in a public house.

'And here I must say a word in praise of the conduct of Irish children towards their parents. Never do they forget them; I have known sons and daughters who have been away in America for ten, yes and fifteen years, and who regularly send home their savings to the old couple in Ireland.'

He refers to Moore Hall as Lake Mount, and part of the account of the journey takes the form of an interview between Moore, in the role of a reporter perhaps, certainly as a stranger and 'the mysterious being of whom nothing seems to be known except that he lives in France and writes French poetry'. He even describes his own appearance at this stage: 'His tiny hat, his long hair, his Parisian-cut clothes and his Capoul-like beard give him a very strange and anomalous air. On the Boulevard he might pass muster, but where he stands, he is an *être de féerie*.'

Speaking again as the reporter, he goes on: 'He told me his story – that on the refusal of his agent to supply any more money, he had come over from Paris with a few pounds and a volume of Baudelaire and Verlaine in his pocket. Of all the latest tricks that had been played in French verse, he was thoroughly master; of the size, situation and condition of his property, he knew no more than I did.'

Then, lapsing once more into his own voice, returns to a description of the place: 'The great stables once filled with thirty or forty racehorses are now for the most part but formless masses of brick and mortar; here a bit of roofing still holds on, and there a young ash-tree forces its way through the rack out of which the winner of the Chester Cup once drew his hay. And the great wide green path of the racecourse that wound in and out of the woods and fields is now overgrown and lost . . . the gate lodge is in ruins, the drive is weed-grown and covered in cow dung and herds of cattle wander through the woods and feed along the terraces.'

Moore offered his tenants a twenty per cent reduction all round; the tenants had been demanding a thirty per cent reduction but finally agreed to settle for one of twenty-five per cent. His final summing up of the whole situation: 'For in Ireland you think of border forays, wild chieftains, and tribes dressed in skins. The graft of civilisation that the Anglo-Saxon has for some seven hundred years striven to bind upon the island has never caught, but whether the Celt will be able to civilise himself when he gets Home Rule, I do not pretend to say. At present, he is a savage, but ill-suited to ply the industry of farming which the law forces as the alternative of starvation upon him.'

And he talks about landlords under police protection, never stirring out except when preceded by a car full of policemen armed to the teeth, with another following to guard against attacks from the rear from the Land Leaguers. The landlord's own property probably yields him no more than £1,000 a year, which is mortgaged to the extent of £700. That £700 must be paid regardless and any further reductions have to come from the remaining £300.

'You would not think it easy to enjoy a shooting party with a policeman walking behind to prevent a Land Leaguer from shooting you while you try to shoot the pheasant – you would not think it easy to enjoy a flirtation with a policeman watching to see that your kissing was not interrupted by a Land Leaguer sticking a knife in you from behind.'

But, he goes on, the landlord has some consolation, for he has one other source of income: he can act as a land agent for absentee landlords; some were collecting rents to the extent of £50,000 a year, for which they were paid a flat five per cent, though collection of so vast a sum of money from such very poor people means the unpleasant business of serving of writs, securing evictions and the constant danger of being shot.

A fair rent, he says, is defined as the sum that remains when the peasant has taken from the price he can raise for his wretched produce what little he needs to keep himself and his family alive in the squalor in which they live; imagine trying to collect rents on the Champs-Elysées or anywhere else in the world on that basis. And the reductions in rents achieved by Parnell and the Land Leaguers did not, he believed, actually benefit the peasants in any way; the money saved all went on subscriptions to the Land League and other political parties, or to the support of evicted members of the League, and what was left went over the counter in the public house. He foresees a time when the native Irish Celts will become peasant proprietors of their own lands, when, he believes, they will immediately start to borrow from the banks and usurers, using their lands as security; he remains convinced that, if an Irish Parliament sitting in Dublin were to be set up, '. . . within five years there would be even more evictions being carried out by order of the banker and the usurer than are carried out by the landlords today'.

While he was in Mayo, Moore renewed the acquaintance of some people he knew in his childhood: among them, Dan, a local landlord and horse trainer, who lived with a peasant mistress, and who used to go racing with Moore and his father. 'Dan. Aren't you going to see your horse run?' he remembered asking him as a boy. 'He'll run the same whether I'm looking at him or not,' was the taciturn reply.

It was never any use asking Dan questions about his horses. 'There he is, quite well, but whether he can gallop or not, I can't tell you. I've nothing to try him with. There he is; go and look at him.' At the post he might advise the Moores to put a fiver on him, if he wasn't in too great a hurry. 'Is your own money on him, Dan?' one of his cousins would cry, and Dan would only turn to say: 'It's all right,' and from his words they guessed, and guessed rightly, that the horse had been backed to win seven or eight thousand pounds (£350,000 or £400,000 today), enough to keep his Dunamon stables going for the next four or five years.

When he called on Dan, the door was opened by his mistress Bridget, and Moore thought it worth putting on record that, despite the fact that he found her very pretty, he refrained from kissing Bridget, as if that were a matter upon which he was to be congratulated.

'The reason I refrained from kissing Dan's mistress was because it has always been the tradition in the West that my family never yielded to such indulgences as peasant mistresses or the esuriences of hot punch: nobody but Archbishop McHale was allowed punch in my father's house; the common priests who dined there at election times had to lap claret. And, proud of my family's fortitudes, I refrained from Bridget.'

The feminists could have had a field day here. As the local landlord, the young master was convinced that it was his right to make love to any servant girl if it pleased him to do so, even if she happened to be the mistress of a neighbour and friend of the family. He muses on Bridget's fate: 'Any day . . . another girl may be brought up from the village, and then Bridget will be seen less and less frequently upstairs. She'll receive ten or twelve pounds a year for cleaning and cooking, and perhaps after a little while drift away like a piece of broken furniture into the outhouses.'

But she didn't; though Dan never married her, he died in her arms. Other servant girls in the area were not so lucky. Moore makes the point that a run of bad luck with the horses might well have forced Dan into marrying one of the neighbouring gentry's daughters, for the sake of the money that would come his way in the form of the bride's dowry; and, if that happened, he would have had to get rid of Bridget somehow. He recalls an occasion when a prospective bride's relations, in a similar predicament, gathered around the fire to debate the fate of the peasant mistress and her children. They were all at sixes and sevens until a pious old lady muttered: 'Let him emigrate them.' Whereupon, Moore says, they all rubbed their shins complacently: the problem was solved.

In those days it was quite common for gentlemen who lived with peasant girls and had children by them to 'emigrate' the lot to America, or elsewhere, whence the sons frequently returned, howling for their fathers' blood.

With others of his friends, Moore went sailing on Lough Carra and visited an island on which there were some late pagan and early

Christian ruins, including a church built, he says, by St Patrick's brother, who was a hermit.

Here is his description of his last evening by the lake: 'The scene is now supernaturally still. The day dies in pale greys and soft pink tints and harmonies in mauve more delicate and elusive than the most beautiful Japanese watercolour; the lake hangs like a grey veil behind the dark pinewood through which we wander, making our way to the yacht . . . and we look on the long wavy lines of mountains that enclose the horizon . . . our eyes follow the black flight of the cormorant along the smooth greyness of the water and our souls are filled and stilled with a sadness that is at one with the knowledge that the dear day we have lived through is now a day that is over and done . . . on the following day I started back for Dublin. The carriage was full of Irish Members and American agitators. They denounce the injustice of the English and proclaim the sweet Irish peace that will follow Home Rule.'

# EIGHT

# Teaching Himself to Write

When Moore returned from Ireland in the spring of 1881, to settle down in London and learn to become a writer, he already had three published works behind him: *Flowers of Passion*, his first book of poems; the play *Martin Luther* which he had written in collaboration with Bernard de Lopez in Paris and which had been published by Remington & Co in London in 1879; and a poem which he wrote while at Moore Hall with his sister Nina in the late summer of 1879 which had been published by the *Spectator* on December 11, 1880, his first appearance in an English periodical. While living at Moore Hall, he had also started work again on a novel, with a central character based roughly on his Paris friend Lewis Marshall, but he found it very tough going for a variety of reasons, principally because he was not, at this stage, fluent in English.

*Martin Luther* was never reviewed; certainly it was never performed, and hardly surprisingly. It has settings ranging from the Piazza del Popolo in Rome, the Vatican Palace, the monastery of Wittenberg and the Diet of Worms, and a cast of characters which includes half the Cardinals in Europe, the Elector Frederick the Wise of Saxony and the Emperor Charles V as well as Pope Julius II and, of course, Martin Luther himself.

The play opens with the sale of some sacred relics in the Piazza del Popolo in Rome, and Luther's first line – which is also the first line of the play – runs as follows: 'At last! I stand in Rome!'

While standing there in Rome, Luther cannot help overhearing two monks discussing the Mass. 'Mass does not take long to read/I read it yesterday in thirteen minutes and a half,' one remarks, and the other replies that during the Mass he had remarked to the host, 'But bread thou art/and bread thou ne'er can cease to be', whereupon the first one says that he addressed the wine thus: 'But wine thou art, and wine/Thou never can cease to be/Till I have drunk of thee.' Luther remonstrates with them: 'God wot, such things are little fit for jest,' and they reply, mocking him: 'Such innocence/is tender as a child's first skin/It soon is rubbed away.'

From a guide called Zoppino, Luther learns that there are seven churches in Rome where you can buy indulgences for all of your sins, even if they happen to include both matricide and patricide, and that there is a priest in Rome called Salvino, who is openly living an incestuous life with his three nieces, and a Cardinal Stricca who always chooses for his palace pages 'the beautifullest youths in Christendom.' All these discoveries are made within the first three or four pages of the drama and Luther laments: 'O Rome, thou art a den of thieves; my soul/Is sick to loathing of thy infamy.'

Luther visits the Papal Court only to discover that audiences cost money and when, as a poor and honest Augustine monk, he puts his case to the usher, the man replies that he 'cannot afford affairs that give me no return'.

He castigates – all in blank verse, of a sort – this infamous city where he sees 'Statues of Venus and the Virgin Mother/receiving here an equal reverence.'

Like St Paul on the road to Damascus – and indeed like Moore himself, later, on the Royal Hospital Road, Chelsea – Luther hears a voice from deep inside himself uttering one word: Reformation! 'Yes, reformation was the word/The word was God/The reformation of all things/Of scandals and of infamies/Abuses that cry aloud Reform!'

And the scene concludes with him addressing himself thus:

'Friar Martin Luther! What! So weak and frail/Can I go forth into the direful fight/Against the prelates of the Church, against/The Kings, the Rulers of the World! Why dream/These dreams impossible. What enterprise/My soul would undertake! To over-throw/This Titan, this Colossus – yet why not/Make the attempt, tho' it be in vain, if it/Be in thy name, O desecrated Christ!/For thou wilt give me David's stone to sling/Against this monster of iniquity.'

Then there is a scene involving a nun called Catherine (and Moore, typically, sometimes spells her with a 'C' and sometimes with a 'K') who approaches him in the woods: 'And turned to himward [Moore for sure, there is no chance that de Lopez penned that line] like/a flower turns into the light.' She confesses her love for Martin Luther without realising that the Augustinian monk to whom she is confessing is none other than Luther himself.

As a direct consequence of his attempt to carry the Reformation into effect, initially by attacking the sale of indulgences, and eventually by an attack on the whole doctrinal system of the Church of Rome in a treatise called *On the Babylonish Captivity of the Church of God*, he is excommunicated, whereupon he proceeds to burn the Papal Bull. During the course of his trial at the Diet of Worms, we are treated to a sample of some of his views about the Catholic Church in verse: 'Luther, the issue of this trial doth/Depend as much upon yourself as us;' and 'Who hostile are to youward; turn this side.' Luther refuses to recant and proceeds to list various (fairly) recent accretions to the Christian dogma, including holy water (from 121 AD); Mass in Latin (348); Purgatory (593); the obligatory celibacy of priests (1015) and Confession (1200).

Nobody could possibly deny that the examples quoted from Moore's first book of poems, *Flowers of Passion*, or the scenes referred to from his* play *Martin Luther* are appalling.

---

* I say *his* play because I find it hard to believe that Bernard de Lopez, co-author with Dumas, *père et fils*, with Gautier and Gérard dé Nerval of countless successful collaborations, and constructor of 160 plays, could have agreed to so naive and

Moore's second book of verse, *Pagan Poems*, was published in 1881, the year he settled in London. To make up a decent-sized volume from what new poems he had written while living in Moore Hall in 1879–80, he was obliged to include some extracts from *Flowers of Passion*, and indeed there is not a hair's breadth of difference between them, so far as quality is concerned. Joseph Hone remarks laconically that Moore's second book of verse failed to attract even hostile attention, and was soon scrapped and sold as waste paper; though he does add that its publication earned Moore the nickname of 'Pagan Moore' when he returned to London.

The immensity of Moore's achievement in refashioning himself as a writer can easily be judged by comparing the extracts quoted from his first book of poems and *Martin Luther* with the extracts from his collection of writings about Ireland, originally called *Terre d'Irlande* and published in France in *Le Figaro* in 1887. Everything Moore wrote in the period between his discovery that he was never going to be a painter and about 1883 was disastrous: derivative in style, full of the most excruciating clichés, and utterly banal in thought content. Yet, by applying himself with a single-minded ferocity, he devoured modern English and French literature, adapted what suited him to his own purposes, taught himself to speak and to write English not just fluently, but with a superb style, and within ten years had become not only a popular author of best-selling novels but also a writer of subtlety and imagination capable of changing – which he did, and well in advance of James Joyce – the whole future pattern and range and voice of English literature. And not only that, he also taught himself to think.

It was a most remarkable achievement.

*

simplistic a plot and such totally banal dialogue as that which characterises the play *Martin Luther*. De Lopez had an English mother, and spoke English perfectly, but it seems, even from Moore's accounts of the collaboration, that he went along with the reckless young Irishman reluctantly.

Moore became aware of what was going to be the main problem confronting him in his attempt to achieve his second aim – of becoming a writer, rather than a painter – long before he left Paris.

'I have heard of writing and speaking two languages equally well,' he wrote in *Confessions*, 'but if I had remained two more years in France I should never have been able to identify my thoughts with the language I am now writing in, and I should have written it as an alien. It was in the last two years [in Paris] that I began to lose my English, and I remember very well indeed how one day, while arranging an act of a play I was writing with a friend [de Lopez], I found to my surprise that I could think more easily and more rapidly in French than in English; but with all this, I did not learn French. I could write a sonnet or a ballade almost without a slip, but my prose required a good deal of alteration, and when I returned to London I could write English verse, but even ordinary newspaper prose was beyond my reach, and an attempt I made to write a novel drifted into failure.'

Education, he believed, should be confined to clerks, 'and it drives even them to drink. Will the world never learn that we never learn anything that we did not know before? The artist, the poet, painter, musician and novelist go straight to the food they want, guided by an unerring and ineffable instinct . . . do they suppose that there is one sort of painting that is better than all the others and that there is a receipt for making it as for making chocolate? . . . It doesn't matter how badly you paint if you don't paint badly like other people.'

Moore was acutely aware that he could make no claim to scholarship: save from life, he wrote in *Confessions*, he could never learn anything. He was a student of ballrooms, streets, arcades. Whatever he reads, he can turn to account, but the fabulous river of gold was for him always in the conversation of living men and women, 'where the precious metal is washed up without stint for all to take, to take as much as we can carry'.

Moore now set out to teach himself how to write in English by reading and studying all the contemporary novelists, and above all by translating all sorts of things from French into English. He had a theory that to be a successful translator required a far greater knowledge of a language than to be a writer, on the basis that if you are writing something original, and cannot find the words in which to express your thoughts clearly, it is very easy to steer around the whole problem and write something quite different. Whereas, on the other hand, if you are making a translation, you are forced to find the words and phrases in which to express the thoughts of the writer of the original material.

Hone says that, when Moore first returned to London from Paris, he took a job on the *Examiner* with Heinrich Felbermann, a cosmopolitan Hungarian also recently returned from Paris, but it is not clear whether this was before Moore went back to Ireland to talk to his tenants or whether it was when he finally settled in London in 1882. The suggestion is that Moore took this job in an effort to acquire some training in journalism, but he does not mention it himself anywhere, so Hone no doubt heard it from Maurice Moore – from whom he got most of the information in his biography – and it is probably true. The job did not, however, last for very long, because Moore proved a total failure as a trainee journalist, and did not refer to the matter himself in any of his writings because he always had to come out on top, in one way or another, in all his reconstructed memoirs of his dead life.

What we do know is that, in the spring of 1882, Moore took lodgings in Cecil Street in the Strand, paying two pounds a week for a couple of rooms. He had a pretty young actress from the Savoy Theatre living above him, who used to play the piano – whenever she could afford to rent one – and who would spend hours sitting on the stairs talking to Moore, on her way home from the theatre. She was Jewish, with large brown eyes and a slim figure, and was hoping for a few lines in Mr Gilbert's next opera; she also informed Moore that she was married but was separated from her husband.

The landlady, who, Moore claims, was always trying to entice him into her rooms, lived on the ground floor, with her children, and there was a maid called Emma who spent seventeen out of the twenty-four hours of every day at the beck and call of the landlady, running upstairs with buckets of coal and breakfasts and cans of hot water, or down on her knees in front of the grates, pulling out the cinders with her hands, scouring, washing, cooking, and looking after the children.

Moore tries to imagine what it must feel like to be a maid (here perhaps is the genesis of *Esther Waters*), to be born in a slum and to leave it only to work seventeen hours out of twenty-four in a lodging house; to be a Londoner and to know only this one lodging house and the few shops around it at which the landlady deals; to live in London and have no notion whatever of the House of Commons. 'To know nothing of London meant in your case,' he writes, addressing Emma directly, as he so often does, 'not to know that it was not England; England and London! You could not distinguish between them. Was England an island or a mountain? You had no notion.'

Emma occasionally had a half-day off, during which she took the landlady's children out for a walk, and bought them sweets, because she did not know there was anything else that you could do. When George Moore told his brother Maurice about Emma, Maurice replied: 'You might as well give a mule a half-holiday.'

He did not, however, find living in the lodgings in Cecil Street any great hardship: 'A young man in a house full of women must be almost supernaturally unpleasant if he does not occupy a good deal of their attention. Certain at least it is that I was the point of interest in that house; and I found there that the practice of virtue is not so disagreeable as many young men think it. The fat landlady hovered around my doors, and I obtained perfectly fresh eggs by merely keeping her at a distance; the pretty actress, with whom I used to sympathise on the stairs at midnight, loved me better, and our intimacy was more strange and subtle, because it was pure, and it was not very unpleasant to know that the servant dreamed of me as she might of a star, or something equally unattainable; the landlady's daughter, a nasty girl of fifteen, annoyed me with her ogling; the house was not aristocratic, it is true, but, I repeat, it was not unpleasant, nor do I believe that any young man, however refined, would have found it unpleasant.'

Here in his lodgings in Cecil Street, Moore did his first journalistic work and started on yet another attempt to write the novel based on Lewis Marshall, *A Modern Lover*, set partly in England and partly in France, writing it out in copybooks from dawn until dusk, when he went out, as he puts it, 'to learn London. It was the *café* that I missed, the brilliant life of the *café*, the casual life of the *café*, so different from the life of the bars into which I turned in search of a companion . . .'

He writes about the eating-houses where he dined between seven and eight on roast saddle of mutton with potatoes and vegetables. Why potatoes *and* vegetables, he wondered; are potatoes not vegetables? After nine o'clock, he lamented, there was nowhere to go. London had lost her taverns.

Some seventy years earlier, he claims, the club superseded the tavern, and since then all literary intercourse had ceased in London. 'Did anyone ever see a gay club-room? Can anyone imagine such a thing? You can't have a club-room without mahogany tables, you can't have mahogany tables without magazines . . . you can't have a club without a waiter in red plush and silver salver in his hand; and you can't bring a lady to a club, and you have to go into a corner to talk about them.' It is no wonder that Moore found the clubs dull.

At first, he was clearly very unhappy. He had spent the formative years of his life – his early twenties – in France and had begun to think of himself as a Frenchman. In *Confessions* he talks about his 'original hatred' of his native country, and his brutal loathing of the religion in which he was brought up: 'I am instinctively averse from my own countrymen [note the *from*: Moore was teaching himself English very thoroughly]; they are at once remote and repulsive; but with Frenchmen I am conscious of a sense of nearness.' He adds that he loves the English better than the French but does not feel so close to them, and wonders whether he might not have some French blood in his veins.

But he feels like a total stranger in England. An Englishman was at that time as much out of his mental reach as an Eskimo would be now [this was written about ten years later]. He believed that English and French women were very similar in their attitudes, but that the men were poles apart, and he was convinced that, if he had spent another two years in France, he would never have been able to become an English writer.

He now set out upon an intensive study of contemporary English literature, being careful to make notes as he went, thereby exhibiting one essential trait of the born professional writer: a dogged determination not to waste a scrap of anything he ever read or wrote or observed or heard about or overheard or experienced in any way. Moore kept all the notes he made during his course of reading, and used them to bulk out his *Confessions*, to provide him with raw material for newspaper and magazine articles, and for other, subsequent books.

He read Henry James. 'Why does he always avoid decisive action? In his stories a woman never leaves the house with her lover, nor does a man ever kill another man or himself. Why is nothing ever accomplished? In real life murder, adultery, and suicide are of common occurrence; but Mr James's people live in a calm, sad and very polite twilight of volition. Suicide or adultery has happened before the story begins, suicide or adultery happens some years after the characters have left the stage, but in front of the reader nothing happens.'

He read Thomas Hardy: '*Far from the Madding Crowd* discovered the fact to me that Mr Hardy was but one of George Eliot's miscarriages . . .'

He read Rider Haggard: '. . . when improbability, which in these days does duty for imagination, is mixed with familiar aspects of life – I mean the combination of Ma and Pa and dear Annie who live in Clapham, with the mountains of the moon and the secret of eternal life, the result is art for the villa. His literary atrocities are more atrocious than his accounts of slaughter.'

There was one institution in England which reminded him of the blithe humanities of the Continent, although it was wholly and essentially English: the music hall. No affectation of language here, 'but bright quips and cranks fresh from the back yard of the slum where the linen is drying, or the pub where the unfortunate wife has just received a black eye that will last her a week'. He sees the music hall as a vigorous protest against the villa, the circulating library and the club.

This was the period when he used to go to the Gaiety Bar because, although the literati he met there were no substitute for Manet, Degas, Pissarro, Renoir, Cabaner, Villiers de l'Isle Adam and the others at the Nouvelles Athènes, at least they talked art and were willing to listen to him. They drank and talked from five o'clock until seven, and a lot of whisky was drunk, which displeased Moore who admits that he 'was always annoyed by drunkenness'. But there was nowhere else he could talk literature, and it was necessary to talk literature to drive the French language and French ideas out of his mind; till that was done a novel of English life could not be written.

At this stage he met Margaret Veley, who had had a novel published in the *Cornhill Magazine*, and who corrected his proofs, 'and with every correction she helped me out of the French into the English language'.

Between times, he went back to his reading. He read Robert Louis Stevenson: '[he] never wrote a line that failed to delight me; but he never wrote a book.'

He read the newspapers: 'The penny paper that may be bought everywhere, that is allowed to lie on every table, prints seven or eight columns of filth, for no reason except that the public likes to read filth.'

But he still hadn't got France out of his mind, or Paris out of his thoughts. 'Sometimes, at night, when all is still, and I look out on that desolate river, I think I shall go mad with grief, with wild regret for my beautiful *appartement* in the Rue de la Tour des Dames . . . I hate with my whole soul this London lodging, and all that concerns it – Emma, and eggs and bacon, the lascivious landlady and her smutty daughter; I am weary of the sentimental actress who lives upstairs . . . I can do nothing, nothing; my novel I know is worthless . . . I am weary of everything and wish I were back in Paris.'

NINE

# The First Novels

As well as feeling homesick for France, Moore was finding that habits of behaviour and even of thought which he had picked up in Paris were hampering his progress in England. He talked about the French wit in his brain, the French sentiment in his heart, the French idiom on his lips. 'I was full of France,' he was to write in *Confessions*, 'and France had to be got rid of, or pushed out of sight, before I could understand England; I was handicapped with dangerous ideas, and an impossible style, and before long the leading journal [the *Spectator*] that had printed two poems and some seven or eight critical articles, ceased to send me books for review. I fell back upon obscure society papers. But it was not incumbent upon me to live by my pen; so I talked, and watched, and waited till I grew akin to those around me, until my thoughts blended with, and took root in my environment.'

He wrote a play or two, he says, dramatised a novel, and read a great deal more contemporary fiction. Hone says that, when the *Spectator* was closed to him on account of his dangerous ideas, he looked around for odd literary jobs, contributing short stories and essays to the sort of society journals with which his brother Augustus was associated.

What Hone referred to as Moore's 'dangerous' ideas were probably his ideas on religion. Hone writes: '. . . Anyone who saw much of him in the eighties, and knew that he had lived a good deal among Frenchmen, would probably have attributed a number of his characteristics to a French formation – his thriftiness, [his] dislike of travel and lack of curiosity about foreign countries and people, [his] contempt for all that did not interest himself. His attitude towards religion then reflected the Paris *boulevardier* of the eighties who talked about Darwin and Renan in much the same way as people nowadays [in the early 1930s] talk about Einstein and Freud. The way he talked about women was French rather than English. For the *boulevardier* of the eighties it was highly creditable to be known as *un homme à femmes* and few deprived themselves of the pleasure of boasting of their conquests. Variations from the truth, for which the listener made allowance, were part of the game.'

Augustus, who had come to London a few years earlier with the same intention of making a living as a journalist, was the dashing member of the Moore family and was known as 'The Masher' Moore. Initially, George Moore spent a good deal of time with his young brother at fashionable restaurants, but whereas The Masher Moore's playboy days were only beginning, George Moore's were really coming to an end, and he felt that the long nights of champagne drinking with other men-about-town, prize-fighters and chorus girls at Romano's – where in those days the big boxing matches were all staged – tended to interfere with his work the next day.

He did, however, collaborate with Augustus in writing an English libretto for *Les Cloches de Corneville*, which earned him £30 (worth £1,500 today); it had a successful run in London and a second company took it on a protracted tour of the provinces.

While he was working on his first novel, *A Modern Lover*, writing it out in penny exercise books, Moore wrote to Zola, reminding him that M. Manet, one of his, Moore's, great friends, had presented him to Zola at a ball given in honour of Zola's novel *L'Assommoir*; but that he had been discreet enough not to annoy The Master by visiting him unnecessarily. He tells Zola of the efforts he has been making to popularise the work of the French

Naturalist School in Britain and asks Zola if he would permit him to accept a commission from a publisher who has asked him to do a translation of the book.

Zola did not bother to reply and although Moore never translated *L'Assommoir*, he must, as Hone remarks, have convinced Zola that he could be of some use to him, because, with his Paris friend Paul Alexis, a young writer of the Zola school, he called on The Master during a visit to Paris in 1882, an incident described in almost excessive detail in a short piece called 'A Visit to Médan', which appeared in a collection of newspaper and magazine articles by Moore published under the title *Impressions and Opinions* in 1891.

He found that Médan was not on the railway line but about a mile and a half from the nearest station, the name of which he had forgotten, and did not even bother to look up, another example of the utter contempt he showed for his readers. The Zola residence turned out to be a cottage which the writer had converted into what Moore, a member of the landed gentry, regarded as a rather vulgar sort of imitation castle.

He was left waiting for a long time in the billiard room, and then had to go through all sorts of tedious explanations of who he was, and where they had previously met, before finally persuading Madame Zola to allow him in to meet The Master.

It is greatly to Moore's credit that, although he had become almost as famous, in his own country at least, as Zola was in his, when he wrote this, that he did not disguise Zola's hostility and his own nervousness. Zola made no attempt to rise from the couch on which he was slumped, to greet Moore: and Moore recounts how he stumbled through some vague pleasantries about the weather and such, wondering if Zola would dismiss him as an idiot without even discovering who he was (a distinguished writer), also wondering how Shakespeare or Homer would behave in a similar situation.

He even endeavours to excuse Zola's failure to recognise him for what he was, by saying that Zola was going through an iconoclastic period, as an 'idol-breaker, a bear that curses the universe'. Moore introduced himself as a fan of Zola's weekly articles in the *Voltaire* magazine, and began to discourse on one of his favourite subjects, the circulating library. They discussed Puritanism and Protestantism in literature, and Zola remarked that Protestantism had never produced any great art, apart from Milton: Shakespeare and the Elizabethans had lived before the Reformation. It could well be that it was this remark which prompted Moore to advance the theory that Catholicism had produced no literature; he probably was not joking when he made the remark, on hearing of Zola's death, that 'that man was the making of me'.

This first conversation lasted about three-quarters of an hour and Moore left feeling that he had made a good impression on The Master.

On his return to London, he worked extremely hard on his first novel, which was published in the summer of 1883, whereupon it was immediately banned by the circulating libraries, including the principal ones, Mudie's and W.H. Smith's, who considered it unsuitable reading for young girls. According to Hone, the manager of W.H. Smith's explained to Moore that two ladies had written from the country objecting to a scene in which a young working girl poses naked for the artist, and after that the firm naturally refused to circulate the book, though it was not banned in the sense that any customers who particularly wanted to read it could order copies.

There can be no doubt that the Modern Lover of the title is none other than Lewis Ponsonby Marshall, also known as Lewis Seymour and in real life Louis Weldon Hawkins, Moore's Paris friend; and the substance of the plot is summarised by Moore himself in his preface to a rewritten version of the book, published in 1917 as *Lewis Seymour and Some Women*: 'Three women undertake to work for a young man's welfare: a work-girl, a rich woman, and a lady of high degree. All contribute something, and the young man is put on a high pedestal, one worshipper retains her faith, one loses hers partially, and one altogether.'

*A Modern Lover* did not make Moore famous overnight, nor were the reviews unmixed in their praise. The *Spectator* commented: 'One is made aware by certain passages that Mr Moore would fain imitate the methods of Zola and his odious school, but two obstacles are in his path – the faith of a Christian and the instincts of a gentleman; the author recognises and respects goodness, purity and disinterestedness, and if M. Zola and any of the hogs of his sty could write such an episode as that with which the story opens, the work-girl's sacrifice for the penniless artist, one could have as much hope for their future as that of Mr Moore.' Moore also had largely appreciative reviews in other newspapers and magazines, including a long one in the *Fortnightly* and he wrote to Zola that he had just published a novel 'which has had success'. The *St James's Gazette* commented that 'Mr Moore has a real power of drawing character, and some of his descriptive scenes are capital.'

*A Modern Lover* provides us with the first example of Moore's extremely parsimonious attitude towards his own raw material: during a *séjour* in Paris, the young artist and his mistress, Mrs Lucy Bentham, go yachting with Mallarmé, and are nearly drowned. The same scene appears again and again throughout Moore's work, though in later versions it is Moore who is in the boat with Mallarmé and who saves the day, and it appears to be fact, rather than fiction, though, with Moore, who ever knows?

There is also a short scene in the book which foreshadows both his interest in the Daphnis and Chloe legend, and his preoccupation with working the same material over and over again, in book after book, fiction or non-fiction.

Despite the comparative success of *A Modern Lover*, Moore was displeased with what he considered to be the weak way in which his publishers, Tinsley Brothers, had handled the objections to his first novel by the circulating libraries; and he approached Vizetelly, former Paris correspondent of the *Illustrated London*

*News*, who had just set up a new publishing venture in London and was making a precarious living printing translations of foreign books. To Vizetelly, Moore explained the idea of a new project he was contemplating, which was to be a Naturalistic novel about the actor-manager of a touring operatic company who rescues the pretty wife of a linen-draper – with whom he lodges while on tour – from her drab existence, looking after a dull, asthmatic husband, only to watch her degenerate into an incurable alcoholic.

In order to find a suitable location for the opening scene, Moore approached his friends at the Gaiety Bar, and then spent some weeks touring with the second company with his own and his brother's version of the operetta, *Les Cloches de Corneville*. According to Hone, Jimmy Glover, later director of the Drury Lane Theatre Orchestra, and at that time conductor for the *Les Cloches* touring company, always claimed that he was the real author of *A Mummer's Wife*; he had been a member of Augustus Moore's circle in London, and had told Moore many stories about touring with theatrical companies; the book, when it appeared, was dedicated to him.

Moore went to Ireland in October 1883 to work on the novel, staying at Moore Hall with his mother. Julian and Nina were both away, and his mother recalled how Moore would work all day on the book, never emerging from the study until tea-time, and even then usually still in a dressing-gown. At this period he neither rode nor shot; his only recreation was an occasional walk by the lake.

He has described, in *Parnell and His Island*, how he found Moore Hall neglected and run-down, the famous stables empty and dilapidated, the walled gardens overgrown with weeds, and the woods abandoned to nature. He spent the evenings with his mother, and a cousin who had been keeping her company, chatting in front of the fire.

While he worked on *A Mummer's Wife*, Moore was already planning his next novel, a book which he always thought of as *The*

*Galway Girls*, though when it was published he called it *A Drama in Muslin*. It was to be a study of the life of a group of well-brought-up, middle-class girls who go up to Dublin to 'do' the season at the Viceregal Court in the hope of finding husbands. Already researching the background for this novel in his mind, he stayed for a time with Edward Martyn at Tullyra Castle in County Galway, not far from Moore Hall. He also visited the Ruttledges at nearby Cornfield – where, Hone claims, a room called The Pink Room was always kept in reserve for him as a writing room – and at Browne's Grove near Tuam.

After Christmas, he travelled up to Dublin and stayed at the Shelbourne Hotel, where he worked every morning on *A Mummer's Wife* and, in the evening, observed the progress of the Dublin season at first hand. During the season, he met again a Miss Maud Browne, whom he had first encountered at Browne's Grove; she became the model for one of the characters in *Drama in Muslin*, a timid, frightened thing, 'the pale martyr of Lord Spencer's private dance, who speaks to no one and hasn't even a brother to offer her an ice'.

There was a suggestion of some sort of unfinished affair between Moore and Maud. Moore was vaguely interested in her plight, and intrigued by the challenge presented by her guardian aunt who strongly disapproved of him; besides, she was an heiress, and Moore was always on the look-out for security, though never prepared, when the moment of decision came, to forfeit his freedom, even for a fortune. However, it came to nothing, though Hone reports that, when a husband was finally found for the girl, she claimed that she always had loved George.

When he returned from Dublin to London in the spring of 1894 – he could not find the time to rejoin his mother at Moore Hall, after the season – he moved from his lodgings in Cecil Street into bachelor chambers in Dane's Inn, in Wych Street on the north side of the Strand. By now, he was much better off; things were quieter in Ireland, rents once again were being collected and he was making some money from his contributions to the French newspapers and to the *Pall Mall Gazette*. He was even able to afford another trip to Paris, where he visited the painter Jacques-Emile Blanche, whom he had first met in Manet's studio, and with whom he became very friendly. Blanche painted him on a couple of occasions, as he recalls in his memoirs *Mes Modèles*: 'I painted two portraits of him, one in 1888, the other in 1902 – one of my best, which the model described as "a drunken cabman" and wished to have me destroy. Yet it was a most dignified picture and psychologically the most true of any that I shall leave behind me.'

On his return from Paris, Moore finished *A Mummer's Wife* at Dane's Inn in the summer of 1884, creating in it two very strong characters, Kate Ede, the linen-draper's wife, a sort of Madame Bovary of the Potteries, who ends up drink-sodden in an asylum, and her seducer, the huge, good-natured, extremely common and insensitive actor-manager and member of Morton and Cox's theatrical and operatic touring company, Dick Lennox; this novel was a determined attempt to apply the French Naturalistic School technique to a depiction of English life, shirking nothing, not even a highly graphic description of Kate vomiting all over her own new dress and the red velvet seat of a four-wheeler, using a kind of candour extremely rare in Victorian times.

Moore had time to correct the proofs before leaving, once again, for Ireland, to spend the last three months of the year with his mother at Moore Hall, where he worked all day and every day, until the sun set behind the hills beyond Lake Carra, on his series of articles on Irish life for *Le Figaro*, and on some preliminary outline sketches for *A Drama in Muslin*.

After Christmas, Moore again went up to Dublin for the season, this time to do some serious research. He wrote to Dublin Castle explaining that he was working on a book dealing with the social and political power of the Castle in modern Ireland, and asked to be invited to the Levée and to one of the big State dinner parties. When he received no reply from the State

Steward – who perhaps had heard him referred to as Pagan Moore
and the Bestial Bard, and considered him, though a large landowner in the West of Ireland, highly unsuitable company for the
Viceroy and his distinguished guests – Moore proceeded to
bombard the Castle with requests for invitations to various State
functions.

When finally the State Steward became exasperated and
informed Moore that the lists for all the State functions connected
with the current season were closed, Moore went to the *Freeman's
Journal*, a Nationalist paper whose principal target at this
particular period was what it always referred to as 'the Castle
hacks'. The newspaper reported the entire affair in detail, even
allowing Moore the last word: '. . . it was as a man of letters, it was
for the purpose of studying, not of amusing myself, that I applied
for an invitation. Was that the reason I was refused? . . . I came to
the Castle, not as a patriot nor as a place hunter, but as the
passionless observer, who, unbiased by political creed, comments
impartially on the matter submitted to him for analysis. I confess I
would like to have seen one of the State dinner parties, but we
cannot have all things, and I am not sure that Lord Fingall was not
right to refuse my application. Fame comes to us in unexpected
ways, and I believe that when this somnolent earl is overtaken by
that sleep which overtakes us all, and for which, it appears, he is
qualifying himself daily as well as nightly, his claim to be
remembered will be that he refused to invite me to dinner at the
Castle.'

The affair attracted a good deal of attention in Dublin and as a
consequence Moore not only became a sort of folk hero with the
Irish Nationalists but also a lot better known to the ordinary
public than he had previously been. It was an early example of his
natural flair for publicity.

*A Mummer's Wife* appeared in January; by March it had gone
into its third edition, despite mixed reviews. Frank Harris, an
influential critic, had welcomed it whole-heartedly but the bulk of

the reviewers disliked the almost savage Naturalism. The *Athenaeum* admitted that Kate Ede was a powerful study of a commonplace character, but regarded the novel as a whole as wearisome and painful, and the *Academy* gave it as its opinion that 'a more repulsive tale had never been told'. The *Graphic* said: 'A *Mummer's Wife* holds at present a unique position among English novels. It is the first thorough-going attempt, at any rate of importance, to carry out the principles of realism in their final, and possibly their only logical, result . . . It comprises the results of close and elaborate observation, of artistic labour, and of a conscientious effort on the author's part to make the very best and utmost of his materials.' And *Society* claimed that Moore might 'fairly claim the title of the English Zola'.

In his *Epitaph on George Moore*, Charles Morgan says that George Bernard Shaw remarked to him that, after his early knowledge of Moore, he lost sight of him for a time, 'until one day Archer came to me and said he had been reading a most wonderful Naturalistic book by a new writer'. It was called *A Mummer's Wife*. 'But who is the writer?' Shaw asked. Archer said that his name was George Moore. 'Nonsense,' Shaw said, 'I know George Moore. He couldn't possibly write a real book.

'But there it was,' Shaw added, 'he had written it, and I then began to understand the incredible industry of the man.'

Moore was delighted with the book's reception and talked about 'an enthusiastic press'. He also profited from his acquaintance with W. T. Stead, the first truly yellow journalist and proprietor of the *Pall Mall Gazette*, to persuade him to run an article attacking Charles Edward Mudie and the literary censorship exercised by his and the other big circulating libraries. This article brought a flood of letters from the readers of the *Gazette* which went on for almost a fortnight, and other papers, including the influential *Saturday Review*, weighed in with articles of their own on the topic. It all added up to a tremendous amount of very welcome publicity for George Moore and his new novel, which everyone now wanted to read.

He had promised his mother that he would spend the whole spring with her at Moore Hall but, with the cuttings from Vizetelly coming in thick and fast with every postal delivery, he had to go to London 'to see the Press in bloom', as he put it in *A Confession to my Friends*. He also wanted to get back to London because he had just read *Marius the Epicurean* and wished to meet Walter Pater.

Of *Marius the Epicurean* he wrote: 'I knew that I was awakened a fourth time, and a fourth vision of life was given to me.' Previous visions had come from Shelley, Gautier and Balzac, and there had been other minor awakenings – to Zola, Flaubert and Goncourt. 'But *Marius the Epicurean* was more to me than a mere emotional experience, precious and rare though that may be, for this book was the first in English prose I had come across that procured for me any genuine pleasure in the language itself . . . Until I read *Marius* the English language was to me what French must be to the majority of English readers. I read for the sense and that was all; the language itself seemed to me coarse and plain . . . *Marius* was the stepping-stone that carried me across the channel into the genius of my own tongue.'

He did manage to meet Pater that summer in the drawing room of his London friends, the Robinsons, and proceeded to pursue him for a time; later, although he continued to admire Pater's writing to the end of his life, and was greatly influenced by his style, he became disillusioned with the man himself, whom he found to be 'a shy, sentimental man, all powerful in the written word, impotent in life'.

Moore followed up the newspaper controversy over the circulating libraries with a pamphlet, *Literature at Nurse, or Circulating Morals*, which Vizetelly naturally enough was very anxious to publish; in this pamphlet Moore listed and quoted a collection of risky passages which could be found in novels which the libraries did freely circulate. He argued that human nature had from the earliest times shown a liking for smutty stories, and what was banished from the novels brought out by publishers anxious to supply 'respectable reading' for the circulating libraries rolled out to the public again through the popular newspapers. And he pondered on the strange idea that our morality is in any way dependent upon the books we read: '. . . even the little children in the street know by this time that the morality of the world will alway be the same, despite good or bad books.'

The pamphlet was greeted with a leading article in *The World* in which Moore was defended and Mudie and his library severely criticised, and by now, as he told his mother in a letter, all London had read *A Mummer's Wife*: 'When I enter a drawing room everyone wants to be introduced to me. I could dine out every night if I care to – I am pestered with invitations.'

To Zola he wrote: 'I am fighting that Englishmen may exercise a right that they formerly enjoyed, that of writing freely and sanely . . . Duret writes to me from time to time – and he has asked me if I was the author of the articles in the *Pall Mall Gazette*. I had nothing to do with that filth . . . All the same I am glad of their appearance from the point of view of literature since it destroys the sweet illusion of English virtue.'

Moore's friend, W. T. Stead, had just exposed what he described as London's 'white slave traffic' (juvenile prostitution) under the general headline THE MAIDEN TRIBUTE OF MODERN BABYLON, in the *Pall Mall Gazette*. This was a personal investigation into vice in London, seemingly carried out with the support of the Archbishop of Canterbury, Cardinal Manning and General Booth of the Salvation Army. Stead had concluded the series in typical tabloid fashion (though the tabloid itself lay still more than a decade in the future) by purchasing a thirteen-year-old girl, Eliza Armstrong, from her mother for £5. Having satisfied himself that she was *virgo intacta* and that he could have had his way with her, had he elected to do so, he handed her over to the Salvation Army.

It did George Moore no harm at all at this stage of his career to be associated in the public mind with a man like Stead and a paper like the *Pall Mall Gazette*. The Bestial Bard had arrived;

inside a year George Moore had become Britain's best-known writer.

TEN

# The Galway Girls

George Moore now began to move into different circles.

When he first returned to London from Paris, he went in search of his old friend Jim Browne, the painter of the crucifix above the altar in Carnacum Chapel in County Mayo, and found him in somewhat straitened circumstances in lodgings in Park Road, near Regent's Park. The Brownes had been obliged to sell their house in Kensington and Jim's sisters, Pinkie and Ada, had gone to live with relatives. Jim Browne's landlord was a dancing-master who lived in the same house, with his wife and daughter.

Moore discovered to his surprise and horror that Jim knew nothing of Manet, nor did he care to hear anything about any of the painters who had frequented the Nouvelles Athènes; and, when Moore invited him out to dinner, he pleaded that his wardrobe was in too wretched a state, and they settled for some cold meat from the larder in Browne's lodgings.

'I felt that he had worn out himself as well as his clothes,' Moore wrote in *Vale*, ' – his hopes, his talent, his enthusiasm for life, all were gone, an echo remained, an echo which I did not try to reawaken. I never saw him again; he was for me but an occasional thought, until one day I found myself sitting next a showily dressed woman at luncheon, the daughter of Jim's landlady, and it was from her [that] I learnt that Jim had died about two years back in Park Road.'

And, although he only heard about it second-hand, he embroiders the account he heard of Jim Browne's death into a rich and marvellously colourful tragi-comical tapestry. And this was Jim Browne, his cousin, the man who first interested Moore in painting, the man who put it into his mind that he should go to France to study art, the man who made Moore, in fact, if you accept that it was his Paris period that transformed him from a County Mayo country bumpkin into the cosmopolitan man of letters he had now become.

Jim had always been interested in lions and had held a theory that a lion invariably lies with one paw tucked under, and never with both forepaws stretched out, like Landseer's lions at the foot of Nelson's column in Trafalgar Square. His landlord and landlady would not allow him to demonstrate his theory by making a sculpture inside the house, but one winter, when the snow was lying several feet deep around the house, it occurred to Jim that he could test his notion just as easily by making a snow lion in the garden:

> . . . now there was snow at the very door, and he began to pile it up, and when all the snow in the garden was exhausted, the neighbours sent their snow in wheelbarrows and he continued to pile up hundredweight upon hundredweight until his lion assumed almost Egyptian proportions, rising above the surrounding walls, attracting the eyes of the hansom-cabmen who drew up their horses to admire [it] and to suggest that the lion should be sent to the British Museum. Perhaps the Governor might have a refrigerator built for him, was a remark, which caused some amusement to the dancing-master, his wife and daughter, and to Jim. But it was not thought worth while writing to the Governor of the Museum on the subject. The suggestion, Why don't you 'ave him photographed? coming next day from the top of an omnibus seemed more practical, and the maid-servant was asked to run around to the photographer, and the evening was spent counting the number of copies that would be required; each neighbour who had sent his snow must get one, and before bedtime it was noticed that the brightness of the stars predicted a fine day. But during the night the clouds gathered, and in the morning the garden was enveloped in a white mist. A messenger came from the photographer to say that he

could do nothing that day, and the following day he failed to keep his appointment, and in a drizzle of rain, Jim set to work to patch up his melting masterpiece. The next day the photographer arrived and got what he hoped would prove a very good impression; but everybody wanted a half-plate; and Jim worked on among the wet snow, Florence begging him to put on an overcoat and a stronger pair of boots. But he trampled about in shoes, and next day he was crouching over the fire, and when the doctor heard the story of the lion, he threw up his hands.

How a man of his age could be foolish enough to risk his life for such nonsense! And you tell me he always goes out without an overcoat? I'll call tomorrow and give him oxygen if required.

The thaw continued during the night, and Jim and his lion dissolved together . . .

Moore was now beginning to make friends among the younger English artists. He met Walter Richard Sickert through Blanche – who had been commissioned to do the frontispiece for Moore's next novel, A Drama in Muslin – and through Sickert he met Wilson Steer and Henry Tonks, a professor at the Slade.

Around this period he translated, with some assistance from his French writer friend, Paul Alexis, W. S. Gilbert's play Sweethearts for the Odéon Theatre in Paris and had a short story published in the Court and Society Review, a struggling periodical edited by Henry Barnett, a friend of Edward Martyn's.

The same periodical also ran some pre-publication extracts from A Drama in Muslin, which were advertised in the journal by an introduction written by Moore himself as 'a picture of Ireland all complete, Castle, landlords and Land Leaguers, and painted by an Irishman'. Barnett's readers were encouraged to look forward to 'the shrill wail of virgins', and 'the thunder of a people marching to manhood', and were informed that one 'out of a hundred delicately nurtured daughters' of the Irish gentry was lucky if she should succeed in marrying a dispensary doctor or a police officer. The advertisement also claimed that A Drama in Muslin contained as vivid an account as existed of social life in Ireland during the Land League . . . 'Nor can any reader doubt that he [Moore] had been animated by a hatred as lively as Ibsen's for the conventions which drive women into the marriage market.'

Edward Martyn had now come to London from Galway, and was living in Pump Court in the Temple, a short walk away from Moore's bachelor apartment off the Strand, and they began to meet fairly regularly; Martyn is the 'dear Edward' of *Hail and Farewell*, a man Moore always mocked gently, but never viciously.

Martyn was seven years younger than Moore, only lately down from Oxford in fact, an eccentric, a big man with a big appetite: Moore described him as 'esurient' and remarked that 'eating procured his death' – he died in 1923, ten years before Moore died, at the age of sixty-four. Like Moore he was full of contrasts. Hone sums him up brilliantly: 'A born celibate without vocation for the priesthood, a Roman Catholic consumed with literary ambition, whose religious scruples had lately caused him to destroy a poem on some classical subject. But literature was again in the ascendant, and he was now engaged upon a vast allegorical satire, modelled on Rabelais. A better educated man than Moore, his devotion to polyphonic music, Wagner and Ibsen and his courteous manners seemed to contradict a blunt-witted and thick-set appearance, a voracious appetite and the religious conformism of an Irish peasant.'

His widowed mother, the daughter of a wealthy stone-mason who had brought a fortune to Tullyra Castle on her marriage to Edward's father, and who wanted to see some grandchildren running around the estate, was always trying to marry dear Edward off, but without any success. Martyn once said to Moore that he didn't hate women, it was just that they seemed absurd to him: 'When I see them going along the streets together, they make me laugh; their hats and feathers, everything about them,' he used to say. Moore added that the exhibition which women make of their bosoms at dinner parties always struck Edward as ludicrous – 'full-blown roses, he used to call them'.

Naturally enough, Martyn strongly disapproved of Moore's

attitude to the Catholic Church, but treated him with a derisive tolerance which probably sprang from his own deep faith, his enormous wealth and his university education. Where his own religious beliefs were involved, he could be very firm; in agreeing to help to arrange for the serialisation of *Drama in Muslin* in the *Court and Society Review*, run by his friend Henry Barnett, he warned Moore that he would immediately withdraw his support if Moore tried to include 'any passages which might contain an offence against faith or morals'.

They went to Paris together in January 1886. Moore wrote to his mother: 'We saw a great many painters and pictures, writers and books. I persuaded Edward to buy two pictures [a Degas and a Manet]. Zola was very kind to me, and I saw a great deal of him. We went to the Salon together on varnishing day and attracted a great deal of attention.' According to Hone, who knew Martyn very well, Martyn's account of the affair was completely different. They happened to meet Zola by chance at the Salon, and Martyn used to recall with quiet, gentle amusement that Moore did not even bother to introduce his friend to Zola, but left him to his own devices as he trotted around the gallery, in The Master's wake, preening himself on being the cynosure of all eyes.

Although still deeply impressed by Zola as a celebrity, as the current giant of French literature, Moore himself had moved away from the literal realism of Zola's novels. As he was to remark later, in one of his characteristic conversations with himself in *Confessions*: 'What I reproach Zola with is that he has no style; there is nothing you won't find in Zola from Chateaubriand to the reporting in the Figaro. He seeks immortality in an exact description of a linen-draper's shop; if the shop conferred immortality [on anyone] it should be on the linen-draper who created the shop, and not on the novelist who described it.'

The style of *A Drama in Muslin*, which came out in the late spring of 1886, was a conscious attempt to escape from the

Naturalism of Zola, and his development of characters like Alice Barton and the handicapped Lady Cecilia Cullen reflects Moore's desire to deal with more complex natures than those that people Zola's most successful works. In many ways, *A Drama in Muslin* is a very modern book; the tentative Lesbian undertones in the relationship between Alice and Cecilia are sensitively handled, and in this novel Moore introduced a technique then new to fiction, though now very familiar, since it is one of the key devices used in making films for cinema and television: the cut-away. There is a scene, for example, in which two events are occurring simultaneously: twenty or thirty tenants are calling on Mr Barton, a County Galway landlord and the father of two of the Galway girls, Alice and the beautiful but simple Olive, to discuss a reduction in their rents, while Captain Hibbert, a dashing young army officer, is calling on Mrs Barton to ask whether he might be considered as a suitable suitor for the hand of her daughter, the beautiful Olive. Moore intercuts back and forth abruptly and very effectively between the two conversations. Although he claimed that he had long since forgotten Jim Browne, he had not, really; the character of the eccentric, artistic Mr Barton is clearly based on him.

Ostensibly, the storyline is very simple. Five young girls are leaving a convent in North Wales at the end of their schooling to enter what Moore calls the marriage mart. But, as Norman Jeffares says in his introduction to a subsequent edition, 'it is also much more than that: it is a portrayal of a disturbed society, an artificial society, and a simmering conflict between riches and poverty rooted in the question of the ownership of the land. In this novel, Moore is portraying his native country in the time of the Land League ... Out of his experience of the glitter and tinsel of Dublin society came the famous decorative passages: the dress-maker's shop, where Alice Barton and Olive, her beautiful sister, are prepared for the Castle Ball; the Castle Drawing Room itself, with the shoulders of the girls described in

terms of exotic flowers. On this battlefield, Mrs Barton manoeu-
vres her troops, but the prize, Lord Kilcarney, falls for another of
the girls, Violet Scully.'

Moore's empathy with women, and particularly young women,
is particularly well illustrated in the way he handles the contrasts
between the five girls: the plain Alice and the beautiful Olive
Barton; May Gould, the sensual one, the bold girl who has an
illegitimate child and is secretly supported by Alice; Cecilia
Cullen, the cripple, who is intensely religious and has tacit
Lesbian leanings; and Violet Scully, the slightly common girl who
manages to carry off the first prize, Lord Kilcarney. Olive makes a
disastrous attempt to elope with her dashing officer, and Alice has
the courage to defy her formidable mother and leaves home for a
happy marriage.

It is through Alice that Moore expresses his own ideas. For
example, on the Catholic Church: 'Alice watched the ceremony
of the Mass, and the falseness of it jarred upon her terribly. The
mumbled Latin, the by-play with the wine and water, the
mumming of the uplifted hands were so appallingly trivial, and,
worse still, all realisation of the idea seemed impossible to the
mind of the congregation. Passing by, without scorn, the belief
that the white wafer the priest held over his head, in this lonely
Irish chapel, was the Creator of the twenty millions of suns in the
Milky Way, she mused on the faith as exhibited by those who
came to worship . . .'

Or on the lead-up to the end of feudal landlordism: 'From afar
the clanging of a high swinging bell was heard, and the harsh
reverberations travelling over the rocky townlands summoned the
cottagers to God. The stone pillars of the chapel-gateway stared
with bright yellow proclamations. The tenant-farmers were called
upon to assemble by thousands and assert their rights . . .

'Now Arthur – do you hear? – you mustn't look at those horrid
papers!' Mrs Barton whispered to her husband, 'we must pretend
not to see them. I wonder how Father Shannon can allow such a

thing, making the house of God into – into I don't know what, for the purpose of preaching robbery and murder. Just look at the country-people, how sour and wicked they look – don't they, Alice?'

'Well, I don't know that they do mamma,' said Alice, who had already begun to see something wrong in each big house being surrounded by a hundred small ones, all working to keep it in sloth and luxury.

Through Alice, he defines the fundamental tenet of feminism, almost a century before Gloria Steinem made it a matter of political correctness: 'How then can we be really noble and pure, while we are still decked out in innocence, virtue and belief as ephemeral as the muslins we wear? Until we are free to think, until we are their sisters in thought, we cannot hope to become the companions, the friends, the supports of men.'

If Moore failed to learn how to paint like a painter, he had certainly taught himself how to write like one. Here is his description of Olive arriving in Patrick's Hall in Dublin Castle for the State Ball: 'What white wonder, what manifold marvel of art! Dress of snow satin, skirt quite plain in front. Bodice and train of white poplin; the latter wrought with patterns representing night and morning: a morning made of silver leaves with silver birds fluttering through leafy trees, butterflies sporting among them, and over all a sunrise worked in gold and silver thread; then on the left side the same sun sank amid rosy clouds . . . She was adorably beautiful and adorably pale; and like some wonderful white bird . . . she sailed through the red glare, along the scarlet line, unto the weary-looking man in maroon breeches. He kissed her on both cheeks; she curtsied to the vice-regal lips, and passed away to the further door, where her train was caught up and handed to her by two aides-de-camp.'

Moore had also, during his Paris period, discovered music: and in *Muslin* he uses musical similes to give depth to his descriptive passages. Here is the dress-maker's shop where Mrs Barton is choosing the material for Olive's ball gown: 'Lengths of white silk clear as the notes of violins playing in a minor key; white poplin falling into folds statuesque as the bass of a fugue by Bach; yards of ruby velvet rich as an air from Verdi played upon the piano . . .'

A bit overblown, perhaps. Obviously his London friends, the Misses Robinson, thought so because they added in the margin a few touches of their own: 'Everything was represented there, from the light clarinet of the embroidered lace handkerchief to the profound trombone of the red flannel pantaloons.'

'Oh how could you write such a thing, Mr Moore?' they asked him on his next visit to the house, reading their own addition out to him.

'He fell into the trap and defended a phrase he never used,' Madame Duclaux, who had been present in the Robinsons' drawing room when it happened, reported in an article on Moore in the *Revue de Paris*. 'We enlightened him . . . but he bore no malice, and was enchanted that we should interest ourselves in his literature.'

This is typical of Moore. In later life, he was quite capable of telling a story which involved someone who was present in the room, and if that person stopped Moore in his tracks and said that what he was saying was completely untrue, Moore showed no resentment at all, but merely continued with his version of the story, with unabated enthusiasm.

Charles Morgan has a note of a conversation he had with George Bernard Shaw about Moore (in *Epitaph on George Moore*). Shaw said: 'Everybody used to laugh at George and no one believed him, but he had an imperturbable good humour and if you said: "But, George, don't talk such nonsense, you are making it all up," he was not in the least put out or angry but just said: "Don't interrupt me," and went on as before.'

A *Drama in Muslin* got very good notices in England. The *Pall Mall Gazette* commented that it stood 'on a very much higher plane than the facile fiction of the circulating libraries . . . The hideous comedy of the marriage-market has been a stock topic with novelists from Thackeray downwards; but Mr Moore goes deep into the yet more hideous tragedy which forms its after-piece, the tragedy of enforced stagnant celibacy, with its double catastrophe of disease and vice. The characters are drawn with patient care and with a power of individualism which marks the born novelist. It is a serious, powerful and in many respects edifying book.'

In Dublin, the publication of the book caused such a sensation that Moore could not go back to Ireland. He had castigated the guests at a dinner party to which he had not been invited, and many people recognised themselves in the assembly of time-servers and panders whom he had so vividly described. And in picturing his five central characters – five young girls coming straight out of a convent school and now looking for husbands – he had opened the book with a performance of a play written by one of the girls for the prize-giving day performance at the convent, at which the nuns 'forgot themselves . . . and gloried in having been at least bride-providers for men'. This comment led to the threat of a libel action from the convent, which was named in the book, and was withdrawn in subsequent editions, and a portrait of a priest, obviously the parish priest of Ardrahan, caused Mrs Martyn to tell her son that George Moore was never to be invited to Tullyra Castle again.

None of this, however, worried Moore, who now felt that he had London at his feet. He spent the summer of 1886 at the Inn, Southwick, near Brighton, after a chance meeting with Colvill Bridger, his friend from the days of Jurles's Academy, the Colville of the *Hail and Farewell* trilogy. Although he had not seen the Bridgers, or indeed thought much about them from the time he went to live in Paris, when Colvill – whom Moore always called Colly – invited him to come down to Sussex and meet the family again, he travelled to Shoreham that afternoon and found that he felt as much at home with them as he had when he first met them, and he was warmly welcomed back by the squire and his wife, the laughing, talkative woman who still insisted on calling him Kant, and Colly's two sisters, Dulcibella and Florence. The old squire – Colly's grandfather – had died and they were now living in Buckingham, his big Italianate house on the downs, surrounded by elms, which Moore was to use as a model for the house in which Esthers Waters first works as a maid; the smaller house, Little Buckingham, where Moore had first stayed with the Bridgers, was now let to a dentist with two sisters who, like Dulcibella and Florence, the two Saxon maidens, liked to flirt with Moore.

Instead of returning to Ireland for Christmas 1886, Moore spent the holiday period with the Bridgers, staying well into the new year. And, although he enjoyed flirting with the girls, Moore found himself strangely attracted to Mrs Bridger, as he was later to explain in *Memoirs of My Dead Life*:

> Above all, I was surprised to find myself admiring her who, fifteen years ago, had appeared to me not a little dowdy. She was now fifty-five, but such an age seemed impossible for so girl-like a figure and such young and effusive laughter. I was, however, sure that she was fifteen years older than when I first saw her, but those fifteen years had brought each within a range of the other's understanding and sympathy. We became companions. I noticed what dresses she wore, and told her which I liked her best in. She was only cross with me when I surprised her in the potting-shed, wearing an old bonnet, out of which hung a faded poppy. She used to cry, 'Don't look at me, Kant. I know I'm an old gypsy woman.'
>
> . . . We looked at each other. There was an accent of love in our friendship. 'And strange is it not,' I said, 'I did not admire you half as much when I knew you first?'
>
> 'How was that? I was quite a young woman then.'
>
> 'Yes,' I said, regretting my own words, 'but, don't you see, at that time I was a mere boy – I lived in a dream, hardly seeing what passed around me.'
>
> 'Yes, of course,' she said gaily, 'you were so young then, all you saw in me was a woman with a grown-up son.'

And he remembers: 'Her dress was pinned up, and she held in her hand the bonnet which she said made her look like an old gypsy woman, and the sunlight fell on the red hair, now grown a little thinner . . . but not a wrinkle was there on that pretty, vixen-like face. Her figure especially showed no signs of age, and if she and her daughters were in the room, it was she I admired.'

# ELEVEN

# An Experiment in Confession

The summer of 1887 found George Moore living at the Inn, Southwick, finishing another short novel, *A Mere Accident*, and working on his first book of memoirs in which he proposed to experiment with a new style of writing recently adopted by one of his French friends, Edouard Dujardin, the editor of *La Revue Wagnérienne* and author of *Les Lauriers sont Coupés*, widely regarded as the first example of the use of the interior dialogue form in modern literature, later to be more fully exploited by James Joyce, among others. Moore had been a great admirer of Dujardin's work, and had said of *Les Lauriers* that it was 'the inner life of the soul revealed for the first time'; he was going to call his new book *Confessions of a Young Man*.

*A Mere Accident* was just ready to go off to the printers. It was a very short novel about John Norton, a young Sussex landlord, heir to huge estates, who happens also to be a religious ascetic without a vocation for the priesthood. He collects Renoirs and Manets, admires the music of Wagner and Palestrina, and reads the Latin Christian authors. He has a mother who is always trying to marry him off to some nice, suitable girl; in short, this is a thinly disguised portrait of his cousin, Edward Martyn, slimmed down a bit, and transformed into an English squire.

The accident of the title which enables Squire John Norton to escape from marriage is the rape by a tramp of the innocent young girl to whom he was to have been married; she conveniently removes herself from the scene by throwing herself out of her bedroom window. It was something of a flop when it came out later the same year; most of the reviewers thoroughly disliked what they regarded as all the unnecessary violence, and George Bernard Shaw, reviewing it for the *Pall Mall Gazette*, said that Moore's 'commendable reticence in avoiding the realities of the rape might have been taken further, even to the point of not writing the book'.

Hone believed that, although the book was a dismal failure, it was an event of some importance in his literary career, in so far as the choice of so unusual a principal character – and Moore was to return to the same basic subject in two subsequent books – represented a break-away from the typical representation of society that was the object of the Naturalistic School. 'The book would certainly never have been written if Moore had not read Huysmans,' he goes on, 'and [if Moore had not] been impressed by the superior breadth of mind and culture of this former disciple of Zola, who was now in revolt against the absolute materialism of Médan.'

Moore certainly put a lot of work into the book. 'I have spent the summer,' he wrote to his brother Julian, while he was writing *A Mere Accident*, 'reading all the Latin authors of the Middle Ages from the second to the eighth century for a chapter in my book.' Quite a formidable task for a man who never had any formal training as a scholar; and, in the process, he must have been forced to acquire some knowledge of Latin as well, though he is bound to have picked up some basic Latin at school at Oscott.

By now Moore's articles on Ireland for *Le Figaro* had appeared in France in book form and in England, too, as *Parnell and His Island*, and it is a measure of the high regard felt for Moore – and in general for men of letters at this period – that he was allowed to dilate at great length, and in enormous detail, in reply to earlier criticisms of his writings in a pamphlet, also published in 1887, by Swan Sonnenschein, called *Defensio pro Scriptis Meis*.

His friend Colly, Colvill Bridger, an officer in the Sussex militia, now decided to take up rabbit farming, inspired by roughly the same mathematical concept based on the predictable fecundity of rabbits which inspired *Jean de Florette* in Pagnol's novel.

Bridger bought a farm on the South Downs and invited Moore to share in this adventure, which he did, though his part in the enterprise, comically described in the trilogy, never amounted to much more than the shooting down of the rabbits when Bridger was ready to sell them. In the event, the system proved slow and inefficient and was eventually superseded by netting.

'The squire and I were fair shots; we could be counted upon to shoot well forward, hitting the rabbit in the head, spoiling him as little as possible for the market; but, in spite of our careful shooting, Colville soon found that the profit that could be made on shot rabbits would not pay the interest on the large sums of money that had been spent on the house and the hurdles.'

Moore had a pony sent to him from Ireland and spent much time riding along the downs and picking locations for scenes he was later to use in some of his novels. The long, peaceful days in Sussex had awakened in him a love of 'dear, sweet Protestant England' to which he confessed in the book he was writing: 'The red tiles of the farmhouse, the elms, the great hedgerows, and all the rich fields adorned with spreading trees, and the weald and the wold . . . The villages clustered round the greens, the spires of the churches pointing between the elm trees. This is congenial to me, and this is Protestantism. England is Protestantism, Protestantism is England.'

He wrote to his mother, just before Christmas, 1877: 'I have now taken up my abode, I hope for good, in Sussex . . . I am very fond of my friends, and have entirely adopted their life – have said in fact thy people shall be my people and thy God shall be my God.

I put on a high hat, take an umbrella and march to church every Sunday. I do not believe, but I love Protestantism. If it is not the faith of my brain, it is the faith of my heart.'

At this period he rejoiced in the thought that the Moores were of English descent, and he congratulated the entire family on its wisdom and discernment when he heard that his brother Maurice had become engaged to a Protestant girl, Evelyn Handcock of Galway. His younger brother, Julian, was now living with his mother at Moore Hall, and doing nothing; George Moore disapproved of this and made no secret of it, but he had nothing but praise at this stage for Maurice, who was about to be sent off to India with his regiment.

However, despite his remark to his mother about settling in Sussex, Moore still had not given up his apartment in Dane Court, and frequently went up to London for several days at a time. But he was still living on the rabbit farm in February 1888, when he sent an advance copy of *Confessions* to Dujardin: 'I am enchanted that you have decided to publish it in the review . . . I hope to see the first instalment in your next number.'

And he was in Sussex when *Confessions of a Young Man* was published. Although the *Academy* reviewer wondered why such a disagreeable young man of such bad education should ever have thought his memoirs worth recording, the book was on the whole well received and sold very well.

It is very largely autobiographical, though in the first edition it was a mythical 'Edmund Dayne' who related the story of his life and gave us the benefit of his views on life and literature and art. Moore was later to remark in a letter: 'I do think I can write autobiography as well as anyone that has yet written it – with perfect candour and complete shamelessness.'

It is dedicated to one of his oldest Paris friends, the painter Jacques-Emile Blanche, in French: 'The soul of the ancient Egyptian awakened in me when my youth died, and I have had the idea of conserving my past, its spirit and its form, in art.

'Thus, dipping my paint-brush in memory, I have painted its

games* so that they take an exact resemblance to life, and I have wrapped the corpse in the finest shroud. Rameses II did not receive more devoted attention! Would that this book would turn out to be as durable as his pyramid!'

In a preface to the 1904 edition, he says that the book is 'a sort of genesis; the seed of everything I have written since will be found herein'. He claims that the book is completely original and that it contains the first eulogies in English, or indeed in any language, of Manet, Degas, Whistler, Monet and Pissarro – all of whom he knew, or had met; and he adds that anyone who reads it will have to admit that time has vindicated his enthusiasm. Which is certainly true.

It is worth noting that Moore has an extraordinary way of breaking off the narrative to give his views on various topics, often quite at random. At one stage he goes into a long and slightly juvenile debate in which he attempts to demonstrate that Balzac is a far greater writer than Shakespeare; the arguments include the curious point that Shakespeare enjoys the unfair advantage of having had three hundred years of stage representation to impress his characterisations 'on the sluggish mind of the world'. Balzac alone, and particularly his *Comédie Humaine*, left an important or lasting impression on his mind. 'The rest was like walnuts and wine, an agreeable after-taste.' In *Confessions*, he explains that he never derived any profit whatsoever and very little pleasure from the reading of Shakespeare's plays; he concedes that some of Shakespeare's verse is melody but adds that Shakespeare does not 'fetch him', and that while Marlowe enchants him 'Shakespeare leaves him cold' – a curiously modern idiom for 1886 or 1887. He was later to revise his opinion of Shakespeare and the Elizabethan dramatists, as he was to revise his opinion on so many other topics.

From time to time, he interjects odd, offhand observations. A sample: 'You must have rules in poetry, if it is only for the pleasure

* Moore uses '*joues*' but probably means '*jeux*'.

of breaking them, just as you must have women dressed, if it is only for the pleasure of undressing them.'

And another: 'The world is dying of machinery; that is the great disease, that is the plague that will sweep away and destroy civilisation; man will have to rise against it sooner or later . . . the great and reasonable revolution will be when mankind rises in revolt and smashes the machinery . . .'

Another, on translating poetry: 'If the translator is a good poet, he substitutes his verse for that of the original – I don't want his verse, I want the original – [but] if he is a bad poet, he gives us bad verse, which is intolerable.'

Another, on Christianity: 'It has brought nothing into the world but chastity, a fraudulent humanitarianism, fear of life, and a code of morality which has made the world an ugly and hypocritical place.'

Sometimes he digresses to tell a story, like the one about his friend Mendès from the Nouvelles Athènes circle, who, when a friend came to him and complained that his mother had gone off to live with a priest, replied: 'With what better man would you have your mother live? Clearly, young man, you have no religious feelings.'

He claims, probably correctly: '. . . pity, that most vile of all vile virtues, has never been known to me. The great pagan world I love knew it not. Now the world proposes to interrupt the terrible austere laws of nature which ordain that the weak shall be trampled upon, shall be ground into death and dust, that the strong shall be really strong – that the strong shall be glorious, sublime . . . hither the world has been drifting since the coming of the pale socialist of Galilee; and this is why I hate Him, and deny His divinity.' He gives him, nevertheless, the benefit of the doubt by bestowing upon him the capital H; unless that was done on the insistence of his publishers, Swan Sonnenschein, who may not have shared Moore's doubts about the divinity of Jesus of Nazareth and wanted to be on the safe side.

He then goes into a diatribe addressed to Jesus: 'I who hold nought else pitiful, pity Thee.' Odd, too, that he should feel it necessary to lapse into biblical language when addressing Jesus, though he tends to move into the thee/thou format fairly frequently in all his writings. The whole passage illustrates his extremely ambivalent attitude towards religion, and possibly indicates why he ultimately became a Protestant rather than remaining an agnostic, though a number of the ideas expressed in *Confessions* sadly lack any hint of the essential charity which is embodied in most forms of Christianity.

What do I care, he asks, that millions of wretched Israelites died under Pharaoh's lash or the heat of the Egyptian sun? It was well that they died so, in order that he, George Moore, could have the pyramids to fill a musing hour with wonderment. He goes on to develop this theme. He is not concerned that a sixteen-year-old model of Ingres should have lost her virtue and died of drink and disease, so long as he, Moore, would later be able to enjoy the painting that was the result. In all sincerity (his words), he would be ready to decapitate all the Japanese in Japan, to save one Hokusai from destruction.

This particular passage ends with the thought that 'England was great and glorious, because England was unjust, and England's greatest son was the personification of injustice – Cromwell'. A strange sentiment for an Irishman later to become deeply involved in the Irish Literary Renaissance, though Moore was always inclined to snatch at random illustrations to back up his cock-eyed theories without ever investigating them fully. His contention that no Catholic country had produced any literature since the Reformation was a case in point.

He disapproves of the Club, expressing his disapproval in horse-breeding terms: '*Club* is out of *The Housewife* by *Respectability*.' And he disapproves of respectability, as exemplified by the villa: '. . . A suburban villa, a piano in the drawing-room, and going home to dinner.' He sees universal uniformity as the imminent fate of the world: 'Today our plight is pitiable enough – the duke, the jockey-boy, and the artist are exactly alike; they are dressed

George Moore, aged 53,
painted by John Butler Yeats,
father of the poet W.B. Yeats.

Colonel Maurice Moore,
George Moore's younger brother:
from a painting by Walter Osborne.

A portrait of A.E. (George Russell),
by John Butler Yeats.

A portrait of 'dear Edward' Martyn,
by Sarah Purser.

A cartoon by Max Beerbohm of W.B. Yeats
introducing George Moore to the queen of the fairies.

Lady Gregory,
painted by John Butler Yeats.

Susan Mitchell,
who was one of Moore's circle in Dublin,
and wrote the first book about him:
a portrait by John Butler Yeats.

A portrait of J.M. Synge,
the Abbey Theatre playwright who was
a member of Moore's circle in Dublin,
by Harold Oakley.

by the same tailor, they dine at the same clubs, they swear the same oaths, they speak equally bad English, they love the same women. Such a state of things is dreary enough, but what unimaginable dreariness there will be when there are neither rich nor poor, when all have been educated, when self-education has ceased.'

He is horrified at the idea of universal education. In the old days, when a people became too highly civilised, the barbarians came down from the north and regenerated that nation with darkness; but now there are no more barbarians, it will be necessary to bring in legislation to ensure that 'no more than one child in a hundred shall be taught to read, and no more than one in ten thousand shall learn to play the piano'.

He swore that he would never bring a child into the world: 'That I may die childless – that when my hour comes I may turn my face to the wall saying, I have not increased the great evil of human life – then, though I were a murderer, fornicator, thief, and liar, my sins shall melt even as a cloud. But he who dies with children about him, though his life were in all else an excellent deed, shall be held accursed by the truly wise, and the stain upon him shall endure for ever.'

For a man who was always advancing outrageous ideas and trying them out on his friends, *Confessions* contains an extraordinary diatribe against ideas: 'Of all literary qualities the creation of ideas is the most fugitive. Think of the fate of an author who puts forward a new idea tomorrow in a book, in a play, in a poem. The new idea is seized upon, it becomes common property, it is dragged through newspaper articles, magazine articles, through books, it is repeated in clubs, drawing rooms; it is bandied about the corners of streets; in a week it is wearisome, in a month it is an abomination. Who has not felt a sickening feeling coming over him when he hears such phrases as "To be or not to be, that is the question". Shakespeare was really great when he wrote, "Music to hear, why hearest thou music sadly?" not when he wrote, "The apparel oft proclaims the man." Could he be freed from his ideas, what a poet we should have! Therefore let those who have taken firsts at Oxford devote their trite souls to preparing an edition from which everything resembling an idea has been excluded.'

Next comes an extensive dialogue between Moore and his conscience. His conscience reminds him that he has passed the Rubicon, his thirtieth year, and asks him whether he is ashamed, whether he repents. He replies in the phrase he learnt from Manet: 'I am ashamed of nothing, but to be ashamed.'

And, later, his conscience asks: 'Since death is the only good, why do you not embrace death? Of all the world's goods it is the cheapest, and the most easily obtained.' And Moore himself replies: 'For at least a hundred thousand years man has rendered this planet abominable and ridiculous with what he is pleased to call his intelligence, without, however, having learned that his life is merely the breaking of the peace of unconsciousness, the drowsy uplifting of tired eyelids of somnolent nature. How glibly this loquacious ape chatters of his religion and his moral sense, always failing to see that both are but allurements and inveiglements.'

And still later: 'For years it seemed impossible to me that women could love men. Women seemed to me so beautiful and desirable – men so ugly, almost revolting. Could they really touch us without revulsion of feeling, could they really desire us? I was absorbed in the life of woman – the mystery of petticoats, so different from the staidness of trousers! . . . I loved women too much to give myself wholly to one.'

Characteristically, for Moore knew himself every bit as well as anybody else knew him, his conscience now asks: 'Yes, yes; but what real success have you had with women?' And he replies: 'I love women as I love champagne. I drink and enjoy it; but an exact account of every bottle drunk would prove a flat narrative . . . Why should I undertake to keep a woman by me for the entire space of her life, watching her grow fat, grey, wrinkled and foolish? Think of the annoyance of perpetually looking after anyone, especially a woman! . . . We punish a man with death for killing his fellow; but a little reflection should make the dullest understand that the crime of bringing a being into the world exceeds by a thousandfold, a millionfold, that of putting one out of it.

'Men are today as thick as flies in a confectioner's shop; in fifty years there will be less to eat, but certainly some millions more mouths. I laugh, I rub my hands! I shall be dead before the red time comes. I laugh at religionists who say that God provides for those He brings into the world. The French Revolution will compare with the revolution that is to come, that is inevitable, as a puddle on the road-side compares with the sea. Men will hang like pears on every lamp-post, in every quarter of London there will be an electric guillotine that will decapitate the rich like hogs in Chicago. Christ, who with his [lower case here, Moore is nothing if not inconsistent] white feet trod out the blood of the ancient world, and promised Universal Peace, shall go out in a cataclysm of blood.'

Moore has a most unnerving habit of suddenly addressing the reader and accusing him (or her) of thoughts which have never once entered the unfortunate person's mind:

> And now, hypocritical reader, I will answer the questions which have been agitating you this long while, which you have asked at every stage of this long narrative of a sinful life.
> You have been angrily asking, exquisitely hypocritical reader, why you have been forced to read this record of a sinful life.

Nobody is forced to read it, and it does not appear to have been nearly as sinful as Moore himself would have wished it to be, nor is there anything in it likely to make us hypocritical readers the slightest bit angry. He comes across as incorrigibly naive, rather than irrevocably wicked.

> Soldier, robber, priest, atheist, courtesan, virgin, I care not what you are, if you have not brought children into the world to suffer, your life has been as vain and harmless as mine has been . . . I hold out my hand to you, we are brothers; but in my

heart of hearts I think myself a cut above you, because I do not
believe in leaving the world better than I found it; and you,
exquisitely hypocritical reader, think that you are a cut above me
because you say you would leave the world better than you found
it.

That Moore got away with what his contemporaries called the
'confounded cheek' of these self-adulating chats with his own
conscience is one thing; but the sheer arrogance of putting words
into an imaginary reader's mind, and then overthrowing that
imaginary reader's arguments with displays of his own verbal
virtuosity is typical of what Walter Pater called Moore's awful
audacity. Later, he was to apply this technique to his own form of
autobiography, rewriting conversations he had had, or might have
had, with people in Dublin, giving them all the duff lines, all the
bogus arguments, and always taking, as his friend AE ruefully
remarked, the best lines for himself.

'The knell of my thirtieth year has sounded. In three or
four years my youth will be as a faint haze on the sea,' he writes
as he enjoins his dear, exquisite readers to admit that they
feel just a little bit interested in his wickedness, to confess that
their mouths begin to water a bit when they think of the rich and
various pleasures that fell to his share in happy Paris, to
acknowledge that if they, too, had had the courage, health and
money to lead such a fast life, like him, they would certainly have
done so.

Around this period he became involved in a row which should
have ended in a duel: Lewis Marshall came over from Paris to act
as his second but nothing came of it, for what reason no one can
say; for, with a typically arrogant lack of consideration for his dear,
hypocritical, and by now perhaps a little less patient, reader,
Moore cuts off the narrative in midstream and concludes: 'At
breakfast next day the duel seemed more tiresome than ever, but
the gentlemen were coming to meet Marshall. He showed his
usual tact in arranging my affair of honour; a letter was drawn up in
which my friend withdrew the blow of his hand, I withdrew the

blow of the bottle, etc., – really now I lack energy to explain it any further.'

And his *Confessions* end with an address to all the young men who will read the book: 'Dear ones, dear ones, the world is your pleasure; use it at your will. Dear ones, I see you about me still, I yield my place, but one more glass I will drink with you; and while drinking, I will say my last word – were it possible I would be remembered by you as a young man: but I know too well that the young never realise that the old were not born old. Farewell.'

Moore soon began to find the evenings with his friend Colvill tedious, and took to spending more and more of them with Colly's family, the Squire and Mrs Bridger, and the two Saxon maidens at Shoreham, frequently staying there overnight because he found it difficult to make his way along the path across the downs in the dark. He was also tending to visit London more and more frequently, and before very long, as he puts it in *Ave*: 'Life, although pleasant at the top and the foot of the downs, was too restricted in view for the purpose of my literature. If one wants to write, one has to live where writing is being done, I said, and again I left my friends, this time for a still longer absence, and I might never have returned to them if the Boer War had not brought me down to Sussex [in 1900] to find out if there were anything in England, in the country, in the people with whom I could still sympathise.'

*Spring Days*, another of Moore's novels, was published in 1888, as well as a French translation of *Confessions*. He himself described *Spring Days* as 'the tale of a city merchant, who is worried about his daughters – a sort of comic King Lear'. It was in fact intended as the prelude to the first part of a projected trilogy which never materialised; the subject of the first part of the trilogy was to be the young men about town in London, amusing themselves; the second part was to be a study of the servants of the rich, written from the servants' point of view, which eventually became *Esther*

*Waters*; and the third and final part was to have dealt with the hopes and disappointments of old people, watching their children grow up. Initially Moore had intended to follow the same characters through the trilogy, including John Norton, his Sussex squire, based on his cousin Edward Martyn, transformed into an English gentleman.

Hone describes *Spring Days* as an English suburban variant on *A Drama in Muslin*, and there are certain superficial similarities. The city merchant, a man called William Brooke, hesitates about dividing his fortune between his three daughters, who ultimately miss out on all chances of marriage. Frank Escott, heir to an Irish peerage, and a university friend of Willie Brooke, is brother to the three girls, Maggie, Sally and Grace, who fight like cats for possession of a pair of sheets between which this young man once slept during a visit to their house. Willie secretly marries a young working-class girl, to whom he refers as 'the missus', and like Colvill Bridger, on whom the character is largely based, he is happiest when going through the account books.

*Spring Days*, like *A Mere Accident*, was a failure; in his preface to a revised edition published in 1915, Moore admitted that all the welcome it got 'were a few contemptuous paragraphs scattered through the Press and an insolent article in *The Academy*'. The reviewer in *The Academy* wrote that he started on the novel with 'distinctly friendly feelings', being under the impression that Moore had been the victim of press persecution, but found himself confronted 'with the worst novel ever written'. Moore was extremely upset, because he genuinely believed that he was recreating Jane Austen in the novel; 'it was an attempt, not to continue, but to recreate *Pride and Prejudice*, *Emma*, etc. . . . Everybody is abusing *Spring Days* . . . Apparently I have failed horribly.'

These remarks were made in a letter to Clara Lanza, with whom Moore immediately developed an intimate correspondence.* What had happened was that a few copies of his *Confessions* had found their way to New York and were on offer in Brentano's bookshop in Union Square. Brentano, who was a publisher as well as a bookseller, was considering the publication of an American edition, and discussed it with a young American novelist, Clara Lanza. Madame Lanza, as Moore initially addressed her, had never heard of George Moore, but took a copy of the book home with her and was, apparently, entranced by its contents. She encouraged Brentano to proceed with the publication of an American edition, and then wrote to Moore to tell him of her admiration for the book, and of the small part that she had played in having it published in the States. Moore was flattered and delighted, all the more so when he discovered – from American friends in London – that his correspondent was not only of good family and extremely rich, but was one of the reigning beauties in New York. A correspondence between them ensued which carried on for years.

In August 1888, Moore spent a few days in Dieppe, where the parents of his painter friend Blanche had a house. He saw Blanche himself, Dujardin and Gervex, another painter. On his return, he started to write *Mike Fletcher*, the first part of his planned trilogy, the novel about the young man about town; the Mike Fletcher of the title is the illegitimate son of a French father and an Irish mother, who edits a magazine called *The Pilgrim*, not unlike *The Hawk*, the journal edited by Moore's own brother Augustus. The book is, in fact dedicated to Augustus.

Frank Escott, of *Spring Days*, reappears in this novel, joining Mike Fletcher on the staff of *The Pilgrim*. One of their friends is John Norton, the Saxon squire, also from *Spring Days*, who is now reading Schopenhauer and is extremely critical of their loose lives and looser conversations.

Mike stays with Norton in Sussex, enjoying the hunting and country-house life generally, and creating havoc everywhere

---

* She was one of the first of many. To the day he died, Moore was in constant correspondence with a number of young women, most of them American.

because he is such a dab hand with the ladies. Wearying of all this, he returns to London, where he visits the Escotts and wins a lot of money from them by cheating at cards. Next he hears he has been left some property in Berkshire by a former mistress, and finally he goes off to Nice – Moore's fictional characters do not behave any more rationally than he himself did, in the course of his own life – in search of Lily Green, his idea of womanly purity, whom he had persuaded, some time earlier, to run away from the convent in which she was training to become a nun. He finds her dying of consumption, goes to Africa in despair, and eventually returns to Ireland to shoot himself. Not surprisingly, the principal critical complaint about this book was that it was, like *Spring Days*, lacking in humour. Moore wrote to his mother to say that he thought it was the best thing he had ever done: 'My novel is a new method. It is not a warming up out of Dickens and Thackeray. It is a method that will certainly be adopted by other writers, but will the first effort meet with recognition? I scarcely think so . . .'

And he was right. Though he was now famous, largely as a result of controversial articles in popular newspapers like the *Pall Mall Gazette*, his novels were not, in general, well received by the press, and he still was not making much money from his writing. Also, the income from his estate in Ireland was uncertain and inadequate, particularly in view of the fact that he was still paying for the upkeep of Moore Hall so that it could be available to his mother and to his brothers and sisters and their children.

The germ of the idea which had first occurred to him as he watched the maidservant Emma in the lodgings in the Strand now crystallised; he forgot all about his proposed trilogy and settled down to work on a novel based on a maidservant, set in his friends', the Bridgers', house in Sussex and incorporating all his memories of his father's racing stables at Moore Hall.

It was an instant success; it made a fortune and Moore never again had to worry about money; and it received instant critical acclaim.

*Esther Waters* was to be the turning point. But it was still six years away in the future.

TWELVE

# GM, Art Critic
# and Journalist

As well as establishing himself as a famous novelist, George Moore – or GM as he was by then widely known in London – was now also making quite a reputation as an art critic and as a witty and controversial journalist. Always a frequent theatre-goer, he had developed a considerable contempt for the acting profession, and he unburdened himself of a number of his thoughts on this subject in an article called 'Mummer-Worship', which was originally published in the *Universal Review*; was then published, in 1891, along with various other of his newspaper and magazine pieces in *Impressions and Opinions*; and later reappeared, among a few other selected pieces, in the Appendix to the 1933 edition of *Confessions*, as well as in his last, unfinished published work, *A Communication to My Friends*.

Since Moore clearly thought so highly of this piece, it is worth examining it in some detail. Moore obviously regarded acting as the lowest of the arts, if indeed it could be considered an art at all, and lamented the fact that actors and actresses were, at this particular period, revered above all other beings.

You can teach a child to act, he says, but you cannot teach a child to paint pictures, to model statues, or to write prose, poetry or music. Acting makes very slender demands on the intelligence of those who practise it. And yet what the mummers really yearn for, in his opinion, is respectability; they covet the top hat, the club and villa, and the suburban respectability which the villa confers upon those who live in one. Some Mummers even aspire to send their sons to Eton, he complains.

Even worse, in his view, was the fact that some of them had taken to writing newspaper articles and books. Books about what? he asks, and answers himself: 'There is but one subject of interest to the mummer, and, like his clothes, his talk, and his virtue, his books excite the curiosity of the public . . . And when not engaged in compiling the stories of their virtuous and successful lives, the mummers discuss their social grievances in the evening papers.'

They aspire to being received into society and, when they are, their wives have the temerity to question the morals of their hostesses. This would not have happened a century earlier, he believes; you would not find Madame Récamier including a mere mummer among her guests, much less among her lovers.

He hates their tiresome conversation about the little bits of stage 'business' with which they succeed in distracting the audience's attention from the principal performers to themselves, and he deplores the way in which the mummer claims intelligence, even genius, by virtue of his office, though neither intelligence (let alone genius) nor even any training is required for success on the stage.

And to back this up he quotes an article in the *Evening News* by one of Mr Wyndham's young ladies, a Miss Mary Moore. 'I began my stage career at Bradford, in Yorkshire,' she writes, 'in the first touring company of *The Candidate*, sent out by Mr Wyndham. I went out as understudy of Miss Eveson in the leading part of Lady Dorothy. At Bradford, Miss Eveson was taken ill, and I had to go on at very short notice. I need not tell you how dreadfully nervous I was. It was a very severe trial, but I managed to get through it. *It was actually my first appearance on the stage. I had no previous experience, even as an amateur.*'

The italics are Moore's, and he adds: 'I would ask those who think I have unjustly deprecated the art of acting in comparison with the other arts, to think – if they can – of a man painting a picture *without previous experience*, or modelling a statue, or composing a sonata, or even playing the piano.'

Miss Mary Moore next received a summons to go to Berlin to play the part in German, a startling proposal since she had not kept up what she calls her 'familiarity' with the German language since her school-days. However, she repairs the omission by taking a passage on the north German Lloyd steamer, *Saal*, to brush up her German en route, as Moore puts it, 'through conversations with ticket collectors'.

'The newspapers told us that they were applauded and rewarded with floral tributes,' he writes. 'But then so would a band of Hottentots who came to Europe to flourish clubs.'

He makes the valid point that 'only those who have lived for ten years abroad and speak a foreign language with fluency and conversational correctness' can appreciate how skin-deep their real knowledge of the language is. He goes on to observe that an ability of some kind is required to compose even a bad opera or to paint a bad picture, but anybody can play Hamlet or Juliet badly, without either any basic ability or any training of any sort.

Our generation is no longer prepared to work, he concludes, we all want to live well and to enjoy life. Twenty years ago farm labourers were paid by the piece and worked on until eight o'clock in the evening; now they are paid by the week and they strike work at half-past five. As a result, the arts are encumbered with young men and women, especially women, since they are currently in surplus. Clearly they cannot all marry, or enlist, or go to the colonies as domestic servants; so they decide to go on the stage.

In the autumn of 1888, Vizetelly was taken to court by the Vigilance Society for publishing English translations of Zola's

*Nana, Piping Hot,* and *The Soil.* Vizetelly, on Moore's suggestion, brought out an anthology designed to show that, on the grounds alleged against Zola, Shakespeare and most of the English classics would instantly qualify for suppression, a *reductio ad absurdum* which became Moore's stock argument against censorship.

Later, referring to the subject in *Avowals,* Moore says: 'It is not true that pornography and literature overlap, that the frontiers are indistinct. Real literature is concerned with the description of life, and thoughts about life, rather than acts. The very opposite is true in the case of pornographic books.'

Moore now gave up his quarters in Dane's Inn, and moved to 8, King's Bench Walk, in the Temple. He continued to visit his friends the Bridgers in Sussex, but was no longer involved in the rabbit farm. He spent a lot of time with Frank Harris, whom he described extravagantly as 'the most brilliant conversationalist who ever lived'. Harris was at this time editor of the *Fortnightly Review.*

Moore's rooms in King's Bench Walk – a sitting room and a bedroom – were very humble, and were described as being 'as dreary as a cheap hotel, without even the melancholy counterfeit of luxury, found in a dentist's waiting room'. His land agent, Ruttledge, described the place as a 'cockloft'. Moore was now thirty-seven, and was corresponding with Madame Lanza about collaborating with her in the task of turning one of her novels into a play.

The Recorder found the Vizetelly translations of Zola obscene, but allowed Vizetelly to go free under a recognisance of £200 and a promise that he would withdraw all Zola's books from publication. Instead of complying with the law, Vizetelly began to reprint the novels in unexpurgated editions, one of them at least translated by Moore, and was sentenced to three months' imprisonment; Moore visited him in prison and the case filled him with disgust at English hypocrisy.

Around this period he went to Paris, where he met the novelist Mrs Gertrude Atherton: she described him in her memoirs,

*Adventures of a Woman Novelist* as 'very tall and very blond, with a long, colourless face that looked like a codfish crossed by a satyr'.

Hearing that Degas had liked his *Confessions*, Moore called at the painter's studio and offered to write about him, but Degas did not appear to want to see him. This was not untypical; throughout his life Moore spent hours waiting to be received by 'great' people (or people whom he considered to be great) who seemed not to want to have anything to do with him.

In March 1889, Mrs Bridger died; quite suddenly, she had become desperately ill and went up to London to see a specialist. Moore wrote a piece about her death shortly after it occurred, though it was not published until 1906 when it appeared as an essay called 'A Remembrance' in *Memoirs of My Dead Life*: 'The little pony carriage took her to the station, and I saw her in the waiting room wrapped up in shawls. She was ashamed to see me, but in truth the disease had not changed her as she thought it had. There are some that are so beautiful that disease cannot deform them, and she was endowed with such exquisite life that she would turn to smile back on you over the brink of the grave.'

She returned and appeared to have taken a new lease of life. 'How nice you look,' Moore said to her. 'You are quite well now, and your figure is like a girl of fifteen.' And he thought: 'She turned to me with that love in her face which an old woman feels for a young man who is something less and something more than her son. As a flush of summer lingers in autumn's face, so does a sensation of sex float in such an affection. There is something strangely tender in the yearning of a young man for the decadent charms of her whom he regards as the mother of his election [two odd choices of word here, *decadent* and *election*], and who, at the same time, suggests to him the girl he would have loved if time had not robbed him of her youth. There is a waywardness in such an affection that a formal man knows not of. I remember that day, for it was the last time I saw her beautiful.'

The disease turned out to be incurable, and Mrs Bridger died a slow, lingering death. Moore spent several weeks with her family, waiting for her to die, deeply shocked by the way life went on as usual: 'Lunch was the meal that shocked me most, and I often thought: She is dying upstairs, and we are eating jam tarts.'

And the funeral: '. . . the querulous voice of the organ, the ugly hymn and the grating voice of the aged parson standing in a white surplice on the altar steps were so hard to bear that I closed my eyes and shut out the sight of old men, impelled by senile curiosity, pressing forward to look into her grave . . . The crowd dispersed quickly; the relatives and friends of the deceased, as they returned home, sought those who were most agreeable and sympathetic, and matters of private interest were discussed. Those who had come from a distance consulted their watches, and an apology to life was implicit in their looks, and the time they had surrendered to something outside of life evidently struck them as being strangely disproportionate. The sunlight laughed along the sea, and the young corn was thick in the fields; leaves were beginning in the branches, larks rose higher and higher, disappearing in the pale air, and as we approached the woods, the rooks reminded us that she would never hear the pleasant sounds of spring-time again, and that our lives would not be the same.'

Bridger married again – to one of the sisters of the dentist who had taken the small house on the estate where the Bridgers had been living when Moore first met Colly – and Moore gradually lost touch with the family, though he continued to write to one of the daughters, Dulcibella, until the end of his life, and he visited them once again, during the Boer War, and before his departure for Ireland.

His thoughts on *Esther Waters* were now taking definite shape. But in the meantime he wanted to prepare a book of essays, and to write a play about a Socialist leader, who falls in love with the owner of a mine, who happens also to be an attractive woman.

While still working on *The Strike at Arlingford*, Moore went to

Paris, where, in the Louvre, he met two women writers, Kathleen Bradley and Edith Cooper, who described him as 'of hue unhealthy, of hair honey-coloured, light eyes sincere, speech candid . . . He has the obstinate tactlessness of speech that comes of his race.'

The novel about the servants (it had not yet acquired the title *Esther Waters*) was again laid aside in August for a visit to Ireland, where his brother Julian was living at Moore Hall with his mother, working on an opera. Augustus was now about to marry for the second time and proposed to take his bride to Moore Hall for their honeymoon. Moore strongly disapproved of this on the grounds that Moore Hall was not a suitable place for the second honeymoon of a divorced man, much less of a man who edited *The Hawk*, which was described as 'a smart journal for men about town', though with characteristic inconsistency Moore was not above contributing to the magazine himself. Moore's sister Nina was now married to a man called Kilkelly, and was about to have her first baby. 'I don't know why she goes on having babies,' he wrote to his mother. 'She can't afford them.'

During his visit, Moore spent some time in and around Dublin, and later, in the first volume of *Hail and Farewell*, recalled a walk through Terenure out into the Dublin Mountains where he looked at a house to let, known as Mount Venus. At the gate lodge, a woman came to the door, as Moore approached:

> 'You've come to see the house?'
> 'Is there any reason why I shouldn't see it?'
> 'No, there's no reason why you shouldn't. If you'll wait a minute, I'll fetch the key.'
> She doesn't speak like a caretaker, I thought, nor look like one.
> 'Is it a lease of the house you'd like, or do you wish only to hire it for the season, sir?'
> 'Only for the season,' I said. 'Is it to be let furnished?'
> 'There's not much furniture, but sufficient – '
> 'So long as there are beds, and a table to write upon, and a few chairs.'
> 'Yes, there's that, and more than that,' she answered, smiling . . .

'These are the drawing-rooms,' she said, and drew my attention to the chimney piece.

'It's very beautiful,' I answered, turning from the parti-coloured marbles to the pictures. All the ordinary subjects of pictorial art lined the walls, but I passed on without noticing any, so poor and provincial was the painting, until I came suddenly upon the portrait of a young girl. The painting was hardly better than any I had already seen, but her natural gracefulness transpired in classical folds as she stood leaning on her bow, a Diana of the forties, looking across the greensward, waiting to hear if the arrow had reached its mark . . .

Several generations seemed to be on these walls, and I asked the caretaker if she knew anything about the people who had lived in the house? It was built about two hundred years ago, I should say, and we wandered into another room.

'I should like to hear something about the girl whose portrait I have been looking at. There's nothing to conceal? No story?'

'There's nothing in her story that any one need be ashamed of. But why do you ask?' And the manner in which she put the question still further excited my curiosity.

'Because it seems to me that I've seen the face before.'

'Yes,' she answered, 'you have. The portrait in the next room is my portrait . . . as I was forty years ago. But I didn't think that anyone would see the likeness . . .'

. . . my thoughts returned to her whom an artist had painted as Diana the Huntress. A man of some talent, for he had painted her in an attitude that atoned to some extent for the poverty of the painting. Or was it she who gave him the attitude, leaning on her bow? Was it she who settled the folds about her limbs, and decided the turn of her head, the eyes looking across the greensward towards the target? Had she fled with somebody whom she had loved dearly and been deserted and cast away on that hillside? Does the house belong to her? Or is she the caretaker? Does she live there with a servant? Or alone, cooking her own dinner? None of my questions would be answered, and I invented story after story to explain her as I returned through the grey evening in which no star appeared, only a red moon rising up through the woods like a fire in the branches.

When he had finished his play, *The Strike at Arlingford*, he submitted it to the actor-manager John Hare (later Sir John), and went off to Paris, where he had his portrait painted by Blanche. He also went with Ludovic Halévy to Antoine's

Théâtre Libre to see performances of Ibsen's *Ghosts* and *A Doll's House*.

When Moore returned to London, he discovered that Hare did not want to produce *The Strike at Arlingford*, and Beerbohm Tree, the actor for whom he had written the principal part, had also turned it down. Partly, perhaps, because of the play, and partly as a result of seeing Ibsen's plays in Paris, he now became involved, with George Bernard Shaw, in the management of the Independent Theatre, dedicated to the improvement of English theatrical taste through the performance of foreign plays. He interrupted work on the novel which was to become *Esther Waters* and spent the winter of 1890–91 writing *Vain Fortune*, a serial for the *Lady's Pictorial*, under the nom-de-plume Lady Rhone – it was rewritten and published under his own name by Henry & Co in 1892 – and on collecting some of the best of his recent journalistic pieces on literature, drama and art for publication in book form.

These appeared under the title *Impressions and Opinions* in 1891 and greatly rewarded his efforts; the book was well received and earned him some badly needed money, as well as good reviews everywhere, including the front page and five columns in *The Athenaeum*.

*Vain Fortune*, published in book form in a limited large-paper edition, as well as the ordinary edition, did not fare very well critically, and scarcely was it published before Moore bought back the rights in order to re-write it and have it translated into French and Dutch. But James Joyce, then aged nineteen, praised it in a review and so did John Freeman, an influential critic.

With the money he had earned from these two enterprises, Moore was able to spend the winter of 1891–2 working on *Esther Waters* and he felt himself that he was now within sight of a masterpiece.

'You ask me to tell you about my book,' he wrote to Madame Lanza. 'Well, it is all about servants – servants devoured by betting. It begins in a house in the country where there are race-horses. Towards the end of the book – past the middle – the servants set up a public house. They cannot get custom unless they have betting. Then come the various tragedies of the bar – the hairdresser who cuts his throat – the servant who loses thirty years' character for six shillings – the woman who pledges the plate to give her lover money to bet with. The human drama is the story of a servant girl with an illegitimate child, how she saves the child from baby farmers, her endless temptations to get rid of it, and to steal for it. She succeeds in bringing up her boy, and the last scene is when she is living with her first mistress in the old place, ruined and deserted. The race-horses have ruined the masters as well as the servants.'

Moore had now published four successive novels without much success; in recreating this period in *A Communication to My Friends* published in 1933, he chose to ignore everything that had happened between the publication of *A Drama in Muslin* in 1886 and *Esther Waters* in 1894, giving the impression that the latter was the immediate successor to *Confessions* and *Muslin*.

Arthur Symons, a fellow-countryman as well as a near-neighbour of Moore's, and at that time a rising critic, reviewed *Impressions* at length in the *Academy*. He talked about Moore's great talent, as well as his tireless industry and a single-minded devotion to art; yet Moore had, he wrote, an inexplicable capacity, not only for offences against literary good taste, but also for astounding incorrectness, the incorrectness of a man who knows better, who is not really careless, and yet cannot help himself. Oscar Wilde had already remarked that Moore took seven years to discover grammar, and then discovered the paragraph, shouting his discoveries aloud from the housetops. 'Moore always conducts his education in public,' he commented.

Moore had now begun to attract great attention as an art critic. He had originally written for his brother's magazine, *The Hawk*, in its early days, and then became a regular critic for the *Speaker*, in which he preached the gospel of the French Impressionists, on the basis of his personal acquaintance with Manet. He now began to cultivate the company of painters and other art critics at the Hogarth Club and published a selection from his art criticisms from the *Speaker* in 1893 in book form, under the title *Modern Painting*.

Towards the end of 1892, he had again interrupted work on the novel, this time because G. R. Sims, the critic and champion of the popular drama, who did not share Shaw's and Moore's admiration for Ibsen, offered the Independent Theatre £100 if the directors would dare to stage a play written by Moore.

Moore took *The Strike at Arlingford* out of the drawer, dusted it off, reduced its length from five acts to three and had it ready for production by the beginning of 1893; it was presented on February 21 at the Opéra Comique in the Strand. G. R. Sims sat in the box for which he had in effect paid £100; among the audience were a number of leading dramatic authors whom Moore had savaged in *Impressions and Opinions* as well as various theatre critics whom he had attacked in the *Pall Mall Gazette*. Moore was so nervous about what would happen that he stayed away.

William Archer wrote in the *World* that he liked the play far better than Shaw's *Widowers' Houses*, and Walter Scott, a new publisher, who had taken over Vizetelly's copyrights, brought out *The Strike at Arlingford* along with new editions of *A Mummer's Wife* and *A Drama in Muslin*; and an offer reached Moore for the serial rights of *Esther Waters*, even though it was not yet finished.

*Modern Painting* also proved to be a great success: 1,000 copies were sold in the summer of 1893; it was reviewed by Walter Pater in the *Daily Chronicle*; and McColl gave it a full-page review in the *Spectator*.

While Moore was closely involved with the Independent Theatre Society of London, which had produced his play, as well as one of George Bernard Shaw's, his journalist brother, Augustus, had also been involved with various London theatres, as a writer, producer, librettist and stage manager. And it was around this period that George Moore attended a performance of the poet W. B. Yeats's *The Land of Heart's Desire*, which had been used as a curtain-raiser for Shaw's *Arms and the Man*, at an Independent Theatre Society performance in 1894.

'It amused me to remember the amazement with which I watched Yeats marching around the dress circle after the performance of his little, one-act play,' Moore wrote. 'His play neither pleased nor displeased; it struck me as an inoffensive trifle, but he himself provoked a violent antipathy as he strode to and forth at the back of the dress circle, a long black cloak drooping from his shoulders, a voluminous black tie flowing from his collar, loose, black trousers dragging untidily over his long, heavy feet, a man of such excessive appearance that I could not do otherwise – could I? – than to mistake him for a parody of the poetry I had seen all my life strutting its rhythmic way in the alleys of the Luxembourg Gardens, preening its rhymes by the fountains, excessive in habit and gait.'

Yeats's appearance so confirmed Moore in his belief that the poet's art could not be anything more than a pretty externality that he declined to meet him.

It was in the same year, 1894, that George Moore, now aged forty-two, first met the future Lady Cunard, then aged twenty-two. Born Maud Alice Burke in San Francisco, and a distant relative of the Irish patriot, Robert Emmet, she had been brought up as one of the many 'nieces' of Horace Carpentier, an American Civil War general who had subsequently amassed a fortune in real estate. One of her favourite authors was Emile Zola, and through reading about Zola and his work she encountered the name of George Moore, and was highly impressed and gratified when, during a visit to London, she discovered that Moore was to be a fellow-guest at a big luncheon party at the Savoy. So determined was she to make his acquaintance that she slipped into the restaurant beforehand and changed the place cards so that she would find herself seated next to him.

During the luncheon he launched himself on one of his favourite topics, his desire to win the same freedom for the English novel as Zola had won for the French novel. As he talked, Maud hung on his very words and, laying her hand (Moore called it a 'fern-like hand') upon his arm, she enthused: 'George Moore, you have a soul of fire!'

Moore was at this period suffering from the after-effects of his first quarrel with Pearl Craigie, mentioned in the introduction to this book; he was, therefore, extremely susceptible to these admiring advances from a very beautiful young girl. It will be remembered that sometime in the 1890s, Moore received a letter from a John Oliver Hobbes asking him whether he would be interested in dramatising a story of his. Moore was not particularly interested until he learned that John Oliver Hobbes was the nom-de-plume of a Mrs Pearl Craigie, a very beautiful, rich, fashionable young woman. But their efforts to collaborate were doomed to failure, possibly because at this period Pearl Craigie's [John Oliver Hobbes's] books were selling far better than his own, and in any dispute, the publishers always took her side.

Years later he told Maud that she had given him what other women had offered, but which he did not want from them: an immense kindness and an extraordinary sympathy. He wrote about 'her brightly coloured cheeks and fair hair, fair as the hair in an eighteenth-century pastel', and remembered how she seemed to him in her beautiful dress at their first meeting, 'like a Gavarni drawing'.

He fell in love with her instantly and continued to correspond with her – and subsequently with her daughter Nancy, born in 1896, after Maud had returned to England from America as the wife of Sir Bache Cunard, the forty-three-year-old grandson of the founder of the shipping line. Nearly forty years later, when he was seventy-nine and she was sixty, he was still writing to her: 'Dearest Maud, Your letter was very welcome; I was beginning to think I had lost you – a familiar dread. But since I have not, let me know when you are in England, for I am longing to see you . . . With the same affection, George Moore.' She had left Sir Bache Cunard in 1911 and, although he died in 1925, she never remarried.

Around this period, too, Moore joined Boodle's, the High Tory aristocratic club in St James's, and had a row with Whistler, whom he had never liked, and who had never liked him, which resulted in a challenge to a duel. It came to nothing because, as Moore pointed out, duelling was not allowed in England, and he was always seasick crossing the Channel.

*Esther Waters* finally appeared in March 1894, and was initially dedicated to his brother, Maurice, to whose son, Rory, usually known as Ulick, he became godfather.

The novel was almost universally well received; among those who praised it were Q (Arthur Quiller-Couch, a leading critic and authority on English) who said in the *Spectator* that it was 'the best book of its kind in the English language'; Lionel Johnson in the *Daily Chronicle*; and Hubert Crackenthorpe of the *Yellow Book*.

His mother died in Moore Hall on May 25, 1895; she had been ailing for some considerable time, and his brother Maurice had been urging him to go to Mayo to see her. He later wrote – again in *Memoirs of My Dead Life* – that he had not mourned for his mother as he might have done in normal circumstances because he was at that time recovering from an unhappy love affair and 'a man cannot lament two women at the same time'.

He also confessed his terror at the thought that he would arrive home in time to see his mother die. The funeral pomp, the shroud, and the Irish keening repelled him.

He describes his mixed feelings at the time of his mother's death in very great detail. His sister Nina told him how his mother died. The specialist had not arrived in time, and someone had blundered, not that it mattered much, for his mother would never have submitted to an operation, anyway. The sofa on which his sister was sitting had been broken years ago; he distinctly remembered that it had been taken away to a lumber room. Now it was back; somebody had obviously had it mended. He began to wonder who; his mother, most likely, for she had always looked after everything in the house. His sister spoke of lunch – he had come a long way – and they went into the dining room, and in the middle of the meal his brother Maurice came in and they did not dare to talk about anything but their mother, so they all tried to keep the conversation going for as long as possible.

'But,' he says, 'my brother and I had not seen each other for years, he had come back from India after a long absence; nor do I think I had seen my sister since she married, and that was a long time ago; she had had children, and it was the first time I had seen her in middle age. We were anxious to ask each other questions, to hear each other's news, and we were anxious, too, to see the landscape that we had not seen, at least not together, for many years; we were tempted by the soft sunlight floating on the lawn, by an afternoon full of mist and sun . . . The day moved like a bride from afternoon to evening, arrayed in white lace and blossom . . . This was our first meeting since childhood, and we were assembled in the house where we had all been born. My eyes were drawn to the way the ivy had grown all over one side of the house, and I noticed the disappearance of one of the hollies on the lawn and a gap in the woods – these things were new; but the lake which I hadn't seen since childhood I did not need to look at, so well did I know how every shore was bent, and the place of every island. My first adventures began on that long yellow strand, and I did not need to turn my head to see it, for I knew that trees intervened; and I knew every twisting path through the woods. That yellow strand speckled with tufts of rushes was my first playground. But when my brother proposed that we should walk there, I found some excuse. Why go? the reality would destroy the dream; but I did not speak my thoughts for shame of them.'

One day the silence of the woods was broken by the sound of a mason's hammer, and, on making an inquiry from a passing workman, Moore 'learned that on opening the vault, there was not room for another coffin. But no enlargement of the vault was necessary; a couple of shelves would be all that would be wanted for many a year to come. His meaning was not to be mistaken – when two more shelves had been added there would be room for my brother, myself, and my sister, but the next generation would have to order that a further excavation be made in the hill, or look out for a new burial ground.'

This, typically, set him thinking about his own end:

> That very morning I had seen two old blue-bottles huddled together in the corner of a pane, and at once remembered that a term of life is set out for all things, a few months for the blue-bottle, a few years for me . . . I thought that nothing that could be said on this old subject could move me, but a boy from Derryanny had brought home to me, better than literature could have done, the thought that follows us from youth to age . . . he had reminded me that Michael Malia, that was the mason's name, had known me since I was a little boy . . . I had only to tell Michael Malia if my heart were set on any particular place, and he would keep it for me; there would be a convenient one, just above my grandfather when they got the new shelf up; and he mentioned that he had heard it said that we were both writers.
>
> . . . In twenty or thirty years I shall certainly join the others in that horrible vault . . . and I thought of my Catholic relations, every one of whom believes in the intervention of priests and holy water, the Immaculate Conception, the Pope's Indulgences, and a host of other things which I could not remember, so great was my anguish of mind at the thought that my poor pagan body should be delivered helpless into their pious hands.
>
> How shall I escape from that vault? I cried out suddenly . . . something must be done to escape, and my eyes were strained out on the lake, upon the island on which a Welshman had built a castle . . . I saw the woods reaching down to the water's edge and thought that a great pyre might be built out of them. No trees had been cut for the last thirty years; I might live for another thirty; what grand timber there would then be to build a pyre for me, a pyre fifty feet high, saturated with scented oils, and the body of me lying on the top of it with all my books (they would make a nice pillow for my head) . . . my pyre should be built on the island facing

me, its flames would be seen for miles and miles, the lake would be lighted up by it, and my body would become a sort of beacon fire – the beacon of the pagan future awaiting old Ireland? Nor would the price of such a funeral be anything too excessive – a few hundred pounds perhaps, the price of a thousand larches and a few barrels of scented oil and the great feast, for while I was roasting, my mourners should eat roast meat and drink wine and wear gay dresses – the men as well as the women . . .

While waiting for his mother's body to decompose sufficiently so that they could bury her with impunity according to her last wishes – she had always been terrified of being buried alive, as a result of one final, false diagnosis on the part of some member of the medical profession – Moore continued to plan his own funeral pyre. He realised that he would have to find out what modern law and Christian morality allowed, in relation to the public burning of human bodies, and for that he would have to wait until he was back in Dublin.

He imagined the interview with the family solicitor: and Moore saw himself as presenting this prejudiced old Catholic with a dilemma – whether he should be guilty of so unbusinesslike an act as to refuse to make a will for theological reasons, or do a violence to his own conscience by assisting a fellow-creature to dispose of his body in such a way as would give the Almighty a great deal of trouble in successfully achieving the resurrection of the body, as guaranteed in the scriptures.

'In order to secure the burial of my body, my notion was to leave all my property, lands, money, pictures and furniture, to my brother, Colonel Maurice Moore, on the condition that I should be burnt and the ashes disposed of without the humiliation of Christian rites,' he writes, and he also provided that, if Maurice could not bring himself to do this, everything should go to his brother Augustus; and that, if he in turn failed to comply with his wishes, all his property should go to his brother Julian.

He was busying himself with these matters, happy that Maurice had 'taken off my hands the disagreeable task of seeing to the

undertakers and making arrangements for the saying of Mass, etc.,
arrangements that would be intensely disagreeable to me to make,
so I had plenty of time to think out details of my burning, and I
grew happy in the thought that I would escape from the disgrace of
a Christian burial ... I could not forego, but loosed my
imagination on the burning I imagined and the vision that had
come to me: a pyre at least fifty feet high sending forth a heat so
intense that the mourners would have to take to the boats – a fine
spectacle that would be, if the law would allow it. But wherever
and however I was burnt, I should have to decide what I would
wish to be done with the ashes, and in a moment of happy
inspiration, I conceived the idea of a Greek vase with a relief
representing Bacchanals dancing.' If the purchase of an original
vase proved too expensive, he would be satisfied with a copy in
granite. In the middle of his mother's funeral rites, none, he says,
would have thought from the smile upon his lips that he was
thinking of a Grecian urn for the little pile of white ashes that
would be the end of him.

He goes on: 'One trouble, however, still remained upon my
mind. Where should the vase be placed? Not in Westminster
Abbey. Fie upon all places of Christian burial!'

For a few moments he considered the possibility of siting the urn
in the corner of the entrance hallway of his home, on the exact
spot where he learned to spin his top. But, sooner or later, a
housemaid might knock it over and spill the ashes, or the house
might become the property of another family, and the strangers
would look upon the vase with idle curiosity or perhaps find it
depressing. and an order for his removal to a garret might be made.

> The disposal of the vase caused me a great deal of anxiety, and I
> foresaw that, unless I hit upon some idea whereby I could
> safeguard it from injury forever, my project would be deprived of
> half its value. As I sat thinking, I heard the noise of feet suddenly
> on the staircase ... They are bringing down my mother's coffin, I
> said, and at that moment the door was opened and I was told that
> the funeral procession was waiting for me. My brother, and various
> relatives and friends, were waiting in the hall; black gloves were

on every hand, crêpe streamed from every hat, all the paraphernalia of grief, I muttered, nothing is wanting. My soul revolted against this mockery. But why should I pity my mother? She wished to lie beside her husband. And far be it from me to criticise such a desire!

The coffin was lifted upon the hearse. A gardener of old time came up to ask me if I wished for any crying. I did not at first understand what he meant; he began to explain and I understood that he meant the cries with which the Western peasant follows his dead to the grave. Horrible savagery! and I ordered that there was to be no keening; but three or four women, unable to contain themselves, rushed forward and began a keen. It was difficult to try to stop them ... And as we followed the straggling grey Irish road, with scant meagre fields on either side – fields that seemed to be on the point of drifting into marshland – past the houses of the poor people, I tried to devise a scheme for the safeguarding of the vase ... Unexpectedly, at the very moment when the priest began to intone the *Pater Noster*, I thought of the deep sea as the only clean and holy receptacle for the vase containing my ashes. If it were dropped where the sea is deepest, it would not reach the bottom, but would hang suspended in dark moveless depths where only a few fishes range, in a cool, deep grave, made without hands, in a world without stain, surrounded by a lovely revel of Bacchanals, youths and maidens and wild creatures from the woods, man in his primitive animality.

But nothing lasts for ever. In some millions of years the sea will begin to wither, and the vase containing me will ... sink down to some secure foundation of rocks to stand in the airless and waterless desert that the earth will then be ... Surrounded by dancing youths and maidens, my tomb shall stand on a high rock in the solitude of the extinct sea, of an extinct planet. Millions of years will pass away, and the earth, having lain dead for a long winter, as it does now for a few weeks under frost and snow, will, with all the other revolving planets, become absorbed in the sun, and the sun itself will become absorbed in greater suns, Sirius and his like. In matters of grave moment, millions of years are but seconds; billions convey very little to our minds.

At the end of, let us say, some billion years, the ultimate moment towards which everything from the beginning of time has been moving, will be reached; and from that moment the tide will begin to flow out again, the eternal dispersal of things will begin again; suns will be scattered abroad, and in tremendous sunquakes, planets will be thrown off; in loud earthquakes, these planets will throw off moons. Millions of years will pass away, the earth will become cool, and out of the primal mud, life will begin again in the shape of plants, and then of fish, and then of animals.

It is like madness, but is it madder than Palestinian folklore? And I believe that billions of years hence, billion and billions of years hence, I shall be sitting in the same room where I sit now, writing the same lines that I am now writing: I believe that again, a few years later, my ashes will swing in the moveless and silent depths of the peaceful ocean, and that the same figures, the same nymphs, and the same fauns, will dance around me again.

# THIRTEEN

## Summoned by Voices

George Moore's interest in at least some aspects of the Irish Literary Renaissance probably dated back to a conversation after dinner in Edward Martyn's lodgings in the Temple, some time around 1894, when Martyn first suggested to Moore the idea of returning to Ireland, learning the Irish language, and perhaps even writing a novel in Irish. By 1894, Martyn had written a couple of plays; he was extremely rich, but he lived most austerely, even at home, in Tullyra Castle, where his bedroom resembled a monk's cell.

When Martyn suggested that he should consider studying Irish, the idea immediately struck Moore as a newsworthy literary event, a novel by a best-seller in a new language, or in an old language revived. What appealed to him most about the notion was its potential for personal publicity, always an irresistible magnet to Moore.

He remembered that the boatmen on Lough Carra, in County Mayo, and the workmen from the nearby village had always spoken Irish, and that, if he had so wished, he could easily have learned the language from them in his childhood. For the moment, however, he put these thoughts away to the back of his mind; it would be time enough to think about Ireland in about ten years, he reckoned. In his opinion, Ireland was not by any means yet ready for a literary, or any other sort of, renaissance.

He always referred to Martyn as 'Dear Edward' and described him at this period 'as great in girth as an owl, and nearly as neckless, blinking behind his glasses'. Although Moore found it impossible to resist mocking even his closest male friends, in Edward's case the mockery was always basically kind hearted and well intentioned, though he despised what he regarded as Edward's abject Irish Catholicism.

And Moore always drew a very distinct difference between Irish Catholicism and every other brand; he had plenty of Catholic friends in England, which tends to indicate that it was far more a matter of class and status than of religion, an innate snobbism, perhaps, which caused him, although still nominally a Catholic, to look down on the religion of the peasants among whom he had spent his childhood and early youth.

Martyn was always desperately uneasy in the company of women. No question of homosexuality was ever involved or even suspected; he was a natural-born Irish bachelor, as Moore realised, and as indeed Moore himself was, too, though he was never uneasy with women. 'We come into the world, Edward,' he said, 'with different minds; that is a thing we can't remember too often . . .'

'The oddest of all animals,' Moore went on, 'is man; in him, as in all animals, the sexual interest is the strongest; yet the desire is inveterate in him [Martyn] to reject it; and I am sure Christ's words that in heaven there is neither marriage, nor giving in marriage, must have taken a great weight off Edward's mind.'

Moore claimed that Edward was never very happy too far away from a Catholic church; he liked to feel that he could go to Mass whenever the mood took him. 'I see,' he remarked to Edward. 'It is the magician and his house that tempts you . . . the desire always to have a magician at one's elbow is extraordinary.'

In a subsequent argument with Martyn, Moore made the point that all the Gods originally came from the East. 'Divinity is like China tea,' he remarked. 'It only grows in the east.' And later he remarked: 'He [Martyn] is a good fellow – an excellent one, and a man who would have written well if his mother hadn't put it into his head that he had a soul.'

Although Yeats's pretentious appearance and behaviour had irritated Moore at the first night of Shaw's *Arms and the Man* and Yeats's *The Land of Heart's Desire*, nevertheless after reading some of Yeats's poems Moore *consented* (his own word) to allow Dear Edward to introduce him to the poet in the Cheshire Cheese pub off Fleet Street one evening in 1895. Yeats was anxious to meet Moore to find out what the chances were of getting a three-act play he had just written put on in London; but, when they parted, Yeats left Moore with the distinct impression that he regarded himself as the more 'considerable' author of the two, and that to meet Moore for dinner at the Cheshire Cheese was something of a condescension on his part. Moore added, grudgingly: 'All the same, I could see that among much Irish humbug there was in him a genuine love of his art, and he was more intelligent than his verses had led me to expect.'

Moore next met Yeats in Arthur Symons's room one evening; he had called on Symons – another Irish expatriate who later became a well-known critic and who also lived in the Temple – and Yeats had opened the door. Symons was out and Moore and Yeats discussed symbolism. Moore claimed that Yeats then told him about a problem he had encountered with one of his short stories which he was rewriting for a book, *The Secret Rose*, and added that he had succeeded in solving the problem for Yeats, who did not exhibit any marked signs of gratitude.

During the evening, Yeats talked to Moore about his search for a different prose style. He could not write in Irish, he explained, because he spoke no Irish, and he was looking for some form of English, an Irish dialect perhaps, certainly not the brogue, but a distinctive dialect in which he could write his stories and plays.

Moore then advanced one of his own pet theories: that very soon there would not be enough 'grammar' left in the English language to accommodate any more literature. English was becoming a very 'lean' language, he claimed.

Yeats argued that even in Shakespeare's time people were already talking about the decline of the language. Yeats said that he regretted that he had no gift, as Lady Gregory had, for capturing the flavour of the talk of the people. Lady Gregory had a knack of picking up the living speech from the peasants, and turning his (Yeats's) prose plays into 'Kiltartan', as she called it, after a village near her home.

When Symons came in, they both listened to Yeats talking about style, and, according to Moore, 'his [Yeats's] strange, old-world appearance and his chanting voice enabled me to identify him with the stories he told . . . and so completely that I could not do otherwise than believe that Angus, Etaine, Diarmuid, Deirdre and the rest were speaking through him.'

This conversation confirmed Moore in his still fairly vague plan to learn Irish and possibly even to write a novel in Irish. Yeats did not think that he himself would ever be able to learn Irish, and did not want to try, preferring to continue to work in his own (or, rather, Lady Gregory's) 'style', which he considered to be an attractive mixture of Tudor English and Irish peasant dialect. Moore, on the other hand, having picked up fairly respectable knowledge of French in a few years, had no doubts at this stage about his own ability to acquire Irish, if he so chose, though a few years later he was to claim that he was far too old to learn a new language.

By now the correspondence with Pearl Craigie had prospered and developed into a collaboration. A play by Mrs Craigie and George Moore, *Journey's End in Lovers' Meeting*, had been produced at Daly's Theatre in June 1895; Moore claimed that the idea, the construction, and the dialogue, were all his, and that she had added only a few epigrams and small speeches. Moore got full credit as co-author on the theatre programme but subsequently, after the collaborators had quarrelled not for the first nor for the last time, when the play was published in book form by Mrs Craigie, Moore got no credit, though they were talking again, and there were even newspaper reports that he was going to marry her, which he strenuously denied.

*Celibates*, a collection of short stories published by Walter Scott in 1895, failed to enhance Moore's reputation in any way; Henry Harland said that one of the stories in the collection, 'Mildred Lawson', would have been worthy of Flaubert if Moore had only known how to write. But the fact that it fell flat did not bother Moore much, because he was already busy on *Evelyn Innes*, a novel about an opera singer who becomes a nun.

Most of Moore's friends were puzzled at this choice of subject, but Moore was already looking for somebody who had been in a convent, and could tell him exactly what it was like; he did not believe in doing his research from books. Through his friend, W. T. Stead, editor of the *Pall Mall Gazette*, he met Mrs Virginia Crawford, a convert to Catholicism who, although born a Protestant, had been educated at a convent school; she was on very friendly terms with a great many nuns, and was able to supply him with exactly the sort of precise information he required. She became his paid researcher, and he entered into an intimate correspondence with her that went on until the end of his life; in his letters, he always addressed her as 'Nia'. She had been married to Donald Crawford, a middle-aged lawyer, and had been at the centre of a notorious divorce case in 1886 when she was about twenty-seven, which involved both the Duke of Marlborough and the head of the London Fire Brigade, as well as Sir Charles Dilke who, if he had not become deeply involved with Nia, might have succeeded Gladstone as premier. She was about thirty-seven when she went to work for Moore.

In the meantime, *Esther Waters* was going from strength to strength. Over 24,000 copies of the book had been sold when he received a card from Gladstone congratulating him on the high moral tone of the book and W.H. Smith's removed the ban on his books in their circulating libraries, which had been in force ever since his first novel *A Modern Lover*.

By now Moore was successful enough not to worry about library boycotts, but he kept up his fight against the prudery of the lending libraries for the sake of the principle involved. He met Havelock Ellis in the Temple and Ellis talked to him about the scandal, then getting headlines in the popular press, of young women being compelled by the hostile attitude of society to get rid of their illegitimate babies. Moore assured Ellis that he had not made any overt attempt to do good in writing *Esther Waters*, but was gratified to think that inadvertently the book might have alleviated more human suffering than any other novel of its generation.

He was referring to the establishment of the Fallowfield Corner Home for Homeless Children which had been founded by a hospital nurse, who had been so moved by Moore's description of Esther's problems as an unmarried mother that she had felt obliged to do something about the situation.

He continued his correspondence with Madame Lanza, hoping that one day they would meet, though throughout his life meeting women with whom he had lovingly corresponded for years often turned out to be a disappointment, and in the case of Pearl Craigie a disaster.

The central figure of *Evelyn Innes* is an opera singer, and Moore's dearest wish now was to meet – and even, he claimed, to have an affair with – an opera singer, and before long he was dining, though not sleeping, with Dame Nellie Melba. He also consulted Arthur Symons, who knew a great deal about music as well as literature, for some of his background details on music which are unerringly correct. Much of *Evelyn Innes* was written during visits to the north of England, particularly to Mr and Mrs Charles Hunter of Darlington.

It is worth noting in passing that it was Mrs Hunter who presented Moore with a copy of the King James Bible; thereafter, he always took it with him on his travels, read it constantly, and soon adopted many of its cadences in his own prose, eventually turning the New Testament into a novel, changing the ending and rendering the biblical dialogue into Irish, Jewish and Sussex vernacular. He also wrote a couple of plays based on the story of Jesus from the New Testament.

He had now decided to leave the Temple, and he first considered the Peckham Rye–Dulwich area (where he had set certain scenes in *Esther Waters*) but eventually chose a flat at 92, Victoria Street. It was there that Edward Martyn brought Yeats in 1897, to discuss their plans for the formation of an Irish Literary Theatre.

Edward Martyn told Moore that it would give him no pleasure any longer to have his plays produced in London; he was done with England. The turn of the century would mark the beginning of a new Irish Celtic Literary Renaissance, he said, and Yeats added that they were thinking of putting on some dialogue in Irish before their plays.

Moore listened to Yeats and Martyn as they told him how they had reached their decision to found an Irish Literary Theatre. Yeats had spent the summer at Coole Park, in County Sligo, with Lady Gregory, a rich 'county' widow; Coole Park was only a few miles from Tullyra, Martyn's Gothic castle in County Galway. Edward often visited Coole Park; Yeats and Lady Gregory frequently called on Edward's widowed mother at Tullyra; and both Edward and Yeats had written plays, and had persuaded Lady Gregory to act as secretary to the new venture. With Lady Gregory's help, as Moore put it, 'the owl and the rook had agreed to build a nest in Dublin'.

Yeats wanted to enlist Moore's support for the theatre as a famous, best-selling author, as well as securing his professional assistance in casting and rehearsing the plays, Martyn's *The Heather Field* and his own *The Countess Cathleen*. Lady Gregory had put up £25 (£1,250 today) towards the expenses of this enterprise and it seems probable that Martyn was picking up the tab for the remainder of the costs.

Before long, Moore had organised a cast for the two plays for

Yeats and Martyn, and had written a preface for Martyn's *The Heather Field*, which he described as the first appearance of humanity in English prose drama of the day, comparing Martyn to Ibsen, translated to the Irish countryside. Moore later claimed that he had only helped Yeats and Martyn because he did not want to see Yeats's *The Countess Cathleen* come out of the encounter better than *The Heather Field*. The two plays were rehearsed in the Bijou Theatre in Notting Hill, London.

At this period the Yeats family, who were then living in Blenheim Road in the Bedford Park area of London, had a house guest, Susan Mitchell, then aged about twenty, who was later to write a book about Moore. She remembered meeting Moore at a rehearsal of Yeats's *The Countess Cathleen* 'in some dark by-way of London' but could recall nothing whatever about him.

More interestingly, she remarks that she read *The Mummer's Wife*, when she was living with the Yeats family, mainly for the reason that she had heard that Yeats had forbidden his own sisters to read it. 'I gulped guilty pages of it as I went to bed of nights,' she wrote, 'and I will agree with anybody that it is a powerful novel; I was impaled upon the point of it, and I know. The fat actor who lures away the poor little woman who becomes his wife lives in my memory as one of the most real human beings in English fiction . . . I understand that the book is regarded as immoral; to me it appeared one of the most gloomy moralities in literature.'

At this period Moore had no intention of going to Ireland on any permanent basis himself; he thought that probably a short visit for the final rehearsals and another for the opening night of the plays would probably suffice, though Yeats later admitted that the work of founding the Irish Literary Theatre could never have been accomplished without Moore and his knowledge of the theatre.

Moore's novel *Evelyn Innes* was published in 1898 by T. Fisher Unwin and dedicated to W. B. Yeats and Arthur Symons – 'two contemporary writers with whom I am in sympathy'. It turned out to be one of the most successful of Moore's books, selling 15,000 copies in the cheap edition.

Evelyn Innes, the central character, is discovered by a rich but very material man, Sir Owen Asher, who takes her to Paris and makes her a star. Later, she meets a Celtic composer, Ulick Dean, a character clearly based on Yeats. Evelyn Innes, torn between two sides of her own character, the spiritual and the sensual, is attracted by Ulick because he can offer an alternative both to her own Catholic leanings and Owen Asher's materialism in the form of the ancient religion of the Druids, in which God is found, not in the host, but in the silence of the soul. Unable to make up her mind between Sir Owen and Ulick, or between either or both of them and the convent, she elects to retreat to the convent to think it over.

This is clearly by no means the end of the story, but by this stage Moore had written more than enough for one book, and it is an indication of how successful he was at this period, that his publishers were prepared to let it go at that, and publish the remainder of the novel as a sequel, *Sister Teresa*. In Germany, the two books were published as one two-part novel, under a translated version of Moore's original idea for a title, *Profane and Sacred Love* (*Irdische und Himmlische Liebe*).

At the beginning of May 1899, Moore went on a visit to Ireland – and to his disgust, though not greatly to his surprise, there was nobody there to meet him either at Westland Row railway station, or at the Shelbourne Hotel, where he was staying – for a performance, at the Antient Concert Rooms (yes, spelt like that, it later became the Palace Cinema) in what is now Pearse Street, of the two plays.

Yeats had been there on the first night, 'listening reverentially to the sound of his verses', Moore reported. The play had been interrupted by what Yeats called the keening, but which were, in fact, cat-calls of protest. And Yeats asked Moore whether a copy had not been put into his hand of *The Cross or the Guillotine*, a pamphlet quoting some of the glaring heresies in *The Countess Cathleen*, and appealing to Catholic Ireland to put an end to all this blasphemy. 'Last night,' Yeats said, 'we had to have the police in, and Edward, I am afraid, will lose heart; he will fear scandal and may stop the play.'

The pamphlet referred to a scene in which the Countess offers to sell her soul to merchants disguised as devils, so that her people, starving in the Great Famine, may be fed. A letter had also appeared in one of the Irish newspapers from a Monsignor attacking the play, and disturbances were expected.

Both Lady Gregory and Yeats had been keeping a close eye on Martyn, who, they feared, might resign his directorship of the theatre if the play should be considered to be in any way 'heretical'. Yeats secured the approval of two priests for his play, to forestall Martyn; and Moore, although relieved – in his capacity as a co-director with Yeats and Martyn of the Irish Literary Theatre – that Martyn had not resigned, was also extremely upset, as a publicity-conscious author, because he had already written an article, 'Edward Martyn and His Soul', which he had intended to publish as soon as Martyn resigned. Yeats (in *Dramatis Personae*) reports Moore as saying: 'It was the best opportunity I ever had. What a sensation it would have made. Nobody has ever written in that way about his most intimate friend. What a chance. It would have been heard of everywhere.'

Cardinal Logue had already condemned the play without either seeing or reading it, and again, on the second night, there were interruptions from the gallery, but it finished its run and Martyn's *The Heather Field*, which followed it, proved popular with the audience.

Moore contemplated going straight back to England, in a protest against Ireland's 'disgraceful Catholicism', as he put it, but added that he had to admit that 'it is difficult to be angry with Ireland on a May morning, when the sun is shining'.

These thoughts came to him as he was shaving in the Shelbourne Hotel, looking out over St Stephen's Green, where, as a child, he had once stolen away from his governess and stripped off his clothes, delighted at the embarrassment he was causing her. This random recollection is at least a refreshing change from Moore's more frequent memories of the succession of attractive young girls who were, apparently, prepared to strip for his pleasure, even in his old age.

In writing about St Stephen's Green, a touch of melancholy intervenes: 'All the same, this much can be said about the winter months, that they are long, and sorrow with us, but the spring passes by, mocking us, telling us that the flowers return as youthful as last years, but we . . .'

The two plays had been extremely well received by the Dublin Press; the review in the Dublin *Daily Express* was particularly glowing. The Dublin *Daily Express* – no connection whatever with the subsequent Beaverbrook *Daily Express* – had been founded in 1851 as a Tory newspaper, with the help of William Howard Russell, the Dublin-born correspondent of the London *Times*, and in 1898 Horace (later Sir Horace) Plunkett, founder of the Irish Agricultural Co-operative Movement, bought the newspaper and appointed T. P. Gill, a former leader writer in the *Freeman's Journal*, as editor.

Of its coverage of the first production of the Irish Literary Theatre, Moore remarked: 'If the entire *Comédie Française* had come over with plays by Racine and Victor Hugo, not the old plays, but new ones, lately discovered, which had not yet been acted, the *Express* could not have displayed more literary enthusiasm.'

And everyone was in great form at a dinner given by T. P. Gill a few evenings later. Among those present were John O'Leary, the old Fenian, whom Moore had met in Paris many years earlier; Douglas Hyde, founder of the Gaelic League and later first president of Ireland; T. W. Rolleston, an authority on the Celtic myths and legends, to whom Moore later dedicated an edition of *Esther Waters*, and many of the others who were to feature so prominently in Moore's trilogy, *Hail and Farewell*.

There also exists an account of the banquet by Yeats. Inevitably, there were some sour notes: the man who spoke after Moore remarked that the Irish now seemed to have reached a level 'which makes it worth while for Mr Moore to return to Ireland . . .'

Edward Martyn was already working on another play, *The Tale of a Town*, a satire on Irish public life; he and Moore had discussed it on one of their annual trips to the Bayreuth Festival, during which Moore met Wagner's widow, Cosima, and wondered whether he should start a serious conversation with her or merely kiss her hand and flirt with her, and wisely decided on the latter course. He also presented her with a specially bound edition of *Esther Waters*, which caused Aubrey Beardsley to remark to reporters in London: 'How like George Moore! And does he think she will read it?'

In September 1899, when the Boer War broke out, Moore was on a visit to Tullyra. Edward Martyn's mother – who had been so offended by *A Drama in Muslin* that she had forbidden Moore to visit the house ever again as long as she lived – was now dead, and there were comfortable quarters for Moore in Dear Edward's Gothic Castle in County Galway whenever he felt like going there, rather than to Moore Hall. At this period, Moore was trying to collaborate with Martyn on a rewrite of *The Tale of a Town*, an extraordinary exercise described both by Moore and Yeats. It did not go at all well, and in the end Martyn told Moore that he could do whatever he wished with the play, he himself wanted nothing further to do with it. The work, under Moore's sole signature, and retitled *The Bending of the Bough*, was produced at the Gaiety Theatre in Dublin on February 19, 1900. It has since, like most of the plays of the Irish Literary Renaissance, disappeared without trace.

Moore's first blow in aid of the Irish language was made at a luncheon party given by the Irish Literary Society early in 1900 at which Moore read a paper, later published along with papers by Yeats, Lady Gregory, Douglas Hyde and others and entitled *Ideals in Ireland*; in it he compared the Irish language to a spring, rising in the mountains, increasing into a rivulet, and then becoming a great river flowing through a plain, and likened the English language to a river which had already arrived in a big city and had to be filtered of accumulated impurities.

He also admitted at the luncheon party that he himself was too old to learn Irish (though he did make a half-hearted attempt a few years later). He returned strongly to this theme on his next visit to Ireland. He had written a paper on the literary need for small languages, to be read at a lunch of the Irish Literary Society: in it he advanced the idea that language after a time becomes like a coin too long current – the English language had become defaced, and to write in English effectively it was necessary to return to dialects. In giving the speech, Moore shouted (or says he did), over the coffee cups, that he had arranged to disinherit his own two nephews if they failed to learn to speak Irish fluently from a nurse who had been brought to Moore Hall from one of the Irish-speaking islands in Galway Bay. At this period Maurice's wife Evelyn was living at Moore Hall with her two sons, while her husband was away at the Boer War.

Ireland's need, he went on, was not a Catholic university, but a Gaelic one. He added that it was being whispered at Edward Martyn's table that he, Moore, had come over to write about the country and its ideas, and would make fun of them all whenever it suited his purpose to do so; which is precisely what he did.

He went back to England, fuming over the fact that the Gaelic League seemed to be showing no great anxiety to avail itself of his services, though within three months he was once again invited over for a meeting in the Rotunda to protest against the continued use of English in Ireland. He took this as a sign that all was forgiven and that his services were now again needed in Dublin.

He had recently become very friendly with a talented lady painter, Clara Christian, whom he calls Stella, and he met her by chance again with her friend Florence, during one of his annual trips to Bayreuth with Edward Martyn. On their way home, they had visited Antwerp, where Florence and Stella were on a painting trip together, and were going on to Holland. Moore admits that he had already started to think of Stella 'perhaps more than was altogether fair to Florence', and had decided to go with the pair of them to Holland, leaving Edward to return to London alone. Edward did not care to visit Protestant countries; he never felt at home in one, though he did not seem to mind living in London.

Moore refers to 'Florence's incautious confession that no more perfect mould of body than Stella's existed in the flesh', as an indication of what he felt about what appears to have been a Lesbian relationship, which he immediately proceeded to break up, though it does not really look, even from his own accounts of the affair, as if he ever offered poor Stella anything very concrete or substantial in return for whatever creature comforts Florence had afforded her. And when Moore and Stella broke up – if that is not altogether the wrong term to use for so tenuous a relationship – Stella almost immediately married an Irishman, Charles MacCarthy, the city architect of Dublin, and died in childbirth in 1906.

When summoned to Dublin to address the Gaelic League, Moore invited Stella, who was then in Wales, painting, as he put, 'flocks and herds', to accompany him. Her telegram in reply to his letter, indicating that she would meet him on board the boat, shows a surprisingly liberated attitude for a young woman in Victorian times. And so it was settled. 'Here you are and here am I and we are going to Ireland together,' Moore remarked. Stella had never been in Dublin before and wanted to see the National Gallery, which seemed to her a sufficient justification for the trip.

At the Rotunda, Moore again met Douglas Hyde. 'Did you come across last night?' Moore reports Hyde as saying. 'You don't tell me so? Tank you, tank you. You'll have a great reception.'

He goes on to talk about Ireland's future president's insignificant nose, the droop of his moustache, through which his Irish frothed out like porter, and adds: '. . . and when he returned to

English, it was easy to understand why he desired to change the language of Ireland.'

Professor Eoin MacNeill, later to found the Irish Volunteers, and to become a minister in the first Irish Free State Government, spoke next, then the two priests, Meehan and Hogarty, and eventually came Moore's own paper. He had arranged for Stella to meet him at the Rotunda after the meeting, and when it was all over he followed the crowd out of the building, wondering what Stella would think of her first Gaelic League meeting; and his own first, too, for that matter. Her tact and affection would save her from the mistake of laughing at the meeting to his face, he thought.

'There was no real reason why I should regret having brought her over, only that the meeting had exhibited Ireland under a rough and uncouth aspect; worse still, as a country that was essentially insincere and frivolous, and this was unfortunate, as I wanted her to like Ireland.

'One of the young priests had said that he was in favour of the Irish language, because no heresy had ever been written in it. He was in favour of the Irish language because there was no thought in its literature . . . there can be no literature when no mental activities are about. Without heresy, there can be no religion, because heresy means trying to think out the answer to the riddle of life and death for ourselves . . . Acquiescence in dogma means decay, dead leaves in the mire, nothing more . . .'

Nobody could say that Moore was not, to use the Irish phrase, 'a divil for punishment'. Although a man of such strong views that the very notion of collaboration must have been entirely foreign to his nature, he was forever trying to write in tandem with someone else. And, despite his dismal failure to achieve any rapport with his old friend Martyn, a few months after he and Stella had returned to England, a letter arrived from Yeats, inviting him to come to Ireland, and stay with Lady Gregory at

Coole Park while they worked together, as Moore had suggested, on the prose play, *Diarmuid and Grania*.

Moore travelled by boat and train, completing the final stage of the journey, from Gort to Coole Park, by push-bicycle. When he arrived, he was told that Yeats was composing and could not be disturbed; they would have to wait breakfast for him, Lady Gregory said. But they began breakfast without him, and the great poet arrived a few minutes later to announce triumphantly that he had succeeded in writing very nearly eight and a half lines of verse that morning.

After breakfast, they discussed the play, or rather the style in which it was to be written. Certainly not, Yeats insisted, in the style of *Esther Waters*. Yeats was not sure whether it should be written in Galway peasant dialect, or in the language of the Bible, though he emphasised that they should take great care to avoid turns of speech which would immediately recall the Bible itself.

'You will not write Angus and his son Diarmuid *which is* in heaven, I hope,' Yeats said. 'For the same reason, we will not use any archaic words, and we must avoid words that recall a particular epoch.' He continued to elaborate: 'The words *honour* and *ideal* suggest the Middle Ages, and should not be used. The word *glory* is charged with modern ideas – the *glory* of God and the *glory* that shall cover Lord Kitchener when he returns from Africa. You will not use it. The word *soldier* represents a man to us who wears a red tunic; an equivalent must be found, *swordsman*, for example, or *fighting man*. *Hill* is a better word than *mountain*: – I can't give you a reason, but that is my feeling, and the word *ocean* was not known to the early Irish, only *the sea*.'

Moore remarked that he felt it was probably far safer to assume that primitive man thought and felt much as we do. 'It seemed to me that I had to come to Coole on a fruitless errand – that we should never be able to write *Diarmuid and Grania* in collaboration.'

A seat had been placed under a weeping ash in the garden for the benefit of the collaborators, and Lady Gregory tried to keep the peace by suggesting that they should confine their collaboration to the construction of the play while they were together, and then let the actual play be written by one or the other, after which the other could go over it yet again.

'I'll try to write within the limits of the vocabulary you impose upon me, although the burden is heavier than that of a foreign language,' Moore told Yeats. 'I'd sooner write the play in French.'

'Then why not write it in French? Lady Gregory will translate it for you,' Yeats replied.

That night Yeats came to him, Moore says, and argued that the idea of writing the whole play in French was a far better one than they had thought at the time. Lady Gregory could translate Moore's French text into English; Taidgh O'Donoghue, a local Irish language expert, would then translate Lady Gregory's English text into Irish; Lady Gregory, who knew Irish, would translate O'Donoghue's Irish back into English; and, finally, Yeats would put his own 'style' on it. Lady Gregory, Yeats assured Moore, supported this plan, and had promised to translate Moore's French version with due deference to his style.

Moore promptly went off to Paris and wrote the first scene of the second act in the cosmopolitan atmosphere of a hotel sitting room.

We can think, he concluded sadly, after this exercise, but we cannot think profoundly in any foreign language.

From the Boer War, Colonel Maurice wrote to his brother George, describing a plan an English General had conceived, which involved trapping de Wet, the Boer General, and his men in a flooded area, between two rivers; and when he was trapped, and the white flag had been raised, the shooting was not to stop. 'A murder plot, pure and simple, having nothing in common with any warfare waged by Europeans for many centuries,' Moore commented.

'It must be stopped and publication will stop it. But is there a newspaper in London that will publish it? One or two were tried, but in vain . . .' In fact, he tried it out on his friend Stead, but Stead told him that no English newspaper would print it, since Moore was not prepared to reveal the identity of the writer who had supplied the information. He decided to take it to Ireland.

'And the next day, in Dublin, I dictated the story to the editor of *The Freeman's Journal. The Times* reprinted it, and the editor of a Cape paper copied it from *The Times*, upon which the military authorities in South Africa disowned and repudiated the plot . . . I looked on myself as having saved England from a crime that would have cried shame after her till the end of history.'

The story in *The Times* was actually reprinted in two Cape newspapers, there were questions in the House of Commons, and two ministers of state were sacked. This was the precise point at which Moore realised that he had done with England, and he seriously contemplated going back to France, which he still felt was his spiritual home.

But first he had to discuss it, as he had to discuss everything, with his circle of friends. He wondered whether these new ideas of his had altered the features of a face that both Steer and Sickert had painted (he had no small opinion of himself and was always having his portrait painted, and trying to negotiate with other authors to write his biography); and that night, at Steer's house, he told them that the Boer War had changed him utterly, and he brought the talk around to the concentration camps which the British had set up in which to intern the Boer women and children.

'No, Moore, it isn't as bad as that,' Tonks argued. 'They couldn't be left out on the veldt,' he went on. 'We had to do something with the women and children.'

'Tonks! I'm ashamed of you. After having burnt down their houses, you had to keep them, and, as it would be an advantage to you to destroy the Boer race, you keep them in concentration camps, where they die off like flies,' Moore replied.

In an effort to get away from London, and think things out,

Moore then revisited his old Sussex friends, those South Saxons as he thought of them, descendants of Hengist and Horsa, the Colvill Bridgers of Southwick.

He told his old Sussex friends that he might never have returned to them if the Boer War had not brought him down there to find out if there were anything in England, in the country, in the people, with which he could still sympathise.

Colly had no sympathy for the Boer women and children: 'My dear fellow, the Boers invaded our territory . . .'

'And Dulcie said that it would be better if I went away and came down again, and Florence seemed to agree with her that I had not been as nice this time as I had been on other occasions.'

Back in London, he again wonders whether it is not time to return to France. And again, there is an interesting aside from Susan Mitchell who happened to be in London at the time of his sudden disgust with what she calls 'a Mafficking' London: 'There is much that is absurd . . . but there is also much that is pathetic. I was living in London at that time myself, and I remember the tin-pot heroics that clanked side by side with real heroism. I remember tawdry and tipsy processions, healed by a whisky bottle in Hammersmith Broadway, and the trays and baths and tin trumpets wherewith respectable suburban London signalised a British victory. I remember the raw boys, under-sized, underfed, filling the departing trains, the anguish, the fear, the shameful joys of victory. England becoming self-conscious, the tipsy bully lashing himself into what he believed was a similitude of Elizabethan greatness. It was very pitiful and very human, and South Africa was very far away.'

'And it was while thinking that England was now behind me, and forever,' Moore wrote, 'that a presence seemed to gather, or rather, seemed to follow me as I went towards Chelsea.'

This was not the road to Damascus, exactly, though it was, in a way, for Moore; it was the Royal Hospital Road in Chelsea:

> . . . walking in a devout collectedness, I heard a voice speaking within me: no whispering thought it was, but a resolute voice,

saying, 'Go to Ireland!' The words were so distinct and clear that I could not but turn to look. Nobody was within many yards of me. I walked on, but had not taken many steps before I heard the voice again – 'Order your manuscripts and your pictures and your furniture to be packed at once, and go to Ireland.'

Of this I am sure, that the words, 'Go to Ireland!' did not come from within but from without . . .

Next morning, as I lay between sleeping and waking, I heard the words 'Go to Ireland! Go to Ireland!' – repeated by the same voice, and this time it was close by me, speaking into my ear . . . Doubt was no longer possible. I had been summoned to Ireland!

# FOURTEEN

## Into the Celtic Twilight

When George Moore had his Damascus experience on the Chelsea Royal Hospital Road, around the turn of the century, he still had nearly two years of his lease on the flat in Victoria Street to run. No suitable tenant had come forward to take it over, and it did not seem to Moore that he could go back to Ireland, leaving the flat empty.

A house in Dublin would have to be part of his equipment as a Gaelic League propagandist, and it would cost him at least £100 a year, though at that time he thought the League would probably pay his rent. By now he was on the look-out for something a bit more ambitious than his flat in Victoria Street.

His decision to leave England was hastened by purely practical considerations: the fact that his flat in Victoria Street was being refurbished, and the presence of the workmen was causing him a great deal of personal inconvenience. He had an almighty row with the builders, which went to law, and in the end the proprietors of the block of flats bought up the remainder of his lease for £100; this sum would pay for the removal of his furniture and pictures to Dublin several times over.

He ordered an overnight trunk to be packed that evening, and the next morning was at a house agent's office in Dublin. He knew that the houses in Merrion Square were far too big for a single man of limited means; his mother had been living in one of them when, as he put it, 'the boycott had brought him back from France'. He looked at houses in Upper Mount Street, Mount Street Crescent, and Baggot Street, as well as in Fitzwilliam Square, where the rents were higher than he wished to pay. Then he tried Leeson Street; 'houses that had once sheltered an aristocracy, now falling into the hands of nuns and lodging-house keepers,' he commented.

He rejected Harcourt Street, but tried Pembroke Road, Clyde Road and Waterloo Road, visited Clonskeagh and Rathmines and ultimately Clondalkin, where he saw The Moat House, and thought again about Mount Venus, that house to let which he had visited high up in the Dublin mountains many years earlier.

He now enlisted the help of the poet and writer AE (George Russell) in finding a suitable house. George William Russell was born in Lurgan, County Antrim in 1867, and was thirty-four when Moore, then forty-nine, met him through Yeats on one of his earlier trips to Dublin. He had studied at the Dublin Metropolitan School of Art, and had then taken a job as an assistant in the accounts department of Messrs Pims Brothers, a well-known Dublin drapery store. By the time Moore met him, he had become, on Yeats's recommendation, assistant secretary of Horace Plunkett's co-operative movement, the Irish Agricultural Organisation Society, a well-meaning West-British attempt to introduce in Ireland co-operative farming practices which had proved highly successful in America.

AE was a theosophist, a form of belief which, so far as I understand it offers an attempt at an explanation of the source and purpose of life by postulating a first cause (eternal, unborn, undying); a created universe, mirroring the primordial source; and thence spirit, matter and the relationship between the two (that is to say, consciousness), and a form of incarnation and possibly even of reincarnation. George Russell began to contribute articles to *The Irish Theosophist* in 1892 and signed his first article Aeon (intended to signify a vast age, an eternity), but the compositer, unable to make head or tail of his signature, solved the problem by signing the article AE.

Russell took a great fancy to this compromise, and so apparently did everybody else; thereafter he always used it as his nom-de-plume. He published his first book of poems (as AE), entitled *Homeward: Songs by the Way* in 1894, and subsequently seven or eight books, including *The Nuts of Knowledge* (1903); *By Still Waters* (1906); *Gods of War* (1915); *Voices of Stones* (1919) and *Vale* (1931), as well as one play, *Deirdre* (1907).

'If I don't find a house,' George Moore said to him in 1901, 'I shall have to return to that inferno which is London . . . There are no houses, AE, to let. I've searched everywhere and can find nothing but The Moat, and Mount Venus, no doubt, is still vacant, but it's a good five miles distant from Rathfarnham, and you won't be able to come to see me very often.'

And AE replied: 'Nature has given you energy, vitality, and perseverance, my dear Moore, but she has denied you the gift of patience, and patience above all things is needed when seeking a house.'

In the end it was AE who found Moore a house, only a few minutes' walk from St Stephen's Green: one (No 4) of five little eighteenth-century houses in Upper Ely Place, shut off from the main thoroughfare, and with an orchard opposite which he could rent for two or three pounds extra a year; its back windows, in the dining and drawing rooms, overlooked the gardens of Loreto Convent.

Moore seems to have had a fairly luke-warm reception from Douglas Hyde, President of the Gaelic League, who dropped a hint that he might have proved far more useful to them if he had stayed on in England, rather than returning to Ireland. And his old friend, Dear Edward, remarked: 'Father Dineen [compiler of the then standard Irish–English dictionary] saw you; I met him in Kildare Street this afternoon and he told me to tell you that the Keating Branch [of the Gaelic League] were saying that you're coming over here to write them up in the English papers.'

His welcome from Yeats did not seem all that much warmer either, and MacNeill (Professor Eoin MacNeill, Vice-President of

the Gaelic League, and founder of the Irish Volunteers), whom
Moore described as 'an honest fellow with a great deal of brown
beard', did not express any opinion regarding his coming to
Ireland, other than to remark that he didn't know what view the
Gaelic League might take of Moore's decision.

'But your subscription will be gratefully received,' he added,
moving away as if to avoid further questioning. Moore, however,
continued to press questions on him. Would the League like to
send him to America to collect funds? What did they think?
Should he become a Gaelic League Missionary preaching the
message of the revival of the Irish language?

How seriously did Moore take his part in the projected Irish
literary and cultural revival? From his own accounts of it in *Hail
and Farewell*, you would think not very, though from what he
wrote and said at the time it seems quite possible that Moore took
it all very seriously indeed, at least initially. This is Hone's view;
and it is also the view of Richard Cave, who edited the most recent
(1985) annotated edition of the trilogy. It could well be that
Moore saw in himself a potential new leader of Irish intellectual
thought, a position for which, for various reasons, Yeats, Lady
Gregory and Edward Martyn were all, in his opinion, unfitted. If
so, he was sorely disappointed, and some of the rancour he felt can
be sensed in *Hail and Farewell*.

To Moore's inquiry as to whether the Gaelic League intended to
finance him on a trip to the United States in support of the cause,
MacNeill answered that, if Moore went to America and succeeded
in collecting some money, the League would naturally be glad to
receive it, but he did not think the League would send him to the
States as their representative. They would, however, be glad to
receive any journalistic help he could offer.

One of the problems then engaging the attention of the Gaelic
League organisers was how to improve their journal, known as *An
Claidheamh Soluis* (The Sword of Light), and MacNeill suggested
that Moore should call upon the editor of that journal at his
convenience and discuss the matter. As his furniture and all his

possessions were still in his flat in Victoria Street, Moore was at this period staying at the Shelbourne Hotel.

First thing the next morning, Moore went to the offices of the Keating Branch of the Gaelic League, where nobody appeared to have heard of him. When he told them that he had been sent to see the editor of their journal by their Vice-President, Professor Eoin MacNeill, they said that they'd certainly tell the editor about him when he came in, and in the meantime, if he'd care to send in an article, they were sure the editor would consider it, though space in the magazine was pretty tight.

'I am George Moore.'

'I'll tell the editor when he comes in, and if you'll send in your article he'll consider it. The next few numbers are full up.' This was not the sort of treatment to which Moore was accustomed: George Moore, the best-selling author who numbered the British Prime Minister among his fans and who had received the highest praise from the foremost critics of the day, a man, moreover, every bit as well known in France as in England, and now making a name for himself in Germany and in the United States.

Moore was bitterly disappointed at his reception in Dublin and made no effort to disguise it in *Salve*: 'Nobody wants me, AE . . . All I had hoped for was a welcome and some enthusiasm; no bonfires, torchlight processions, banners, bands, céad míle fáilte's, nothing of that kind [though clearly that is exactly what he had been expecting], only a welcome. It may be that I did expect some appreciation of the sacrifice I was making, for you see I'm throwing everything into the flames.'

He went straight back to England that night, and shortly afterwards managed to persuade Stella to come to Ireland with him, for the sake of her art, though the question of living with him did not seem to arise. He assured her that the Irish mountains were every bit as beautiful as the Welsh ones and talked to her about the Moat House which he had seen near Clondalkin, a secluded dwelling, built around the time of Queen Anne, which would suit her down to the ground.

Everything apart from his personal luggage went by coasting steamer, and arrived about three weeks later, and AE was there to help him unroll his Aubusson carpet and unpack his paintings, which included two Manets, a Monet, a Gainsborough and a Berthe Morisot. AE did not much like the carpet: 'the purple architecture and the bunches of roses shocking him so much that I think he was on the point of asking me to burn the carpet'. Moore persuaded AE to withdraw his eyes from it and look at the pictures: 'I would conceal the fact if I dared, but a desire for truth compels me to record that when he first saw Manet's portrait it seemed to him commonplace, even uncouth.'

He expresses the extraordinary opinion (coming from him) that AE recognised in him 'the spiritual influence that Ireland had been waiting for so long', and had endless discussions with AE about the identity of the gods (or voices) that had inspired his coming to Ireland in the first place. Hard as it is to believe, it almost seems that Moore was prepared at this stage to embrace Yeats's and AE's muddled ideas about the ancient Celtic deities. Maybe they seemed closer to the pagan gods he celebrated in his youth in Paris than SS Peter and Paul.

From his earlier writings, one might have assumed that Moore was an atheist or at least an agnostic. It is true that he was always passionately interested in religion, but far more from a historical and sociological, than from a doctrinal, point of view. You would not have thought, from his attitude to things as expressed in *Confessions of a Young Man*, that he would have had much time for AE with his belief in the Druidical gods and goddesses, and yet he devotes a long section of *Salve* to his conversations with AE about the nature of his 'voices', and the identity of the three pagan gods who had come, AE claimed, to stand at the foot of his bed one morning.

Surprisingly, ghosts seem to have been accepted as one of the inescapable facts of life at Moore Hall. The ghost of Augustus, younger brother of George Henry Moore the Politician, was reputed to have appeared at the wicket gate of Moore Hall about the time he died after a racing accident during the 1841 Grand National, and, in view of the fact of Augustus's death, that looked as if it might have been a genuine ghost. On the other hand, the ghost of Colonel Maurice Moore also duly appeared at the same wicket gate, while he was away fighting in the Boer War, and in circumstances in which he might well have been killed; but in this case it turned out to be a false alarm, or a ghost impostor, because Maurice survived the Boer War and died of old age in 1939.

After discussing the matter at length and in depth with AE, Moore seems to have come to the conclusion that it may have been one of the ancient Celtic deities who had bidden him to return to Ireland – Diarmuid himself, no less, he reckons – and he arranged to spend three or four days with AE cycling around Ireland's cromlechs and dolmens and visiting various of the old sacred places of the Celtic gods and goddesses. From a letter he wrote to Nia Crawford from the Shelbourne Hotel, it seems that this trip took place before Moore moved into 4, Upper Ely Place, but Moore is quite specific about it. Possibly there was more than one trip to New Grange and Dowth with AE, and Moore ran them together for the sake of a tidier narrative.

According to Moore's own account of it in *Vale*, he had arrived back in Ireland in March 1901 and the first fine day was April 15, when he and AE set out together on bicycles in search of the ancient Gaelic divinities … Moore himself on a brand-new bicycle, bought expressly for the purpose of the trip, and AE on an old one he had ridden all over Ireland, in the interests of Plunkett's co-operative movement.

They cycled together to Amiens Street railway station, took second-class tickets to Drogheda, and made their way to the Boyne valley, where AE showed Moore the monument erected in commemoration of a battle won by the British and the Ulster Scots planters under the Protestant King of England, William III. The latter had proved victorious over a mixed force of Irish, French and other troops supporting King James II, the last

Catholic King of England, in a battle which 'secured forever the Protestant Ascendancy in England'.

This was a notion which might have appealed greatly to Moore a little later, though at the time he longed, with AE, for the honours in the battle to have gone to the Irish. 'The beastly English won the battle,' he reports himself as having remarked. 'If only they'd been beaten.'

When they arrived at Dowth, one of three tumuli or barrow graves, near Navan, which are in effect artificial hills under which the ancient Celts used to bury the ashes of their dead captains and kings, AE told Moore to buy a candle and a box of matches and follow him across a stile, and down a field until they came to a hole in the ground, in which there was a ladder. They climbed down the ladder, and at the bottom, about twenty feet below the surface of the earth, AE went down on his hands and knees and started to crawl into a passage as narrow as a rabbit burrow. Moore followed him and eventually found himself in a small chamber, about ten feet in height and ten in width. A short passage connected it with a larger chamber, perhaps twenty feet in height and about the same in width, built of great stones, all leaning together. It was here, Moore learned from AE, that the ancient tribes came to do homage to their great divinities; AE also revealed to Moore the meaning of the strange designs inscribed upon the walls.

The spot within the first circle, he explained, was the earth, and the circle the sea. The second circle represented the heavens, and the third circle Lir, the god over all gods, the great fate that awaits both mankind and godkind. The Druids, he went on, refrained from committing their mysteries to writing, because writing was traditionally the source of all heresies and confusions, and it was not good for the plain people to discuss divine things among themselves; their lot was to concern themselves with such matters as war and hunting and gathering and to leave it to the Druids to meditate on eternal matters.

The plain truth, of course, was that all the ancient Celts, as AE very well knew, including their Druids and *filidh* (poets or bards), were illiterate in the sense that they never learned to read or write, though they cut notches in the edges of standing stones to indicate something to one another, and they carved mysterious patterns on the surface of the stones they set up to mark the entrances to the communal graves at New Grange and Dowth, and elsewhere, all over Ireland.

St Patrick brought not only Christianity, but also literacy, to the Irish Celts; he and his Breton assistants not only taught the Irish Latin, but they also managed to find a way of writing down the spoken Irish Gaelic which the Celts spoke, and then succeeded in teaching the Irish Celts to read and write their own language, as well as Latin, a fairly formidable exericse.

Having explained the meaning of the markings on the stones to his own satisfaction, if not to anybody else's, AE tucked his legs under him like a Yogi, in preparation for the vision he was confidently expecting, and Moore decided that it would be better if he were to leave AE to his meditations and wait for him at the top of the ladder in the outside world. He had hardly reached the top of the ladder and emerged into the spring sunshine before two Presbyterian ministers hoisted their bicycles over the stile, propped them up against the hedge, and climbed down the ladder into the enchanted cavern; in *Vale*, Moore wrote:

> The gods will not show themselves while Presbyterian ministers are about, AE will not stay in the tomb with them. And at every moment I expected to see him rise out of the earth. But it was the ministers who appeared a few minutes afterwards, and, blowing out their candles in the blue daylight, asked me if I had been below.
> 'I have been in the temple,' I answered.
> 'Did you see the fellow below?'
> 'I'm waiting for him; a great writer and a great painter.'
> 'Is it a history he's brooding down there?' one of them asked, laughing . . .

And Moore lay down on the warm grass thinking of the pain their coarse remarks must have caused AE, who came out of the hill soon after.

It was as Moore expected. AE explained that the vision was just about to appear, but the clergymen had interrupted the process, and when they had left, the mood had passed.

Next, they cycled to nearby New Grange, where AE was confident that the gods would show themselves if they deemed them (GM and AE) worthy. And Moore adds: 'And if we were not worthy – AE at least – who were worthy amongst living men?'

When they arrived, AE pointed to the entrance of the temple – a triangular opening no larger than a fox's or a badger's den and, at AE's bidding, Moore went down on hands and knees, and crawled into the tumulus, where they remained for upwards of an hour without any sign being vouchsafed to them that the gods were listening.

After that, they returned to their bicycles, debating Darwinism, with AE strenuously repudiating the ape theory, as Moore calls the theory of natural selection, all the way down the hillside, and arguing that the world was not old enough to make the theory of evolution possible; he held that unless the planet happened to be a billion years older than it was then believed to be, it could not be else than that man had been evolved from the gods.

Moore sees – or imagines he sees – a vision of Tara from the hills above New Grange, but AE thought they would be more likely to meet the gods elsewhere; he did not recall that the gods had ever been seen at Tara, which had been destroyed by, as he put it, an ecclesiastic (none other than the patron saint himself).

On this trip, Moore seems to waver between behaving as a visionary, trying to catch a glimpse of AE's vision of the pagan gods and goddesses through his own, unworthy eyes, and as an enthusiastic canvasser trying to sell advertisements for the Gaelic League's newspaper, the *Claidheamh Soluis*, to local shopkeepers.

It was also on this trip that Moore developed one of the half-baked theories with which he subsequently plagued every dinner table he graced with his presence: that a nation needs to change its language to produce a new literature. Italy, he argues, trying the argument on himself as he writes the book, produced a new literature because Italy changed her language (from Latin into modern-day Italian), whereas Greece had not changed hers and therefore there was no modern literature in Greece (though modern Greek is as different from classical Greek as Italian is from Latin).

They next visited the cromlech under which Diarmuid and Grania are believed to have slept during their flight from Finn, the super-giant of all the giants of Irish mythology, and Moore walked around it three times praying (though he does not indicate what he was praying for, or to which gods) while AE did a sketch of 'the great rock, poised on top of three or four upright stones, nine or ten feet high'. It is odd that Moore did not count them and establish whether it was three or four stones, and whether they were nine or ten feet high; later he went to enormous trouble to amass precise details of scenes in the Holy Land and in Northern France for books like *The Brook Kerith* and *Héloise and Abélard*.

When the expedition was interrupted by a second puncture, AE became convinced that the gods did not wish to see Moore on the top of their mountain, and had his work cut out to persuade him to go to a nearby cottage for a basin of water, with the aid of which he could locate the puncture. Needless to say, AE had to repair all punctures encountered during the course of this expedition; Moore was utterly useless at doing anything practical. As another Irish landlord, Lord Brownlee of Brownlee Hall (now the headquarters of the Black Preceptory, the élitist top echelon of the Orange Order), remarked when being assisted to his feet by his friends after a fall occasioned by far too much strong drink: 'No, don't bother to trouble yourselves. I have people to do that kind of thing for me.' Moore always had people to do, on his behalf, all the practical little things that this life demands.

So, as AE worked away in the scorching sunshine, 'heaving the tyre off the wheel with many curious instruments, which he extracted from a leather pocket behind the saddle of the machine', Moore talked to him, 'hoping thereby to distract his attention from the heat of the day'.

A sample of the distracting conversation: 'Two millions is the

ideal population for Ireland and about four for England. Do you
know, AE, there could not have been more than two million
people in England when Robin Hood and his merry men hunted
Sherwood Forest? How much more variegated the world was then!
At any moment one might come upon an archer who had just split
a willow wand, distant a hundred yards, or upon charcoal-burners
with their fingers and thumbs cut off for shooting deer, or jugglers
standing on each other's heads in the middle of sunlit inter-spaces.
A little later, on the fringe of the forest, the wayfarer stops to listen
to the hymn of pilgrims on their way to Canterbury!'

Next they visited Slievegullion, leaving their bicycles with a
woman who lived in a cottage three miles below the summit, but
Moore proved unable to make it to the summit, and went to the
cottage for a drink of water while AE strode on to the top of the
peak, confident of encountering Finn, one of the legendary Celtic
god-heroes. Leaving a message for AE at the cottage to the effect
that he was cycling slowly on into Dundalk, Moore rode off,
hoping that AE would overtake him. It was fully two hours before
AE did so. He had not actually encountered Finn, but had done a
drawing of the cairn on the summit for Moore, which he would
show him as soon as they reached Dundalk.

On their way into Dundalk, they met the Presbyterian
clergymen again, and spent the evening with them in an inn,
where AE entertained them with stories about Slievegullion. It
was there, he assured them, that Finn saw a vision rise above the
waters of the lake, and precipitately plunged in after the beautiful
young nymph. Whether he captured her, or whether, as Moore
characteristically speculates, and for how long, did he spend
enjoying her there under the water, AE did not reveal, only the
fact that, when Finn rose to the surface again, he was an old man,
as old as the mountains and the rocks of the world. But his youth
was given back to him, by means of some magical process, which
did not extend to his hair, however, and, as a result, it remained
snow-white.

AE also entertained the Presbyterian clergymen with tales of

Cuchulain and Mananaan Mac Lir, the most spiritual and remote of all the ancient Gaelic divinities, and assured them that the folk-tales of Connaught lay far closer to the hearts of the Irish people than any of the tales from Galilee, a remark which must have confirmed the non-conformists in their worst fears about the Celtic Irish.

Moore and AE said goodbye at Ely Place and AE went back to work. 'He is an adept and can lead both lives, and is on such terms with the gods that he can come and go at will, doing his work in heaven and on earth. Yesterday he was with Finn by the crescent-shaped lake on Slievegullion; tomorrow he will trundle his old bicycle down to the offices of the I.A.O.S. [Irish Agricultural Organisation Society] in Lincoln Place.'

Horace Plunkett had initially talked to Yeats about his co-operative idea, and Yeats had suggested AE – then working as an accountant in Pims drapery store in Dublin – as the right man for the job. AE was given a bicycle and employed by Plunkett to cycle around Ireland preaching the doctrine of co-operation in dairy-farming from village to village. He did this with such success that soon co-operative creameries were springing up all over the countryside, and Irish small farmers began to prosper for the first time since the arrival of the Anglo-Normans in the twelfth century. Unfortunately, the creameries were all burned down during The Troubles, for the sole reason that Plunkett happened also to be a Unionist, a landlord and a Protestant and the Irish farmers would have nothing further to do with co-operatives until Ireland entered the Common Market when they readily co-operated with anyone and everyone to wring every last possible penny out of the European Common Agricultural Policy.

Moore had written to Nia: 'I have just returned from a bicycle tour. I have visited all the sacred places, great Druidic remains, and have pondered the wondrous beauty of gods whose names I admire, but cannot spell . . . The rocks that these great people piled together for the celebration of their mysteries fill the heart with awe, and the carvings of the sun symbol carries the thought out into those far times when man stood nearer to nature, and therefore nearer to the gods by far, than he does now.'

In his next letter to her he is down to more mundane matters: 'I had been intending to write to you, but I have not written anything since I have been in Dublin, neither literature nor letters. Troubles here press hard on me – the trouble of cooks especially. I had six cooks in three weeks and as you know I am not fond of changing. You can imagine the worry it has been.'

Even as early as this, the dream of the Celtic Twilight was beginning to turn sour.

# FIFTEEN

# The Green Door

Despite all his problems with cooks, neighbours and tradesmen, as soon as he settled down in Ely Place, George Moore started to entertain in a way common enough in Paris and London, but not then all that usual in Dublin. He frequently had guests for lunch (he had almost stopped calling it breakfast by now) and dinner, normally preferring to entertain one guest at a time, and began a season of 'open' Saturday nights, when any of his friends and acquaintances could feel free to drop in for a chat. He also held small garden parties in the little orchard opposite, which he had rented, along with the house, and even arranged for a production of one of Douglas Hyde's plays there.

His regular guests during the early part of his Irish Period included W. B. Yeats, whenever he was in Ireland; AE almost always; very often W. K. Magee, a librarian in the National Library, Dublin, who wrote under the pseudonym of John Eglinton, the name by which Moore always refers to him in *Hail and Farewell*; John Healy, editor of the *Irish Times*; Richard Best, also from the National Library; and Susan Mitchell, by then working as a sub-editor (in those days almost exclusively a male occupation) for a magazine called *The Irish Homestead*, edited by AE, and now becoming well known in her own right as a caustic observer, often in verse, of the Dublin scene.

Initially, Moore seems to have been well pleased with Dublin.

In June 1901, he wrote to Virginia Crawford, who was collaborating with him by supplying research material about convent life for *Sister Teresa*, to say that he was in love with the city: 'I think it is the most beautiful town that I have ever seen, mountains at the back and the sea in front, and long roads winding through decaying suburbs and beautiful woods. Dublin dwindles so beautifully, there is no harsh separation between it and the country; it fades away; whereas London seems to devour the country.'

But he was already having troubles with the neighbours. When he first rented No 4, Upper Ely Place, it had a white door like all the other houses in the street; indeed, although one of the features of what little now remains of Georgian Dublin, exuberantly exploited in posters and on postcards, is the wide variety of unlikely colours of the Georgian doors, it was the tradition, when the houses were built, that all the houses in any one street or square would be painted in the same colour; in fact it was a requirement in the leases of many of the houses.

However, and totally typically, as soon as he moved in, Moore had the front door of his house painted a defiant, Irish Nationalist green; and when two sisters, neighbours of his, threatened a lawsuit, and followed it up by buying a copy of the cheap edition of *Esther Waters*, tearing it into strips and posting the fragments through his letter-box with insulting comments, he retaliated by going out late at night and rattling his walking stick along the railings, to awaken the dogs in the neighbourhood and disturb the sleep of all the other residents of Ely Place.

One night, while he was doing this, he was bitten by a dog belonging to the two sisters, and had to call on Sir Thornley Stoker – a well-known Dublin doctor and collector of antiques and brother of Bram Stoker, the author of *Dracula*, who also lived in Ely Place – and get him out of bed to give him an injection against tetanus.

The sisters, according to one version of the incident, as related by Moore himself in *A Story-Teller's Holiday*, then enlisted the help of another resident, an eccentric called Cunningham, who employed an Italian organ-grinder to play his music under Moore's windows, during the hours when Moore was trying to write. Moore next decided to set a trap for the sisters' cat, which was in the habit of using his garden as a lavatory, on the grounds that the animal was threatening the life of a blackbird which sang there. But his plan misfired; the trap caught and killed the blackbird instead. Both parties appealed to the Society for the Prevention of Cruelty to Animals, and the whole affair ended in total confusion.

Sir Thornley frequently pretended that he did not even know Moore. 'There is a ruffian in our street,' he once remarked to his fellow-doctor, Oliver St John Gogarty, when he in turn came to live in Upper Ely Place. 'He will presently try to make your acquaintance and expect free medical treatment. Remember your apothecary's oath.'

By 1901, Moore had rewritten *Evelyn Innes* and had *Sister Teresa* ready to go to the publishers; both were psychological novels in the sense that, instead of revealing his characters through their actions and environment, he attempted to outline their thought processes; together they constitute a study in what Moore called 'that most terrible of all forms of sensuality – the religious'. Certainly Evelyn Innes, the opera singer who becomes Sister Teresa, is forever torn between her sensual desire for men and her equally torrid if less understandable passion for the religious life, a very curious choice of subject for a former agnostic just about to become (or, as he would have put it, 'discover himself to be') a Protestant.

In the rewrite of *Evelyn Innes*, he replaces W. B. Yeats with AE as the role model for the Celtic composer, Ulick Dean. Ulick and Evelyn, in the new version, go on a cycling tour of the holy places of the old Irish Celtic Pagan civilisation, paralleling the trip Moore had made with AE; indeed, they even have an encounter with some Presbyterian ministers.

Moore had by now completed his part in the collaboration with

Yeats on *Diarmuid and Grania,* and had asked Edmond Elgar to compose some music for it; it was performed by Frank Benson's company in the Gaiety Theatre in October 1901. It was moderately well received at the time, but never became a part of the regular Abbey Theatre repertoire.

Moore was also continuing to do his bit for the Irish language. The Irish-speaking nurse whom he had instructed his sister-in-law, Maurice's wife Evelyn, to employ, at his expense, to teach his nephews Irish, had proved a dismal failure. All she did was rattle off long sentences in Irish to the two boys who had no idea what she was talking about and failed to pick up a single word of Irish; and a Mayo schoolmaster who replaced her never got any further than the letters of the alphabet. Moore was informed of these disasters in letters from his brother Maurice, from the Boer War; Maurice had taught himself Irish during the campaign and was practising it in conversation around the camp fire in the evenings, with Irish-speaking members of his regiment, the Connaught Rangers. 'I dare say Evelyn does her best,' Colonel Maurice Moore wrote to his brother, '[But] I wish you would take the matter up . . . you are nearer the scene of action than I am.'

Moore immediately wrote to Evelyn at Moore Hall: 'I have today revoked the will which I made in their [the children's] favour. If I die now, your children will have lost £1,000 a year, and you will be responsible for it. However, the matter can be remedied and the remedy is in your own hands. If you write me a letter within the next few days, assuring me that you have taken steps to have your children taught Irish as their [first] language – mind you, no smattering of Irish will do; I wish their first impressions to be conveyed to them in Irish – I will revoke the will which I have just made; and I will agree to give you a year to make up for the time which you have wasted.'

It is not surprising – though Moore appeared to find it so – that poor Evelyn did not reply to this peremptory and, in view of the fact that Moore hardly knew her, extremely impertinent letter, nor did she accept nor even acknowledge any of Moore's repeated invitations to her to visit him at Upper Ely Place.

In the early spring of 1902, he offered his orchard to the Gaelic League for an outdoor performance of Douglas Hyde's play in Irish, *The Tinker and the Fairy*, and wrote to Nia: 'My attention was fixed on the weather – for three whole days and nights I thought of nothing else. Think of it. Two hundred dripping delegates coming to my tiny house to ask if there would be a play . . . but Monday was a fine day here – a heavy shower fell at twelve and then the sun came out; a few drops fell while the play was being acted, but only a few drops, and the party was an extraordinary success.' In another letter to Nia, he mentions that an old theatre had been discovered in Abbey Street which could be bought for £800 and mentioned to her that they were trying to raise £300 and, if they succeeded, would take out a mortgage for the remainder; they did not succeed in raising enough money, and it was not until 1904, when Yeats had found a new patron in Miss Annie Fredericka Horniman, a Manchester heiress, that the old Mechanics' Institute became the Abbey Theatre.

As part of his work for the language movement, Moore was now writing a series of short stories, 'about the priests and their people', which were to be translated into Irish by the Gaelic League and published in their magazine. Some of these stories were published in English and Irish in the *New Ireland Review*, and by the spring of 1902 Moore was gathering a collection of them together and rewriting them for publication in London under the title of *The Untilled Field*. George Moore was delighted to see his name in Irish – rendered as Seorsa O Mordha – on the title page of the Irish version, and was equally pleased with the result when he had his friend, T. W. Rolleston, the Gaelic scholar, translate one or two of the stories back into English from the Gaelic League version, and reported that he found them much improved after their bath in Irish – 'She had a face such as one sees in a fox' was, he thought, a great improvement on 'She had a fox-like face'.

Moore regarded Trinity College and particularly its staunchly Unionist professor of Greek, Dr John Pentland Mahaffy (later Sir John, and Provost of the university), as the prime enemies of the Irish-language movement, and wrote articles in the nationalist press attacking him, though later he regretted this; he would like to have been part of Mahaffy's circle, the most intellectual in Dublin.

By now the Irish Literary Theatre movement was beginning to fall apart at the seams. Yeats wanted to vary poetic legendary dreams with peasant comedies, and his discovery of the Fay brothers – who earned their living working as clerks, and ran several amateur dramatic societies in their spare time – decided the issue. The Fays' Irish National Dramatic Company became the successor to Edward Martyn's Irish Literary Theatre, and henceforward it was dominated by Yeats and Lady Gregory; both Martyn and Moore soon severed all connections with it.

'An Irish audience always likes to be reminded of the time when Ireland was a nation', Moore wrote in *Salve* 'and the Fays [were] determined that some organisation must be started to keep the idea alive; the Presidency of the National Theatre was offered to AE but he seemed to have considered his dramatic mission over, and contented himself with drawing up the rules and advising the members to elect Yeats as their President . . . Oh, the wise AE, for Yeats, as soon as he was elected President, took the Fays in hand, discovering almost immediately that their art was of French descent and could be traced back to the middle of the seventeenth century in France. Some explanation of this kind was necessary, for Dublin had to be persuaded that the two little clerks had suddenly become great artists, and to confirm Dublin in this belief, the newspapers were requested to state that Mr W. B. Yeats was writing a play for Mr William Fay on the subject of *The Pot of Broth* . . .'

Next, Moore attended a *féis* (a language and musical festival) in Galway with Yeats, Edward Martyn and Lady Gregory: 'A lovely day it was, the town lying under a white canopy of cloud, not a wind in all the air, but a line of houses sheer and dim along the river mingling with grey shadows; and on the other bank there were waste places difficult to account for, ruins showing dimly through the soft, diffused light, like old castles, but Yeats said they were the ruins of ancient mills, for Galway had once been a prosperous town . . . we stopped by the broken railings of a garden . . . and followed him [Martyn] through some crumbling streets to the town house of the Martyns, for in the eighteenth century the western gentry did not go to Dublin for the season. Dublin was two long days' journey away; going to Dublin meant spending a night on the road, and so every important county family had its town house in Galway. . .

'By Edward, one is always safe from adventures, and it would have been well for me not to have stirred from his side. I only strayed fifty yards, but that short distance was enough, for while looking down into the summer sea, thinking how it moved against the land's side like a soft, feline animal, the voices of some women engaged my attention, and turning, I saw that three girls had come down to a pool sequestered out of observation, in a hollow of a headland. Sitting on the bank, they drew off their shoes and stockings and advanced into the water, kilting their petticoats above their knees as it deepened. On seeing me, they laughed invitingly; and, as if desiring my appreciation, one girl walked across the pool, lifting her red petticoat to her waist, and forgetting to drop it when the water shallowed, she showed me thighs whiter and rounder than any I have seen, their country coarseness heightening the temptation.'

It had to happen to Moore; if it had not happened – and maybe it did not – he would have made it up.

Moore's next problem arose when, in a search for other stories that might be translated into Irish to provide reading matter for people who had taken the trouble to learn the language, he suggested *The Arabian Nights* as a collection of ancient stories which had stood the test of time.

All hell broke loose, naturally, and one letter to the *Freeman's Journal* thundered: 'Mr George Moore has selected *The Arabian Nights* because he wishes an indecent book to be put into the hands of every Irish peasant. We do not take our ideas of love from Mohammedan countries; we are a pure race.'

'The Irish are a cantankerous, hateful race' was Moore's reaction: '. . . Every race gets the religion it deserves . . . only as policemen, pugilists, and priests have they succeeded, with here and there a successful lawyer . . . They were that in the beginning, when the greater part of Ireland was forest and marsh, with great pasture lands through which long herds of cattle wandered from dawn to evening, watched over by barbarous men in kilts with terrible dogs; and since those days we have lost the civilisation that obtained in the monasteries. We have declined in everything except our cattle, and our herdsmen, the finest in the world, divining the steak in the bullock with the same certainty as the Greek divined the statue in the block of marble.'

By 1902, when both Martyn and Moore had dropped out of the Irish Literary Movement, Moore's anti-clerical attitude, in Hone's view, had grown so strong as to render him unfitted to undertake an executive part in any public enterprise in Ireland. He mildly admired the talents of the Fay brothers but thought they would be far better employed by the Gaelic League, going up and down the country doing plays in Irish for the benefit of the peasants, an attitude he was later to take in relation to the Welsh Revivalist movement in his 'Epistle to the Cymru', included as part of his *Memoirs of a Dead Life*.

The completion of *An Untilled Field* at the end of September 1902 left him tired and disillusioned; he went to Paris and visited Dujardin who had since become Professor at the Sorbonne, specialising in the history of primitive Christianity, and had just written a book called *La Source du Fleuve Chrétien*, a title that enchanted Moore and may well have aroused his interest in exploring the Christian *fleuve* himself.

Colonel Maurice Moore returned from South Africa and stopped off for a few days at Ely Place before continuing his journey to Moore Hall. The two brothers talked amicably enough about publishing their grandfather's history of the French Revolution, but the first shadows of the row that was to divide them fell across their discussions; Colonel Maurice was in many ways a simple soul, and a pious and devoted Catholic, and George Moore had now become convinced that it was the Catholic Church, and above all its priests, which had barred and blocked every prospect of Irish progress since the Reformation.

In England and abroad, his fame was spreading; *Evelyn Innes* proved to be a very fashionable novel and *Sister Teresa* received extremely enthusiastic reviews; Moore was planning another Irish story, initially intended to be part of *The Untilled Field* collection, but now emerging as a novel in its own right. He had got the idea from an incident that happened in Dublin around that time. A Protestant clergyman, formerly a Catholic priest, left his former life behind him, along with his clerical clothes, when he swam across a lake to start a new life. Moore decided to set the novel in Lough Carra, the lake on which Moore Hall was built, and he decided to use the name of his new neighbour, the Dublin doctor, Oliver Gogarty, as the name for his fictional priest.

Gogarty wrote: 'George Moore had refused my mother's request to exclude my name from *The Lake*.

' "But, Madam, if you can supply a name with two such joyous dactyls, I will change it."

'It caused her much pain. And I came in for a lecture on the company I was keeping: "Show me your company, and I'll tell you who you are." '

In December 1902, Moore had a bad fall. He had been cycling

around Dublin when the front wheel of the bicycle caught in the tramlines, and he fell heavily, breaking his right arm near the shoulder; 'it is extraordinary the fall that these little machines can give one,' he wrote to Mark Fisher, a painter friend of his, 'worse than any fall from a horse . . . I shall ride no more bicycles; a more treacherous thing than a bicycle does not exist upon the earth.' However, with typical energy and determination, he immediately set about teaching himself to write with his left hand and before long he was able to report to Nia from Paris that he liked his left-handed writing better than his right-handed. 'I have seen too much of it,' he added.

In fact, the accident which had made handwriting extremely difficult for him, mattered far less at this stage in his career than it would have done a couple of years earlier, for since coming to live in Ireland he had adopted a new system of dictating all his work, which he continued to the end of his life. It was later to become a specific technique which enabled him to explore the stream of consciousness approach to fiction. At this stage, however, it was largely a matter of convenience; he would dictate all of his work and most of his letters to stenographers who would take them down in shorthand; Moore would then later work on the typescript, and if necessary repeat the process again and again, until he got it to his satisfaction, though it was by no means unusual for him to continue editing and rewriting even up to the final proof stage, a habit which led to terrible rows with the publishers and exorbitant bills for corrections.

Moore's interest in his friend Dujardin's *La Source du Fleuve Chrétien* inspired him to re-read the Bible presented to him by Mrs Hunter, and while he found himself repelled by much of the Old Testament he was enchanted by the gospels and, by St Paul's epistles. In the process of studying them, he discovered himself to be a Protestant. And, for Moore, such a discovery could never be allowed to remain a secret, a personal matter between himself and his maker; he had to shout it from the rooftops. When asked why he could not have remained an agnostic or a lapsed Catholic, he replied that his spontaneous sympathies had always been with the open-minded Protestant, ever prepared for religious discussion, and unwilling to accept dogma. According to Hone, his main motive was a desire to dissociate himself from Irish Catholicism, 'and this, he argued with some reason, could only be done in Ireland by taking steps to become a Protestant: in Ireland, where the distinction embraces so much more than religion, one must be either a Catholic or a Protestant'.

So Moore – although by no means a convinced believer in any feature of the Christian myth, much less the fundamental acceptance of Jesus of Nazareth as the son of the creator of the universe – suddenly decided to become a Protestant. Without consulting anybody, he wrote to the Protestant Archbishop of Dublin, Dr Peacocke, explaining that, since he had come to live in Ireland, he had found his thoughts directed towards religion, and he now realised from his readings that the purest form of the Christian religion was to be found within the Anglican community; and would His Grace kindly advise him as to how he could become a member of the Church of Ireland.

The Archibishop happened to be away at the seaside on holiday, and Moore was referred to a Dr Gilbert Mahaffy – no relation to the Trinity professor – who lived in Ely Place. This clergyman called on Moore, they discussed the project, and kneeled at a table together to recite the Lord's Prayer.

Moore frequently contributed to the correspondence columns of the *Irish Times* as well as to the London newspapers, airing his views on a number of matters about which he had strong feelings; they included censorship, vaccination, religion, Home Rule, hand-set books and electric signs. He now decided to explain his reasons for his decision to become a Protestant in a letter to the editor of the *Irish Times*, which was published in the correspondence columns of the paper on September 24, 1903:

I decided to leave the Church of Rome when I read the announcement that the Roman Catholic Archbishop had attended the King's Levee [during a Royal visit to Dublin by King Edward VII and Queen Alexandra, in July and August 1903], and that Maynooth was preparing to receive the King in spite of the opinion of Irish Nationalists. I am not a politician, and hold no opinion whether it would be better that Ireland should cheer the King or make a silent way for the King to pass. It was said at the time that the Catholic Archbishop had consented to attend the King's Levee in order to get a Cardinal's hat.

At the time I did not credit this rumour. I was willing to attribute his desertion to weakness of character, but I read in the *Freeman's Journal* that he is to be raised to the Cardinalate at the next Consistory.

When will my unfortunate country turn its eyes from Rome – the cause of all her woe? Rome has betrayed Ireland through the centuries. In the fifth century a Roman Archbishop cursed Tara. In the eleventh century a Roman Bishop invited Henry II to invade Ireland. In the eighteenth century the Irish Bishops expressed their willingness to accept salaries from England. In the nineteenth century, when Ireland stood victorious on the threshold of freedom, the priests pressed forward together – shoulder to shoulder – and struck down Parnell. In the first years of the twentieth century, Maynooth and the Roman Catholic Archbishop deserted the Irish Parliamentary Party, one in the hope of getting a Catholic University, the other in order to get a Cardinal's hat. But we should feel no surprise at these acts of treachery. Rome has been anti-national in every country. Rome has no care for any country. Rome is not national, even in Italy. Rome aims at a wider corporation than nationality, and an English duke is no more to Rome than the entire province of Connaught. These truths are no new truths – they were not even new truths to me; but I suddenly became aware of these truths more clearly than before, and no choice was left to me, if I wished to remain an Irishman, but to say goodbye to Rome.

The Roman Catholic Archbishop will get his hat, but he will pay dearly for it. It may gain him the admiration of some sycophants, perhaps, but Ireland will look upon him with contempt; and Rome will pay for his hat, and dearly, for that hat will be the beginning of an anti-clerical movement which will not be slow in coming. But it has come! The emigration of the Celt is an anti-clerical movement. America is the danger, not

England. English rule has not prevented the Roman priests from absorbing all the wealth of Ireland. Why should Rome desire change? Home Rule cannot better Rome's position in Ireland. Home Rule will only serve Protestant interests, and, for this reason, will be resisted by the Roman Hierarchy; when the time comes, a pretext will be found. But if the Protestants do not insist upon Home Rule they will be forced by intrigue out of the country.

Yours etc, George Moore.

# SIXTEEN

# A Farewell to Ireland

By now, Moore was in regular correspondence with a great many people, most of them young ladies, among them Lady Cunard; Mrs Pearl Craigie; Lena Milman, daughter of the Governor of the Tower of London, and something of an authority on Russian literature; and Clara Lanza (the 'foreign countess' of Hone's biography though her claim to a title seems to have been slightly tenuous), whom he initially addressed as Madame Lanza but, when he got to know her better, insisted on calling Gabrielle, much to her annoyance. 'Don't call me Gabrielle,' she wrote, 'I am not a courtesan.' In most cases the correspondence was initiated by the ladies, who wrote to him to tell him how much they admired his books, though in Lady Cunard's case they had met at a public lunch. His correspondence with Lady Cunard and the Marquise Clara Lanza – who wrote to him after reading the Tauchnitz edition of *Evelyn Innes*, which she had picked up in her local bookshop – soon developed into a sort of tantalising, teasing flirtation on paper, which was possibly the only type of flirtation that Moore enjoyed, or perhaps the only type of which he was capable: love affairs, conducted in carefully chosen words, from a great distance. In the early days, he wooed his lady pen-friends in his own handwriting, execrable spelling and all; but, from the time he went to live in Dublin, they usually had to put up with letters typed by a stenographer, or by one of his many secretaries.

Among the first was Margaret Gough, who worked full-time for him later in London, and in 1912, when she was leaving to get married, published – with his full approval and co-operation – a George Moore calendar containing quotations from his works to grace the passing months. There is no evidence as to where she stayed while she was in Dublin, working for him, nor for how long, but it was widely known that Moore trusted her sufficiently to allow her to be alone in the house in Ely Place to continue typing out her transcripts of his dictation in his absence.

Another secretary employed by Moore was a Miss Jugge, a single lady who, according to Oliver St John Gogarty's *It Isn't This Time of Year At All*, was sacked by Moore when she became pregnant, and in retaliation stole some of his manuscripts from the house when she was collecting her things, and sold them.

By the spring of 1904, Moore was back in Paris for a visit 'to be regilded', as he himself expressed it, and writing ecstatically to the Marquise: 'The weather is beautiful and it inspires love . . . I could love you, Gabrielle. I understand so well when you say that life is dry and empty when one hasn't a lover.'

Moore had decided that, as soon as he had finished *The Lake*, he would work on a sort of history of his literary life, and had already, in 1903, found a title for it: it was to be called *Avowals*. In 1904, he began another sort of history – of his real or imagined love life – writing a few pieces that became the opening chapters of *Memoirs of My Dead Life*, including 'Spring Days', an account of an encounter with Lady Cunard, whom he calls Elisabeth, and 'Flowering Normandy', as well as 'The Lovers of Orelay', in which Lady Cunard may again feature as Dora. Hone claims that it was Moore's friend W. K. Magee (John Eglinton) who devised the name Orelay for the town in France where the lovers finally consummate their passion; and a few of the opening chapters of *Memoirs* appeared in *Dana*, a Dublin literary magazine founded and edited by Magee. Hone says that Moore gave them to Magee free, as a gift to a friend, and adds that 'the editor sometimes made a wry face' as the scandalous contents of the next offering were disclosed to him during the course of one of Moore's Saturday-night gatherings in Ely Place. He also believes that it was Richard Best, Magee's colleague at the National Library, who gave Moore the title of 'Resurgam' for the final chapter in the book, originally titled 'My Own Funeral', which was greatly influenced by, if not based on, Nietzsche's poem about what he called the 'eternal return'. The same extracts from Moore's uncompleted *Memoirs* appeared in America in *Lippincott's Monthly Magazine* between July 1903 and February 1904.

In 1904, also, Werner Laurie published a third edition of Moore's *Confessions of a Young Man*, with a preface by Walter Pater, whom Moore described as 'the last great English writer'; actually, the preface consisted of a letter to Moore from Pater, acknowledging receipt of a presentation copy of the first edition, addressed to 'My dear, audacious Moore', and opening: 'Many thanks for the *Confessions*, which I have read with great interest, and admiration for your originality – your delightful criticisms – your Aristophanic joy, or at least enjoyment, in life – your unfailing liveliness.'

Moore once again jumped on the publicity bandwagon, and in August of that year the *Pall Mall Magazine* carried an article he had written about his personal relations with Pater, and his pleasure, on re-reading the *Confessions*, to discover that his views on *Marius the Epicurean* were exactly the same as they had been twenty years earlier, thereby drawing attention, in a popular magazine, to the new edition of his own book.

Moore was now spending more and more time away from Ireland. He had been in Paris for several weeks in November 1903; he was in London in June 1904, and then in the autumn of 1904, when he once again encountered Pearl Craigie; and, when she agreed to collaborate with him on a play he was thinking of writing, he accepted her invitation to spend a month working on it at her father's residence, Steephill Castle, at Ventnor, on the Isle of Wight. The play, at this stage called *The Peacock's Feather*, was published in July 1913 as *Elizabeth Cooper*; it was produced under that title at the Haymarket Theatre in London the previous month and was considered a great success; and eventually it was published, in 1922, as Volume 4,587 in the Tauchnitz collection of British and American authors, under a new title, *The Coming of Gabrielle*. This new version contained much fresh material and bore his name only; Pearl Craigie had died in August 1906.

The final version of this play is a very good example of the way Moore used to interweave incidents and characters from his own books and from his own life into a mixture of fact and fiction and fantasy; the plot, such as it is, concerns a famous writer who has an Aubusson carpet and who lives in an English provincial town called Rockminster, which could well be Dublin. The author, Lewis (that name again; Moore seems still to be mesmerised by memories of his Paris friend) Davenant, is just about to leave on the Orient Express for Vienna where his play, *Elizabeth Cooper*, is about to be performed.

There is a youngish (about thirty) admirer of Davenant's work who invites him and his secretary to stay with her in her nearby stately home – she is called Lady Letham but the character is clearly based on Lady Cunard; and Lewis Davenant, or perhaps his secretary, Sebastian Dayne, has been conducting an epistolary love affair with Gabrielle, Countess von Hoenstadt, who lives in Vienna, is a great admirer of Davenant's work, and has arranged the German production of *Elizabeth Cooper*.

Moore wrote to Nia from Steephill Castle on September 7, 1904, to tell her that he was sorry he had missed her in London, but Mrs Craigie kept wiring him to come down to the Isle of Wight to write the comedy. He says that he dictated the whole of the first act in one day, and was well into the second act on the second day, when the stenographer whom Mrs Craigie had employed begged him to stop because he was getting cramp in his wrist. The whole play was, apparently, dictated inside three days, and indeed it reads as if it was. He also tells Virginia Crawford that he is going to Leeds for the music festival, leaving Mrs Craigie to go through the play again and polish the dialogue. He ends the letter: 'She walks about in expensive robes and millinery. Goodness knows why.'

He was soon quarrelling bitterly with Mrs Craigie again, and the play was put on one side until after her death; and it was probably at the end of this final attempt at collaboration that the famous row in Green Park occurred which ended with him giving her a kick in the behind, 'nearly in the centre of the backside, a little to the right', as he explained in a piece called 'Lui et Elles' which appeared in the first edition of *Memoirs of My Dead Life* and was dropped in subsequent editions. 'It was inevitable,' he commented, 'part of the world's history, and I lost sight of all things but the track of my boot on the black crêpe de chine.'

In December 1904, he referred to the row in a letter to Virginia Crawford: 'I have done with Pearl and hope one day to dissolve that pearl in vinegar . . . I have been working all day and have not the energy to write out a full account of our quarrel.' On the other hand, Nancy Cunard says that Moore told her that this famous kick in Green Park occurred during one of her mother's not-infrequent rows with GM. No one will ever know the truth of the affair, if indeed it was not merely an invention of Moore's.

On February 4, the first production of John Millington Synge's *The Well of the Saints* was staged in the Abbey Theatre. Although Moore had by now broken all connections with Yeats, Martyn and Lady Gregory, he still took a keen interest in the venture and, when Synge's play was poorly received by the critics, wrote a letter to the *Irish Times* praising it, and urging the public to go to see it. He was apt to claim that it was from him that Synge got his ideas for his very distinctive version of the vernacular English spoken by Irish-speaking Celts, but Susan Mitchell, in her book about George Moore, says this is nonsense; it all stemmed, she claims, from Douglas Hyde's rendering in English of *The Love Songs of Connacht*. Hyde, she gently reminds us, and indeed them, was the only one of the entire group who spoke and understood Irish, and he was able to isolate the bony Gaelic sub-structure underlying

Anglo-Irish speech, and identify it and imitate it in English, and it
was this discovery that led to Lady Gregory's Kiltartan and Yeats's
subsequent use of it, as well as to John Millington Synge-Song.

But if Moore did not invent John Millington Synge-Song, he
could mimic it brilliantly, and did so in the preface to the 1914
edition of *The Untilled Field*. Here is a sample: 'It was just as if on
purpose to make an omadahun [Moore's attempt to reproduce
*amadán*, the Irish for fool, in phonetics] of me that Yeats brought
him over from Paris in the year 1903, though he had no English on
him at the time, only the like that's heard in the National Schools,
and if you don't believe me, will you be throwing your eye over the
things he wrote in them days for the weekly papers, and faith you'll
see the editors were right to fire them out . . . 'tis little of the taste
of sugar-candy he got into his articles, and his book about the Aran
islands has more the tang of old leather, like as if he'd be chewing
the big brogues he did be always wearing on his feet. And,
morebetoken, his language in the same book is as bald as the coat
of a mangy dog, and traipsed along over a page of print like the
clatter of a horse that was gone in the legs. It's many a heart scald
this same must have given to my bold Yeats, for it's the grand judge
entirely he is of the shape and the colour and the sound of words.'

One of the major events of 1905 in Dublin was a large exhibition
of modern paintings, most of them for sale, arranged by Hugh
(later Sir Hugh) Lane, which was opened by George Moore, both
in his capacity as a distinguished art critic and because he was
probably the only man in Ireland who knew many of the painters
in the exhibition personally. Hugh Lane, Lady Gregory's nephew,
was a highly successful art dealer, of whom it was said that if he
were ever in need of money he only had to buy a picture from some
art dealer in Bond Street, London, and sell it to another dealer five
doors down for twice the price. By 1905, he had already amassed a
substantial private collection of Impressionist paintings, which he
had promised to leave to the Irish nation, to form the nucleus of a

National Gallery of Modern Art, provided that a suitable building could be found or built to house them.

The exhibition which Moore opened early in February had been arranged by Lane with a view to providing more pictures for the proposed Gallery of Modern Art. The pictures on view included Lane's own collection, which were not for sale; a large collection of modern paintings which had been the property of a late and wealthy American financier, Mr Staats Forbes; and others borrowed by Lane from Durand-Ruel, a Bond Street dealer who had bought many paintings by the Impressionists in the 1870s and '80s when the prices were extremely low. Several committees had been formed in Dublin to raise money, through subscriptions and various other activities, to purchase for the nation as many of the pictures as possible; and, in addition, several wealthy patrons and friends of Hugh Lane bought paintings at the exhibition and presented them to the nation for the Gallery of Modern Art.*

Moore's lengthy and entertaining address on the subject of the Impressionists was published in 1906 under the title *Reminiscences of the Impressionist Painters*, and reproduced in full in the first edition of *Vale*, the final volume of *Hail and Farewell*; for later editions, he edited it down considerably.

The lecture, predictably enough in view of Moore's prevailing mood at this period, ended with a bitter attack on the clergy, which, coming so hot on the heels of his 'conversion' to Protestantism, did little to enhance his popularity in Catholic Ireland: 'Life is a rose that withers in the iron fist of dogma,' he said, 'and it was France that forced open the deadly fingers of the Ecclesiastic and allowed the rose to bloom again. He [the Ecclesiastic] started to crush life out about two thousand years ago, and in three centuries, humility, resignation and obedience were accepted as virtues; the shrines of the Gods were abandoned; the beautiful limbs of the lover and the athlete were forbidden to the

* Lane was drowned when the *Lusitania* sank in 1915, and the legal wrangle between Dublin and London over the ownership of the Lane Collection has only recently – and only partially – been resolved.

sculptor, and the meagre thighs of dying saints offered to them instead. Literature dies, for literature can but praise life. Music dies, for music can but praise life, and the lugubrious *Dies Irae* was heard in the fanes.'*

Towards the end of February 1905, because of his family's long connections with the area, Moore was nominated for the unlikely post of High Sheriff of Mayo. It was an honour which he did not feel he could turn down, and it entailed little more than meeting the judge who arrived in Mayo for the Castlebar Assizes, escorting him to the court, carrying a ceremonial sword, and entertaining him to dinner while the Assizes were in session. He referred to it in letters as a 'wearisome business' and 'an annoyance', but in fact he seems to have rather enjoyed it. He stayed at the best hotel in Castlebar while the court was sitting, with his agent, Tom Ruttledge, as his sub-sheriff, and spent a lot of his spare time reading Wagner's letters to Mathilde Wesendonck.

He returned to Dublin in July 1905, after the Assizes had finished, and completed *The Lake*. By August, he was in Paris again, reading the proofs, and writing a dedication to his friend Edouard Dujardin, with whom he stayed. In this dedication, he acknowledges the larceny, as Hone phrased it, which he had committed by using a straight translation of Dujardin's *La Source du Fleuve Chrétien* as the title of an imaginary work written by Ralph Ellis, a fictional character in the novel, and he remembers his attachment to Valvins, in the Forest of Fontainebleau, where their old friend Mallarmé had lived. The dedication is written in French and, in it, Moore recalls how it was at Valvins that he read parts of *The Lake* aloud to Dujardin. 'In order to explain the sadness of this beautiful country,' he writes, 'strewn with empty castles, and haunted by the memory of festivals of yesteryear [*fêtes d'autrefois*], it would be necessary to have a whole orchestra. I hear first the violins; later other instruments are added, horns, without

---

* It means a temple and comes from the Latin; Moore had a passion for odd words.

doubt; but to render the sadness of my poor country over there [*là-bas*], you wouldn't need all that. I hear it very clearly on a solo flute, playing on an island surrounded by the waters of a lake, the flute-player seated on the hazy [*vagues*] ruins of a Gallic or maybe a Norman redoubt. But, dear friend, you are Norman, and perhaps it could well have been your ancestors who pillaged my country; that is yet another reason why I dedicate this novel to you.'

*The Lake* represented a turning point in Moore's literary career, a stage at which he became as interested in the prose style as in the content. It foreshadowed all the work of his later period; books like *The Brook Kerith*, *Héloïse and Abélard* and *Daphnis and Chloe*. It is set in County Mayo, on and around the shores of Lough Carra. Moore had not visited Moore Hall at all while he was writing the novel. He did not need to; he remembered every tiny detail of the landscape. But he did write to his brother Maurice, asking him for details of the history of the old castles and the islands in the area, and when Maurice called on him at Ely Place on his way home from the Boer War they talked for hours about their home and their childhood and the family.

These conversations frequently turned into arguments about religion, which Maurice always tried to avoid; but Moore disliked the thought that his nephews, who were also his heirs, and for whose education he was at least partly paying, were being brought up as Catholics. Nevertheless, for the moment, the arguments usually ended amicably enough, and it was around this period that it was agreed that Maurice, who was about to retire from the army, should take over Moore Hall and live there with his family for as long as he wished to do so.

It was also decided to dispose of all the other Moore property under Wyndham's Land Act, which offered extremely favourable terms to the landlords in order to encourage them to sell their lands to the Government for redistribution among the tenants. All details of the sale were left to Colonel Maurice and Moore's agent, Tom Ruttledge, and Moore was not at all surprised when the sale fell through; he thought that Maurice and Ruttledge were

asking far too high a price for the land. 'Twenty-two years
purchase of second-term rights,' he wrote to his brother on April 5,
1905, 'is quite sufficient, and if the landlords do not settle on these
terms I assure you that it is my firm conviction that within the next
ten years, they will lose half of their properties.'

*The Lake* was published in November 1905 and was an
immediate critical success. It is the story of a priest who [before the
novel opens] becomes very friendly with a young unmarried
schoolmistress and then denounces her from the pulpit and drives
her from the parish when she becomes pregnant. The girl – called
Rose Leicester in the first edition and Nora Glynn in subsequent
editions – emigrates to England where she works as a secretary/
housekeeper to a famous writer, who also has an Aubusson carpet:
another thinly disguised self-portrait, by Moore, of Moore. As a
result of a series of chance occurrences, Father Oliver Gogarty is
again put in touch with her and a long, intimate correspondence
ensues. Their relationship is very delicately handled but it soon
becomes clear that the priest, Oliver Gogarty, has fallen in love
with the girl; and unable to reconcile his clearly carnal desire for
her with his position as priest, and realising how ambivalent his
feelings about her have always been, he finally accepts the fact that
it was jealousy of the man who had made her pregnant, far more
than any concern for morality, which had caused him to denounce
her. He leaves his clerical garb at the side of the lake, and swims
across it to set out on a new life as a layman in America. Put like
that, it sounds very bald. The whole novel takes place, as it were,
within the mind of the priest who, through a process of self-
analysis, as he walks up and down the lake shore, as Cave puts it in
his introduction to the one-volume edition of *Hail and Farewell*,
'comes to perceive his insensitivity to the natural world and to his
own instincts and emotions. Feeling that his present life is aridly
intellectual and that in repressing his emotional life he has starved
his spiritual life of joy, he emigrates to start a new life abroad rather
than continue dishonestly to preach a faith whose principles he
finds questionable.'

He is fleeing from Ireland and from the priesthood because 'there is a lake in every man's heart, and he listens to its monotonous whispers, year after year, more and more attentive, until at last he ungirds'.

The lake in Moore's heart was now whispering to him urgently that it was time for him to leave Ireland; but he could not, because he had just had an idea for a new book, indeed three new books, a trilogy no less, an autobiographical fantasy woven around his failed mission, a monumental work which would not only reveal the disastrous results of the domination of European civilisation by Rome and its dogmatic priests but would also expose the pompous and hypocritical nature of Irish society wth a fine, satirical irony.

His real mission was to become Ireland's Voltaire; and his trilogy was to be called *Hail and Farewell*, the separate volumes to be entitled *Ave*, *Salve* and *Vale*.

It was another six years before he had collected enough material for this trilogy and to be able to bid his final farewell to Ireland.

SEVENTEEN

# Moore's Memories

Once he had made the decision that he needed a further period in Dublin to assimilate more material for his projected saga, Moore settled down happily enough into the routine described by Hone: '. . . day after day passed quietly at Ely Place with his secretary; the day went by, every day the same as the previous day. On summer evenings, he would mount his bicycle or play a little lawn tennis in his garden. He was fond of a game of lawn tennis and was quite a useful player but his style was now a little cramped by a shoulder dislocated in a fall and badly set because he refused an anaesthetic. He wore his bowler hat while on the courts, a survival of a custom from the early eighties which looked odd.'

Moore never encouraged casual callers at No 4, Ely Place. Although he was living in one of the most informal cities in Europe, and had spent his formative years in another free and easy environment, among the artists and writers of Montmartre, Moore had adopted, and had brought to Ireland with him, the slightly stiff etiquette of polite English society. In addition, he took his art far more seriously than most of his fellow-artists in Ireland – with the possible exception of W. B. Yeats – and rigidly refused to be interrupted when he was working, though he himself took full advantage of the amiable informality of Dublin to call on other people casually, whenever it suited him.

He was still learning most of the things he wanted to know

through reading and conversation, and was always asking questions, and frequently inviting people to supply him with all sorts of
details which he required for the books he was writing; and most of
them were highly surprised when the notes they sent him in
response to these requests appeared unchanged – and unacknowl-
edged – in one or other of his books.

As a rule, Moore worked from nine o'clock in the morning until
four, five, or even five-thirty in the evening, and, after he had had
a cup of tea, would go for a walk, which usually ended up at the
*Irish Times* offices in Westmoreland Street, or at the rooms of E. V.
Longworth, a young barrister, or at the offices of the Co-operative
Society where AE worked, or at the house of the Italian musician,
Esposito, a close friend of his. Edward Martyn was now becoming
involved in politics, and in providing the Palestrina choir for
Dublin's Pro-Cathedral, and Moore saw him only rarely. From
time to time, he visited Lady Ardilaun's country home in
Clontarf, or often spent an evening at Stella's house in the Dublin
mountains above Rathfarnham, or at Sir Walter Armstrong's villa
in Howth.

He also spent a lot of time in the reading room of Dublin's
National Library in Kildare Street, which remained open until ten
o'clock in the evenings, and was a pleasant place to spend an hour
or so after dinner. In the library he often met his friends Magee and
Richard Best, and they would talk together until the library closed,
and then continue the conversation, walking around the Dublin
streets, or along the Grand Canal.

It was in the course of one of these conversations that he heard
from Magee of a book that had just come into the library on the
subject of the Crucifixion. The author, a doctor, took the view
that Christ might not have been dead when he was taken down
from the cross, but merely in a sort of coma, from which he could
well have recovered in the coolness of the tomb. Moore had heard
this theory advanced before; he also knew it was a widely held
belief that, before his ministry in Jerusalem, Jesus had been a monk
in an Essene monastery, somewhere in Jericho.

Immediately, yet another idea for a book occurred to him: nothing less than a rewrite of the New Testament, with a different ending. What would happen if, after his recovery from the coma, Christ had returned to the Essene monastery? And suppose, many years later, after preaching a new religion based on the resurrection, St Paul were to call at the monastery and discover that Christ had not in fact died on the cross but was alive and well and living in Jericho? He went straight home and sketched out a rough scenario for a story he called *The Apostle*, in which Paul kills Christ, because he feels that, by surviving the Crucifixion, Christ has made a nonsense of the whole, central Christian message.

Sometimes he would discuss English grammar with Best, and Hone says that it was from Best that Moore first heard of the subjunctive. 'But what is the subjunctive?' Moore asked. 'Give me an instance.' And when the uses of the subjunctive mood had been fully explained to him, he replied: 'Oh, I would give *anything* to be able to use the subjunctive. If it be; if it rain; how wonderful! But I will *always* use the subjunctive mood.'

On Saturday nights he entertained his group of special friends which now included Oliver St John Gogarty, whom Moore described as 'the author of all the jokes that enable us to live in Dublin'; Gogarty had taken the house next to Moore's garden, on the opposite side of Ely Place, and some of Gogarty's jokes were practical ones; on one occasion, when they were travelling together in a train along Dublin Bay, Moore pompously remarked to Gogarty that he would give ten pounds for five minutes of that view. Gogarty immediately pulled the communication cord and stopped the train. 'You can have it for half that price,' he said, five pounds being the fine for improper use of the piece of equipment in question.

During these Saturday evening gatherings, Moore liked to discuss his current projects with his friends, sometimes reading aloud extracts from forthcoming books from the typewritten sheets prepared by his secretaries, or from the proofs. Synge was among Moore's guests on several occasions, and of the younger writers whom Moore encouraged were James Starkey, the poet who wrote as Seamus O'Sullivan, Padraic Colum and James Stephens. James Joyce was never invited because, in Moore's opinion he was 'rather common', and he resented it bitterly. But Moore remained convinced that his *Confessions* was a far better book than *A Portrait of the Artist as a Young Man*, and was probably a bit galled at Joyce's success in what was essentially the same vein.

The final chapters of his *Memoirs of My Dead Life* were ready at the beginning of 1906. It was published in May and got a rather cool reception from the English reviewers, though it sold extremely well. It consisted of a series of sketches in which he recalled memories of London, Paris, the French countryside, Sussex and Mayo, and wove fictional-factional fantasies around events that happened, or did not happen, or might possibly have happened, if things had been otherwise. The best known of them all, 'The Lovers of Orelay', appears, on the surface, to be a factual account of an affair he once had, as an elderly beau, with a young nymphet in the south of France, though it could equally well be a fantasy woven around his long-distance love affair with Lady Cunard.

In his dedication to Gosse – who had in turn dedicated a collection of his *Sunday Times* pieces, published under the title *Books on the Table*, to Moore – Moore refers to their mutual love for France and Paris, and includes accounts both of the incident when Mallarmé and he were nearly drowned in the Seine and of a more recent visit he had paid to Mallarmé's house at Valvin.

'The Lovers of Orelay' opens with Moore saying that he had come a thousand miles, or nearer to fifteen hundred, in the hope of picking up the thread of a love story that had been broken off abruptly. A character whom he calls Doris had given him a great deal of herself, he admits, while denying him much, and he had fled from a one-sided love affair. Doris had been younger then, seventeen years younger (so that if she was sixteen then, she must have been at least thirty-three at the time of the visit to Orelay, and not eighteen), though Moore does not find her at all changed and she talks of herself as having the figure of a young girl of sixteen.

After seventeen years, Moore decides to break the silence, and writes to his old friend Doris. The note is sent by a messenger to her old address in Cumberland Place in London and the messenger is instructed to wait for an answer. The answer is that the lady is away, but Moore's letter will be forwarded to her.

In reply he receives a telegram saying that she is delighted to hear from him again, and telling him that she had been ill, but is better now, and that she is writing. A letter follows, from a town in the south of France, containing one phrase which puts black misgivings into Moore's mind. She tells him that, if he visits her, 'virtue must be its own reward', whatever that may mean.

He is dismayed: '. . . and this would seem that you are determined to be more aggressively Platonic than ever. Doris, this is ill news indeed; you would not have me consider it good news, would you?' Other letters follow and we soon find him in a train, en route for the south of France and for Doris. He describes the journey very colourfully and in great detail.

The place where she is staying, which he calls Plessy, is 'a difficult place to get at', but he has sent her a telegram announcing when he is arriving, and she is there on the platform to meet him, and turns out to be 'the same pretty girl whom I so bitterly reproached for selfishness in Cumberland Place five years ago'. (Less than ten pages earlier he has assured us that it was seventeen years ago.) She invites him to her hotel to take supper with her but Moore has already eaten on the train, so they talk for a while, and then they part, she going to her hotel and he to his. After a good night's sleep, Moore awakens to a sensuous Mediterranean morning and conveys all the magic it meant to him. 'It seemed a wonderful thing that at last I should see oranges growing on the trees,' he remarks.

They met for lunch (he calls it breakfast again) the next day, and he takes her in his arms, but any further progress in that direction is interrupted by the arrival of the waiter. And, during the meal, it is quite clear, even from Moore's own account of the conversation, that he has been boring her rigid with talk about nymphs and satyrs and logistical details of his journey. 'Forgive me,' he says. 'Remember that three days ago I was in Ireland, the day before yesterday I was in England, yesterday I was in Paris,' and he goes relentlessly on and on: '*Le Côte d'Azur* has become to you only palms and promenades. To me it is still antiquity.'

Understandably, she is far more interested in her own appearance: 'It is provoking, that you should see me when I am thin. I wish you had seen me last year, when I came from the rest cure. I went up more than a stone in weight. Everyone said that I didn't look more than sixteen. I know I didn't, for all the women were jealous of me.'

Then, inexplicably, given a broad hint like that, unless Moore is poking fun at himself, he proceeds to bore the daylights out of her yet again, recounting a tedious tale which seems highly unlikely even within its own very generous terms of reference, about a forty-year-old lady called Gertrude who wrote to him and who, when they met, suggested that he should be her companion on a six-month cruise around the Greek islands in a yacht which she had hired, captain, crew and all, provided, of course, that he would pay one-third of the costs of the expedition.

He goes on and on, boring Doris even further by telling her how Gertrude had made it plain to him that she did not mind him making love to her, but she did not like anybody claiming any rights over her, as if at this stage Doris could possibly care about anything that Gertrude had said. The boredom in Doris's plea is so audible – 'But, dear one, please finish about the yacht . . .' – that you wonder whether Moore is not once more having a little laugh at his own expense.

The yacht, if it ever existed, was wrecked off the coast of France, while Moore and Gertrude waited for it at Marseilles, if there ever was a Gertrude, or if Moore had ever been in Marseilles at this stage, which is unlikely. Not surprisingly, Doris remarks: 'Good

Heavens, how extraordinary! And what became of Gertrude? Were you ever her lover?'

'Never. We abstained . . .' [another awful word] 'while waiting for the yacht. Then she fell in love with somebody else; she married her lover; and now he deplores her; she found an excellent husband, and died in his arms.'

Unbelievably, he comments: 'Whether Doris agreed tacitly that my admiration of Gertrude's slender flanks and charm of manner and taste in dress justified me in agreeing to go away with her, I don't know.' In sheer desperation, Doris tells him about her own life: that she had been engaged to be married, that she fell in love with a friend of her betrothed's, that she sent him away 'before yielding to him'.

Next, they go for a drive to what is clearly a perched village, probably Eze. And in the shade of the ilex-trees, he kisses Doris, and, carried away by the sensation, confesses to her that he shouldn't ever have sent her a telegram saying when he was arriving; if he hadn't, she would have been fast asleep in her hotel when he arrived, and he could have gone straight to her hotel.

'But, darling, you wouldn't compromise me. Everyone would know that we stayed at the same hotel.'

'. . . then I have come a thousand miles for nothing . . . This is worse than the time when I left you in London for your strictness. Can nothing be done?'

'If you're not satisfied, you can go back.'

He comments: 'There was nothing to do but to wait, and hope that life, which is always full of accidents, would favour us; for Doris was clearly anxious that an opportunity should occur, only she did not want to compromise herself.'

They visit the perched town again, which he calls Florac, and they visit the perfume factory at Grasse and he keeps begging her – unconvincingly, because it is clearly the last thing that he wants – to allow him to spend a night at her hotel and she keeps refusing him and, eventually, they decide to go back to Paris via Orelay, which is a sizeable town somewhere between the south coast and

Lyons. By now, he thinks he has persuaded her to consider a closer measure of intimacy, but when they finally stop for the night at Orelay all sorts of problems present themselves.

First, he does not like the bedroom, and thinks it would be an insult to them both if they were obliged to make love for the first time in such a tall, narrow bed. Next, he manages to secure a far better room – which may well be a fantasy inside a fantasy, as it were – and then discovers that his valet has not packed his pyjamas, and how could he possibly think of approaching her, in her boudoir, in a nightshirt? They try all the shops and boutiques in Orelay but can find no pyjamas, and he is finally reconciled to the thought that he might have to confront her, when and if the time comes, in a nightshirt.

He goes on: '. . . but the fears of the lover were not ended yet. The great fear lest the eagerness of his desire should undermine his bodily strength was upon me; and had not Doris proved all that I had imagined her to be, my fate might have been a sad one . . . the colour of the rooms, their shapes, the furniture, all is seen by me today as truly as if the reality were before me; the very wood we burned in the great fireplace, the shape of one log, how it fell into ashes at one end, leaving a great knotted stump at the other, the moving of the candles into shadowy places so that their light should not fall upon our eyes – all these details are remembered, only the moment of ecstasy is forgotten.'

Doris seems to be made of sterner stuff, however, and after he has given his all and bade her goodnight in her own bedroom, she visits him again in the morning in his bedroom, and, as he puts it, 'our intimacy was completed as she sat watching me while I shaved, laughing . . .'

'These stories are memories, not inventions,' he says. Who knows?

Then there is the sketch called 'Spring in London', which clearly concerns Lady Cunard, referred to in this tale and in others sometimes as Elisabeth with an 's', and something with a 'z', even in the same story.

He is in King's Bench Walk, watching spring come to London – better to see it on a Sunday, viewed from a hansom, lying back against the cushions – and it is typical of Moore that, when he wants to view London on a spring Sunday morning, he does not take a walk, he takes a hansom cab. In an echo of 'Oh, to be in London, now that April's there', he says that one must be in London, to see the spring properly. He lovingly describes Park Lane, once a country lane, and of Elisabeth he says: 'For six months our love story was lived out in Paris and elsewhere . . . It was in one of those nooky little drawing-rooms that our last love scene was enacted in view of the Chelsea shepherds and shepherdesses, happy in their powers.' There are heavy suggestions of intimacy that might be of his own imagining, because he also talks about going to meet her husband when he returned from Ireland to London. 'My Elizabeth, now alas! a married woman. I saw her standing on the hearth rug. I have often thought since that I should have done well to take her in my arms, ignoring her marriage altogether, which I think she expected me to do, but one never knows.' This smacks very strongly of the shy, awkward Mayo youth who seemed to loom so large beneath Moore's thin disguise as a cosmopolitan, sophisticated man of the world; it certainly would have qualified for entry in the New Yorker's 'Faint Hearts Department' column.

He muses about what has been, or might have been. 'With the intellectual detachment of genius, we [men] have carved our dreams of women in marble, built palaces for her and wonderful tombs – indeed have loved women so well that women should forget to complain that there are fools among us who chase them round the furniture . . . and I think, too, that it ill behoves them to praise sexual virtue, which has cruelly enslaved them, turning them into kitchen-maids, laundresses, nuns or wives.'

Whilst driving in a hansom through the deserted streets around Kensington he saw Elizabeth coming towards him in another hansom, but instead of asking her in for tea, which was his first impulse, he invites her to go for a drive with him, down the Fulham Road. I could tell of other incidents, he adds, equally odd, but one should be enough. Once, when she called to see him, instead of inviting her in, he took her to a restaurant, a strange piece of stupidity, and in almost the next sentence he reveals the source of this stupidity, his own innate innocence and lack of self-confidence.

On another occasion, whether by accident or by design (and, if by design, it must have been on her part; it certainly would not have been on his), he finds himself sharing the coupé (two-seater, half-compartment at the rear end of a coach) with her, and finds, to his amazement, that she allows his hand to remain upon her knee. But not only that. She even remarks to him: 'Well, you've got me again, after all these years.' But, instead of following up this promising overture with some action, he falls to musing about the incident: 'There is doubtless something marvellous when a woman allows your hand to rest upon her knee . . . All the love I received from her since that day we journeyed in the coupé together, has been richer, more resplendent, mayhap, than our earlier love, but in the autumn sky there is always a hue of death, and in the stillness, a dread of the lean winter coming. Spring love is but a tremor, laughter, and a little ecstasy; an autumn love is enriched with memories; and its fear of the lean winter exalts it.

'. . . and that night Elisabeth seemed to me a very Fragonard maiden as she sat up in bed, her hair in plaits and a large book in her hand. Had I asked her what she was reading [who but Moore would have bothered about her literary tastes at a moment like this?] we might have wasted a while in literature, but throwing the vain linen aside, she revealed herself. . .'

All the time he was in Dublin, Moore wrote regularly to Lady Cunard, frequently stayed with her in their vast mansion, Nevill Holt near Great Easton in Northamptonshire, and was constantly inviting her to meet him for trysts in Paris and Ireland. It seems likely that she did meet him from time to time in Paris, but equally

unlikely, from their correspondence, that she ever went to Ireland
to meet him. According to Daphne Fielding's *Emerald and Nancy*,
some of the happiest days of George Moore's life were spent at
Nevill Holt, during the summer of 1904, where Lady Cunard's
husband, Sir Bache, made him very welcome, apparently unaware
of Moore's passionate feelings about his wife.

Moore believed that he had discovered divinity in the women
he fancied. It was par for the course. The little Catholic boy from
Mayo, forever on the look-out for some sort of a divine revelation
– an expectation instilled in him from earliest childhood, however
much he may have denied it – was always liable to mistake one
kind of ecstasy for another. On the other hand, Moore was by then
no longer a young man, certainly not by Victorian standards; he
was in his fifties.

'Seekers of divinity we all are in secret – in secret, for a middle-
aged man walking down Park Lane, buttoning his frock coat, lest
he should catch cold, would be sent to Bedlam if he were to tell
that one night in his London hotel, he discovered divinity in his
mistress.' He would not, of course; he would merely be accused of
immaturity, a disease that dogged Moore all his life, right up until
his far from immature death at the age of eighty.

Another of the sketches, 'In the Luxembourg Gardens', is an
extraordinary illustration of George Moore's curious relationships
with women; it demonstrates how sensitive he was, how sympathetic, in the French sense, not only to their moods, but also to all
the nuances of their dialogue. A far better title would have been
'A Portrait of a Flapper', and it is hard to believe that it was written
as early as 1905, at the latest; one would be tempted to imagine the
girl Mildred to have been based on Nancy Cunard, perhaps, or
someone of that period, but although Moore knew Nancy Cunard
extremely well at this period, she was still only a child, so Mildred's
dialogue cannot have been based on Nancy's.

Structurally, the sketch is very simple. He begins by recounting
how he had visited the Place des Vosges in Paris with a young

English girl called Mildred, whom he had met on the cross-channel steamer, en route for France, and whom he finds to be staying in the same hotel as he is, in Paris.

He tells her about the Place des Vosges, that it had once been the habitation of the French nobility: 'As I spoke, its colour rose up before my eyes, pretty tones of yellow and brown brick, with wrought-iron railings, high-pitched roofs, and tall clustered chimneys. I tried to remember if there were any colonnades; and failing, fell to thinking how the mind of a nation shapes itself like rocks, by a process of slow accumulation, and that it takes centuries to gather together an idea so characteristic as the Place des Vosges.'

After the Place des Vosges, they visit Notre Dame together, exploring the quays and the old streets of the Ile de la Cité, but, as he puts it, Mildred appears to lack the historical sense, and as they return in the glow of the sunset, remarks that Paris wasn't bad for such an old city.

In the hotel that night, where she is staying with 'mamma dear' and also, though mamma dear does not know it, with her betrothed (if it comes to that, her dear mamma does not even know she considers herself betrothed to Donald, and would never approve, because Donald is penniless; he has taken time off from the office where he works, without leave, and has borrowed a few pounds from Mildred to enable him to join her in Paris), Moore listens to her mother playing a sonata in the salon and has retired to his private sitting room when Mildred comes in, tells him about her betrothed, and adds: 'Isn't it awful? I was in the dining room with my young man, and the waiter caught us kissing. I had to beg of him not to tell mamma.' And, when Moore offers her his sitting room, she replies: 'Oh, no, I wouldn't think of turning you out. I'll see him in my bedroom – it's safer, and if one's conscience is clear, it doesn't matter what people say.'

In the course of the next few days the candour of her confidences to Moore, and her attitude to conventional morality, must have been shattering to a man who was basically a prude, though he obviously had the sort of approach that encouraged such revelations. On the other hand, if he made it all up, what a brilliant example it is of his ability to catch all the tones and inflections of a young girl's defiantly cheeky dialogue.

A day later, as he was shaving, there was a knock on the door. '*Entrez*,' he called.

'Oh, I beg your pardon, but I didn't want to miss you. I'll wait for you in the salon.'

When he went downstairs, she showed him a wedding ring. She had married Donald, or said she had.

'He came to my room last night. Oh, I am tired. I did have a fluffy night, and now mamma wants me to go shopping with her.'

'So your mother knows nothing of your marriage?'

'Nothing. He ought to go back but he's going to stay another night. I think I told you. Poor dear little Mamma, she never suspected a bit. Donald has the room next to mine. He was asleep in my bed this morning when the maid brought in the hot water. But she won't say anything.'

Moore takes her to a museum where she becomes fascinated by a picture of a young naked man sitting amid some grey rocks. 'He has got big muscles, just like Donald,' she says. 'I like a man to be strong; I hate little men and Donald is over six feet. Donald's chest is covered with hair and his legs and arms are rough. Lovely! Last night we stood side by side before the glass without a stitch on. I did look a little tot beside him, and it is jolly to put one's hand in a shaggy chest. I wonder why I speak to you like this; I never dared to speak to a man like this before, but you're so sympathetic. And somehow I feel that you've had a good time, yourself; you wouldn't be so sympathetic if you hadn't.'

Looking at some Rodin sculptures, he wonders if her mind is in some way inaccessible to art, and whether her interest in the sculpture 'were entirely in the model who had posed before Rodin', and at the same time the thought arose in his mind that one so interested in sex as Mildred was could not be without interest in art.

She then goes on to tell him about her courtship with Donald, in delightful detail: 'We used to meet twice a week, and in a month or so, all the lodgings in Bloomsbury were exhausted, for we never went twice to the same place. We often spent half-days together. At twelve I arrived in a hansom and stayed till five. Once the tray was on the floor; we had forgotten it; the room was dark, and I jumped out of bed and put my foot into the marmalade.'

Moore did not realise it, how could he, but he had discovered, or invented, long before Christopher Isherwood and Truman Capote, a curiously irresistible type of outspoken, outrageous girl, like Sally Bowles and Holly Golightly, who fascinates audiences and readers with a shockingly cool and calm acceptance of promiscuity as one of the prices one has to pay for progress in the world of men.

She goes on: 'Did you ever see a picture called *Vertige?* – a woman lying back on a sofa, with a man behind the sofa leaning over kissing her? Donald says I shut my eyes to be kissed, just like that.'

Moore now asks her how many men preceded Donald.

'I don't believe a man thinks any the worse of a girl for having done it, and I'm always quite honest. I admitted to Donald that there had been two ... but, of course, I've been a devil. It happened first when I was sixteen. A friend of my brother's, a hunting friend, used to ride every day to see us; and he did look nice in his hunting breeches, and coat; he used to kiss me – of course I liked that, and one day in the loft ... Oh, it was so hot, that hay! After that, we more than did it ... I've had some awful frights. And I'd rather marry anyone than have a baby without being married. Sometimes I pray, I get so frightened, and I tell God that if I get off safely this time, I'll never do it again. But somehow I always do.'

And the end of Mildred? After Donald had to leave for London, she came down the stairs of the hotel to Moore and, standing at the door, she said to him: 'I want to tell you something that happened yesterday, when I was out with Mamma. It was in

Cook's. When we went in I saw a Yank – oh, so nicely dressed! Lovely patent leather boots, and, I thought, Oh, dear, lovely man, he'll never look at me. But presently he did, and he made me a sign, just a little one, with his tongue, you know. Then he took out his card-case, and folded up a card, and put it on the ledge behind him, and gave me a look and moved away. So I walked over and took it up. Mamma never saw, but the clerks did, and I'm afraid I got very red. He has a flat in the Avenue de l'Opéra; he must be rich. When I got home I wrote to him. I said that, as he was an American, I would forgive his extraordinary behaviour, that had so much surprised me. I was leaving Paris tomorrow for Rome, and if by any chance his lines should ever fall in that direction, c/o Thomas Cook would always find me – but of course, he'll never come.'

In between the flights of fantasy, *Memoirs of My Dead Life* contains some delicious glimpses of the landscape and the cityscape: here he is describing Dieppe:

> A curious, pathetic town is Dieppe, full of nuns and pigeons, old gables and strange dormer windows; courtyards, staircases testified that French nobility had once met where fish was now being sold ... there is no such journey in the world as the journey from Dieppe to Paris on a fine, May morning [though Moore does not say so, it is the fact that Paris is the destination, not the journey itself, that gives the journey its distinction for him].
>
> No one forgets his first glimpse of Rouen cathedral in the diamond air, the branching of the river with tall ships anchored in the deep current ... The shutters were not open when the train went by, those heavy French shutters that we all know so well, and that give French houses such a look of comfort, of ease, of long tradition.

And describing the walk from the Boulevard Clichy up to the summit of the Butte-Montmartre:

> In the Rue Blanche there are *portes-cochères*, but in the Rue Lepic the narrow doors, partially grated, open on narrow passages, at the end of which, squeezed between the wall and the stairs, are small rooms where *concierges* sit *en camisole*, amid vegetables and sewing.

The wooden blinds flung back on the faded yellow walls reveal a strip of white bed-curtain and a heavy middle-aged woman looking into a tin pail in which a rabbit lies steeping; her man, a cobbler, sits hammering in the window, and the smell of leather follows the passenger for several steps. A few doors up the street a girl sits trimming a bonnet. The girl is pale with the exhausting heat. At the corner of the next street there is a *marchand des vins*. Opposite a dirty little *charbonnier* stands in front of a little hole he calls his *boutique*. A group of women in discoloured *peignoirs* and heavy carpet slippers go by with baskets on their arms . . .

As the street ascends, it grows whiter, and at the Butte it is empty of everything except the white rays of noon. Some bygone architecture attracts my attention, a dilapidated façade and broken pillars; and, standing in the midst of ruined gardens, circled by high walls crumbling and white, and looking through a broken gateway, I see a fountain splashing, but nowhere inhabitants that correspond to these houses – only a workman, a grisette and a child crying in the dust. But grand folk must at some time have lived here, and I fall to wondering if the hill-top had once been country . . . in Montmartre I find a literature that is mine without being wholly mine, a literature that is like an exquisite mistress, in whom I find consolation for all the commonplaces of life! The comparison is true, for although I know these French folk better than all else in the world, they must ever remain my holiday rather than my daily life . . . I cannot look upon this city without emotion; it has been my life, for did I not come hither in my youth like a lover, relinquishing myself to Paris, never extending once my adventure beyond Bas Meudon, Ville d'Avray, Fontainebleau, thereby acquiring a fatherland more true, because deliberately chosen, than the one birth impertinently imposed?

This is George Moore both at his worst and at his best; at his worst when he is trying to demonstrate to the world what a wicked, wicked life he used to lead, and at his best when setting the scene or reproducing the light, inconsequential, irresistible chatter of young girls – with whom he seemed to have such a fundamental empathy – with a deadly, often hilarious, sometimes heart-breaking accuracy.

His next three books, the three parts of the trilogy *Hail and Farewell*, are almost aggressively masculine; hardly a woman is mentioned from start to finish. He must have realised, as soon as he started to write the first volume, *Ave*, that he would have to leave Ireland before they came out, because he had relentlessly plundered all his relationships with all his Irish friends, relations and neighbours for the raw material for this extraordinary chronicle.

# EIGHTEEN

# Quarrels and Arguments

Moore's stray thoughts over the years on the subject of the disastrously restricting effect of the Catholic Church and its bishops and priests upon art and literature seem to have crystallised into what he announced as a great discovery, during the course of a conversation with Edward Martyn around 1906 or 1907.

> 'What, another! I thought you had come to the end of them. Your first was the naturalistic novel, your second impressionistic painting . . .'
> 'My third was your plays, Edward, and the Irish Renaissance which is but a bubble.'
> 'Oh, it's only a bubble, is it?' he asked, his jolly great purple face shaking like a jelly.
> 'You may laugh,' I said, 'but it is no laughing matter for the Catholic Church if it can be shown that no Catholic has written a book since the Reformation.'

He had already referred to this Great Discovery of his in a letter in 1906 to Clara Lanza, who had become a Catholic and had written to him to say that she did not much like *The Lake*. In his reply, he said: 'I am sorry to say that I shall not be able to feel much interest in your new book. The intellect of the world, you see, has drifted away from Catholicism; intellectually it is a desert. Since the Reformation Catholics have not produced a book . . . That is hardly an exaggeration. Spain produced some literature that was written by Catholics – all the Italian writers since Dante (nearly all) were agnostics. Protestant Germany has produced a great literature, Catholic Germany nothing. North America Protestant, South America Catholic. How can you feel an interest in a religion that degrades the human mind? The only Catholics who produce books are all converts, for they retain something of their original liberty. Clara, Clara, Clara, for shame!'

This idea now became an obsession with Moore, and it is the main central theme of the trilogy he set out to create from his own life and ideas and from the lives and ideas of his friends. He made the point about *Hail and Farewell* that it took the form of a novel without women. 'I have been so long occupied with the eternal feminine that I dwell with pleasure (in literature) upon the eternal masculine.' He said that he would place events where they 'composed best' but nowhere did he invent out of nothing.

But, first, he has to explore the theme, and find a devil's advocate to state the case for the Church, and he decides to cast his brother Maurice in that role.

'Justice demanded that a good Catholic should be heard,' he writes in *Vale*, 'and the Colonel would be able to put up as good a defence as another; and a letter to him began in my head, half a dozen lines, reminding him that he had been away a long time in the country, and asking him to come up to Dublin and spend a few days with me.'

When Maurice arrives, Moore finds that he presents 'an incongruous spectacle of sport', standing there on the Aubusson carpet in his riding boots, against a background of Impressionist pictures, and, typically, he insists on plunging straight into the subject before his brother has had time to draw breath. Maurice is naturally angry at being dragged away from the important – in his eyes – work he has been doing on the estate, and all the way from Mayo, merely to argue the merits of Catholicism versus Protestantism.

But, like his brother George, Maurice cannot resist an argument and this one seems to have gone on for hours, if not for days, ranging over such topics as whether dogma and literature are compatible; whether there was anything in Shakespeare contrary to Catholic dogma; whether England was completely and entirely a Protestant country in Shakespeare's time; whether Shakespeare was expressing his own views when he wrote that life is a tale told by an idiot, full of sound and fury, and signifying nothing; whether a Catholic could have written the *Rubaiyat of Omar Khayyam*; whether Milton, who was a Unitarian, or Bunyan, who was a Puritan, could properly be described as Protestants; whether anyone can be *born* a Catholic; whether Cardinal Newman, a convert, brought some of his original freedom of thought as a Protestant into his Catholicism; whether the Creator and the Catholic Church are at cross-purposes on the matter of Newman's contention that it would be 'better for the sun and moon to drop from heaven, for the earth to fall, and for all the many millions on it to die of starvation in extremest agony, as far as temporal affliction goes, than that one soul . . . should commit one single venial sin, should tell one wilful untruth, or should steal one farthing without excuse', George Moore's argument on this final point that, if the Creator held the same view as Newman attributes to the Catholic Church, he would have destroyed the world long since.

On his return to Mayo, Colonel Maurice sent his brother George some notes on the Gothic cathedrals of Europe to forestall any claim in his book that the Church had made no contribution to architecture. Moore thanked him in a very friendly note.

But they return to the argument again and again, during subsequent visits which the Colonel pays to his brother, and inevitably it becomes personal. George Moore does not at all like the idea that his heirs, the Colonel's two sons, are being educated – partly, at least, at his expense – in Catholic schools.

'And do you claim the right to seek my children out and destroy their faith?'

'Can you define the difference between faith and superstition? The right I claim is that of every human being to speak what he believes to be the truth to whomever he may meet on his way. Brotherhood doesn't forfeit me that right . . .'

And later: 'But if you think like this, you'd have done better not to have married a Protestant. I suppose your children believe their mother will go to hell; and if you love Ireland as well as you profess to, why did you go into the English army? . . . Why shouldn't their mother have as much voice as you have in their education? Why shouldn't I have a voice?'

'In the education of my children?'

It was a typical Irish row. And Moore comments: 'We haven't an idea in common. We are as much separated as though we came from the ends of the earth; yet we were brought up together in the same house, we learnt the same lessons.'

When he was not arguing with his brother about religion, George Moore was working on a complete revision of *Evelyn Innes* for a French translation to be published by Hachette, or visiting the Cunards at Nevill Holt where, in 1907, as he wrote to an Irish friend, Mrs Murray Robertson, he read the lessons in the local church on Sunday, 'charmed by the beautiful Protestant service', and went for long walks in the fields with Lady Cunard's daughter Nancy, now aged ten or eleven.

Nancy Cunard, who remembered him from when she was aged about four or five, wrote (in GM: *Memories of George Moore*) that the first thing that impressed her about George Moore was his appearance, and the fact that he spoke differently from everybody else: '. . .the sound of that rich voice, filled now and again with the rolling billows of brogue, the use he made of his hands when talking, especially when breaking into French, were extraordinary . . . A great joy it was to see his round, plump, white hands – his very arms, indeed – fly up to heaven in surprise, alarm or expostulation.'

She recalled that he had great charm, something that people who found him unsympathetic, egotistical and self-willed in his opinions could not understand. And she noticed, even at that early age, that he was much more 'difficult' in general with men than with women, and concludes that the right word for him at this period of his life would have been 'winning'.

'He would be funny without knowing it, pretty soon would see how funny he must appear, and then came some mumming on top of that. The *Tea and Salt* [routine] for instance. Could that wonderful voice but be revived, all plumped out with its rich bits of brogue, I think no one present could keep a straight face when GM, once more, would set down his delicate cup of Earl Grey Mixture and suddenly clamour for *kitchen* tea, or be glaring down the lunch-table with cold annoyance and a ceremonious bow: "I thank you, no. I do not wish for any of that salt. Oh, of course, if you insist, go ahead. *But you will be eating the bones of your ancestors.*"

'Salt should come from the salines, not from Cerebos, he said. The *gros sel de France.* Ah! Or that given sheep to lick, rock salt, never mind its red marble appearance – pure both of them, not refined with detestable chemicals and powdered bones for whiteness.'

At the end of that particular recollection of George Moore from around 1907, Nancy Cunard attempts to reproduce his accent, in a reference to a wasp: 'Wel-le, if you will leave him a-lone, hee will go a-way.'

And here she is, in her middle-fifties, remembering a walk in the grounds of Nevill Holt with George Moore, in 1907, when she was about ten, and he was fifty-five: 'Stop and listen to the rooks he would. There was a lot of interest in those rooks (or were they choughs, he asked, remarking that chough is a wonderful word, but of course it means jackdaw). All of a sudden the rooks would come across the lawn homing from their pickings on the ploughlands – caw, caw, caw, – making a very great fuss. As for the starlings and their whirling, wheeling multitudes, what makes them fly like this, why do they congregate and follow each other in such hosts? His questions rang with mine and were as numerous, there being so much of why? in nature, he said, before you get as far as wondering about people. As for the skylarks, ah, that is another mystery. The time will come, Nancy, when Shelley's poems will be a great joy to you.'

In September 1907, he met a Miss Viola Rodgers who had come to Dublin to write some articles about Ireland for the American magazine *Cosmopolitan*, and who commissioned an article from him on art. He decided instead to send the magazine a short story about an imaginary painter and two art collectors which was published towards the end of the year, by which time, captivated by her vivacity and beauty (he always fancied young American women enormously, throughout his long life), he had entered into a regular correspondence with her that lasted almost until his death. 'Indeed,' Hone says, 'he came to have for her a feeling much warmer than friendship, especially in the years just after the war, when he generally saw her on each of his visits to Paris.' He was pleased to think that they were fellow-contributors to *Cosmopolitan* and referred to it as being '*sous la même couverture*'.

One is tempted to wonder whether it was this invitation to join her between the sheets, so to speak, of *Cosmopolitan* magazine, which led Moore to embroider their first meeting into the extraordinary fantasy called 'Euphorion in Texas', in his *Memoirs of My Dead Life*.

He is in his writing room in Ely Place musing about all the invitations from women to which, for one reason or another, he had failed to respond, when he remembers a moment when Agnes, his parlourmaid, came into the room with a letter which had been sent around from the Shelbourne Hotel. It was from a woman he calls Honor, who had come from Texas in the hope of making his acquaintance.

But ever cautious, before agreeing to meet her, he decides to find out what she looks like. So he writes her a note, inviting her to visit him next day and then summons the maid, Agnes, and says to her: 'I want you to go to the Shelbourne [and meet this lady] and if she should strike you as an intelligent and sprightly woman, who is not likely to bore me, give her this letter . . . A good description of her is what I should like; you will be a better judge than I. She will not be able to take you in!'

'And if she's an old woman, sir?'

'Then tell her I am leaving town and am very sorry . . .'

Agnes returns to tell him about the lady's full shoulders, with a plait of yellow hair falling over them. 'She had her dress off, sir, and I don't think she can be more than five and twenty.'

He describes her arrival at Ely Place, and his own pathetic efforts at small talk which the girl he calls Honor interrupts by saying: 'Your books have meant more to me than any other writer.'

She tells him that she had decided to become a nun when she was eighteen but, after she had taken the veil, she discovered that she had no vocation. He learns that she is not married, because she has been unable to find in Texas any man worthy to be the father of her child. She passionately desires an exceptional child, a man of talent, a painter, a poet, a musician.

'I have never thought of anybody definitely, only that I would like to give Texas a literature; and when I read your books – '

He goes on: 'She had paid me the compliment of thinking of me as a possible father for her son, as a man who was likely to beget a son who would give literature to Texas.'

Looking back on the episode, it did not seem to him that he had met her more than seven or eight times during the six weeks which she spent in Dublin, and during which, Moore indicates, her mission was successfully accomplished:

> 'The seed must never know whence it came,' she told him, as they said goodbye. 'We must both sacrifice something for our child. I am sacrificing the common respect of society in Texas, and you must forgo all knowledge of your boy. Your name has been too intimately connected with art and literature. Swear.'
>
> 'I swear,' he replies and goes on: 'We spent our last evening crooning names over the fire in Ely Place, for it was necessary to discover a name that would go with Honor's surname. At last one flamed up in my mind – a name more likely to inspire painting than poetry.'

'But how do you know your child will be a boy?'

Always sure of herself, she smiled and went away, and this letter announcing his birth is all I have. Were it not for this letter the visit might have been a dream of yester-night.

And now I'll doze an hour in this comfortable armchair, and dream that I am on my way to Texas to seek out Honor and her boy.

Moore was busy throughout 1908 working on what he later described in a letter to Dujardin as 'my Messianic book *Hail and Farewell*', as well as on the new version of *Sister Teresa*. He used the same word, messianic, usually with a lower-case 'm', in letters to many of his lady pen-friends including Emily Lorenz and Virginia Crawford.

One explanation as to why he regarded *Hail and Farewell* as a 'Messianic' work is provided by Richard Cave in his introduction to the one-volume paperback edition of *Hail and Farewell*: 'The Renaissance, the rebuilding of Tir-na-nOg, becomes, for the ardent neophyte, an intellectual crusade. Eagerly Moore reviews the deeds and lives of the leaders. Who is the chosen one, the Messiah? Though many are called, no one has yet fulfilled all the conditions of the task, not even Horace Plunkett, despite his dealings with the Judas-like figure of T. P. Gill. In a final audacious conceit, Moore is suddenly enlightened: he is himself the One, the Hero. To triumphant strains of Wagner's music, Moore sees himself as a reincarnation of all his heroes from the past: he is Parnell, Siegfried, St Paul, Christ. *Hail and Farewell* is the Holy Book of the New Ireland, the Gospel of Moore's life and thought.'

The extent of the revisions Moore had made in *Sister Teresa* became clear when Fisher Unwin published it in 1909, along with the third version of *Evelyn Innes*. These were the last of Moore's books to be published by Fisher Unwin; Moore had moved to Heinemann with *The Lake*. His relations with his publishers had always been very stormy – Fisher Unwin, understandably, objected to the enormous amount of rewriting Moore did on almost all of his books, right up to the final proof stage, and tried to charge him for the extra cost of all the resultant resetting; they also disliked the fact that he wrote to them almost daily, complaining about something or other. Moore, equally understandably, mistrusted their accounting system, was forever accusing them of trying to do him out of money which they owed him, and at one stage even insisted on sending in his own accountant to audit their books to ensure that he had not been cheated.

Throughout almost the entire year of 1905, he conducted a bitter argument with them about whether their publication of a version of the play *Journey's End in Lovers' Meeting*, on which he had collaborated with Pearl Craigie, was a libel on him. When the play had been performed, back in 1895, his name had appeared as co-author both on the programme and the posters, as well as in the reviews, but when the play was published in book form by Fisher Unwin Mrs Craigie withdrew his name, and, despite all sorts of threats and demands from Moore, the publishers resolutely refused to allow him to write a preface to the play explaining his part in its composition. Whether, as Mrs Craigie claimed, she withdrew his name on the condition that he would be allowed to appear as the sole author of a second play they had written together in collaboration, *The Peacock's Feathers*, subsequently known as *Elizabeth Cooper*, and finally as *The Coming of Gabrielle*, or whether she did it against his wishes, will never be known, because Mrs Craigie died before the matter had been finally resolved. The publishers appear to have taken her side in the matter, and Moore finally wrote to them to say that, unless they agreed to 'issue *Journey's End in Lovers' Meeting* with my name on it and with a few lines of preface stating the facts – the undisputed facts', it would be impossible for him to consider publishing any further books with them.

When Fisher Unwin refused to give way, Moore then tried to buy back the rights to *Evelyn Innes*, *Sister Teresa* and *The Untilled Field*, so that his new publishers, Heinemann, could bring out a collected edition of his works; by this time the publishers were so irritated with him that they refused to relinquish the rights, and went ahead with a simultaneous publication of the new versions of *Evelyn Innes* and *Sister Teresa* in 1909.

The changes Moore had made were very considerable, particularly in *Sister Teresa*. The first version of *Sister Teresa* had been a quiet, contemplative book, similar in general mood and tone to *The Lake*. In the new version, Moore included a series of colourful descriptions of Edwardian society and introduced such novelties as Sir Owen Asher's hawking expedition in North Africa; on this point Hone remarks that Moore had himself gone hawking with Lord Howard de Walden, and presumably was reluctant to waste the material with which the experience had furnished him. Owen's anti-Catholic feelings have become much stronger and more strident: 'They have got her, they have got her!' he shouts, at one point, referring to the fact that Evelyn has returned to the convent. 'But they shan't get her as long as I have a shoulder to force open a door . . . They will get her, I tell you! Those blasted ghouls, haunters of graveyards . . .'

He has also given the book a new ending. In the 1909 version, Evelyn decides that she has no vocation, leaves the convent and becomes a social worker. Owen sees her from time to time, and they eventually develop a sort of platonic relationship – 'peace between old lovers, an idea dear to Moore,' Hone remarks.

In 1909, Moore is again in Paris, reading extracts from the second play on which he had collaborated with Pearl Craigie to friends like Blanche and Dujardin. She had died in 1906, and he was now free to do what he wanted with it. There was some talk of a French translation; and his pen-friend in Germany, the Boston-born Marquise Emily Lorenz, was already working on a German translation. He had also been in correspondence with Yvette Guilbert, who wanted to play Esther Waters in a projected dramatisation of the novel which never materialised at that time, though *Esther Waters* was later produced both on the stage and on the screen.

There had been another notable death in 1906; Stella (Clara

Christian), Moore's painter friend who had come to Ireland with
him in 1901, had died that year at Tymon Lodge in the hills above
Rathfarnham. Moore gives two or three different fictional-factional accounts of their break-up in *Hail and Farewell*, on which he
was working for about eight hours a day, throughout most of 1909.

The first version in *Vale*, goes like this:

> 'I shall never forget that rainbow, Stella, and am glad that we saw
> it together.'
> In every love story lovers reprove each other for lack of affection,
> and Stella had often sent me angry letters which caused me many
> heart-burnings, and brought me out to her; in the garden there
> were reconciliations, we picked up the thread again, and the
> summer had passed before the reasons for these quarrels became
> clear to me. One September evening Stella said she would
> accompany me to the gate, and we had not gone very far before I
> noticed that she was quarrelling with me. She spoke of the
> loneliness of the Moat House, and I had answered that she had not
> been alone two evenings that week. She admitted my devotion.
> 'And if you admit that there has been no neglect – '
> She would not tell me, but there was something she was not
> satisfied with, and before we reached the end of the avenue she
> said, 'I don't think I can tell you.' But on being pressed she said:
> 'You don't make love to me often enough.'

A bit further down the page, he makes his excuses:

> She had told me that she had refrained from a lover because she
> wished to keep all of herself for her painting, and now she had
> taken to herself a lover. She was twenty years younger than I was,
> and at forty-six or thereabouts one begins to feel that one's time for
> love is over; one is a consultant rather than a practitioner.

And he asks himself whether, if he had been twenty years younger,
he would have acted any differently and replies:

> It seemed to me that the difficulty that had arisen would have been
> the same earlier in my life as it was now, and returning to the
> window I watched the hawthorns blowing under the cold grey
> Dublin sky.

A couple of pages later, he says that, when she returned from a

painting trip to Italy, he brought many friends to see her, thinking
they would interest her.

> 'If you don't care to come to see me without a chaperon, I would
> rather you didn't come at all,' she said, humiliating me very deeply.
> 'It seemed to me,' I answered, blushing, 'that you would like to
> see – ,' and I mentioned the name of the man who had accompa-
> nied me.
> 'If I am cross sometimes it is because I don't see enough of you.'

The passage ends with them standing at the gate of the Moat
House, having walked together down that long avenue of trees,
and with her saying: 'I am no more to you than any other woman.'
This is immediately followed by yet a third account of the same,
or another, similar conversation:

> She went away again to Italy to paint and returned to Ireland,
> and one day she came to see me, and remained talking for an hour. I
> have no memory of what we said to each other, but a very clear
> memory of our walk through Dublin over Carlisle Bridge and along
> the quays. I had accompanied her as far as the Phoenix Park gates,
> and at the corner of Conyngham Road, just as I was bidding her
> goodbye, she said:
> 'I want to ask your advice on a matter of importance to me.'
> 'And to me, for what is important to you is equally important to
> me.'
> 'I am thinking,' she said, 'of being married.'
> At the news it seems to me that I was unduly elated and tried to
> assume the interest that a friend should.

So what really happened between Moore and Clara Christian
back in September 1904, shortly after she returned from a stay of
several months in Rapallo? In his extremely thorough footnotes to
the one-volume paperback edition of *Hail and Farewell*, Richard
Cave writes: '. . . in view of subsequent events, it is possible that in
reality Clara and not Moore took the initiative in causing the
separation either by revealing her wish to marry and have a child
or by telling Moore of her growing affection for another man. Had
Clara asked Moore to marry her, he would certainly have refused.
With his reputation as a naughty, flamboyant bachelor-lover,
Moore was by now too much a part of Dublin mythology to be

taken seriously in the role of a married man. He and Clara would have been a laughing-stock. Moore was not irresponsible but he valued the freedom to change his life-style on impulse; marriage and a family would have curtailed this . . . On January 11, 1905, Miss Christian married Charles MacCarthy, the City Architect of Dublin, in the Church of Our Most Holy Redeemer, Chelsea. Clara retained her former home, Tymon Lodge, Tallaght, after her marriage; and she died there in childbirth on June 7, 1906.'

The year 1910 found Moore in Paris again, delivering a lecture on Balzac and Shakespeare to a distinguished audience in the Salle de l'Agriculture; it was published in two issues of the *Revue Bleue* and subsequently he included it in *Avowals*.

He went straight from Paris to the Munich music festival with Lady Cunard – they were chaperoned, in the style of the period, by an American friend of hers, Josephine Marshall, and all three were involved in a dramatic motor accident on the last evening before their return to Paris. There was a report of the accident in the *Continental Daily Mail*:

> Mr George Moore, the well-known English author, who is at present on his return from Munich, where he had been attending the music festivals, has told a representative of the *Daily Mail* of a remarkable accident which took place the other day in the Bavarian capital in which two ladies were killed and the novelist himself very narrowly escaped death, while Lady Cunard and another American lady, Mrs Marshall, were injured.
>
> The accident occurred through the chauffeur leaving a large touring automobile by the side of the road just as the crowd was coming out of the opera late at night. The chauffeur told his fellow-servant to look after the car while he went on an errand. The servant, to gain time, apparently attempted to move the automobile which ran with great speed into the crowd outside the opera. Mr Moore tells the story in his characteristic style: 'We had arranged to go to supper with Mr and Mrs Perry Belmont after the opera. There was a drizzle of rain in the air, and Lady Cunard was walking quickly in front. Fearing to lose her I called her to come back, and she returned to us, that is, Mrs Marshall and myself. A cry went up – a piercing, animal-like cry – and, turning to see what had

happened, I saw an immense motor surge up and on to the crowded pavement. I was struck down instantly ... Never was anyone nearer death, of that I am sure. I was under the machine for a few moments, unable to rise, and when I was pulled out and it was found that my legs were not broken and that I could stand on them, I staggered off in search of Lady Cunard, attracted by the sight of men carrying women away.

But I did not follow far; in my dazed mind the thought passed that I could not speak German and could get lost, so I came back to the motor and found Lady Cunard, who had just recovered consciousness. A few feet away, some men supported Mrs Marshall. I saw shreds of women's dresses – the blood and finery of the women I had seen borne aloft like Sabine women by Romans. One of these poor creatures died a few moments after. The doctors fear that there will be many cripples. Mrs Marshall is in hospital too. She will recover in some months. Lady Cunard was sorely shaken and bruised and had to keep to her bed for a couple of days, but is now well and bore the long journey from Munich to Paris better than I expected.

By the middle of the year, Moore had *Ave*, the first volume of his trilogy, ready to go to the printers. Heinemann were anxious to publish the book as soon as possible but Moore was determined that it should not be published until after he had left Ireland for good.

Around this time, too, he began to hear rumours that legislation would soon be introduced to force Irish landlords to surrender part of their private demesnes for sale to land-hungry Irish peasants; if this ever happened, he would quit Ireland straight away, he decided, and he wrote to his brother Maurice: 'You may live there [in Moore Hall], but no other Moore will ever live there. I divine these things. I don't know how I know them, but I do know them.'

The sale of his other properties, postponed in 1905, was now taking place; he sold the greater part of the outlying land to the Land Commission for £25,000 (£1,250,000 today), and became involved in yet another row when his inquiries into his financial affairs confirmed that he was contributing towards Maurice's elder son's education at Downside, a Catholic public school run by the Benedictines.

In December 1910, news reached him of the serious illness of his younger brother, Augustus, in London, but Moore could not face the thought of seeing his brother on his death-bed. So the Colonel went instead, but although a sum of £150 was raised for an operation, to which Moore contributed generously, Augustus died before the doctors could operate. Augustus was described in an obituary in the *Irish Times* as a member of 'an old Roman Catholic family long established in the West of Ireland'.

The next day George Moore's protest appeared in the newspaper: 'I take this opportunity of telling you that my family was Protestant until my great grand-father went to Spain. He settled in Alicante, and by successful trading amassed a fortune of three or four hundred thousand pounds. It would not have been possible for him to do this if he had remained a Protestant . . . My grand-father was a man of letters, a very cultured but unsuccessful man of letters . . . He was a disciple of Gibbon, and many passages in his published writings show him to be an agnostic. Of my father's belief, I know nothing; he went to Mass on Sundays, so I suppose he was a Catholic.'

In February 1911, Moore paid the long-deferred visit to his brother Maurice at Moore Hall. The Colonel's wife was perturbed about the Great Author's fussiness over food and drink and did her best to find some real coffee for him, but nothing was available in Castlebar or Westport but coffee essence. In the event she made it extremely thick and Moore was delighted. 'My dear Evelyn, your coffee is wonderful, you must give me the name of the brew,' he said.

Hone clearly had this from Maurice. It is very hard to believe that a man who had lived in Paris for almost ten years could have been impressed by Camp coffee essence; probably George Moore was merely being polite to people he secretly regarded as fairly undiscerning in such matters.

All the disappointment and bitterness he felt about what had happened to Moore Hall in the years that his brother Maurice had been living there spill over at the close of *Vale*. He finds in the old house nothing but disaster and decay. The gardens and deer park are overgrown, the outhouses and stables are in ruins, the woods are being cut down, and the fields sold off.

His brother's plans for restoring the house – which included a sawmill to turn some of the surplus forest into firewood – were constantly curtailed for lack of funds; Maurice, trying to run a big house on an army pension, was always strapped for cash, and his elder brother was forever writing to him to instruct him not to spend any more money on the family home. 'I don't want to speculate on sawmills, I speculate in literature,' he wrote, citing, with characteristic inside knowledge of the entire situation, the case of a man called McCann who had started a sawmill in County Meath which did not even pay the wages of the workmen and another case of a baronet in Galway 'who tried sawmills and lost a great deal of money on it'.

While he was at Moore Hall, he had another row with Maurice – who was still angry about Moore's recent letter to the *Irish Times* – over the fact that he was paying £100 a year towards Maurice's eldest son's education. He did not mind paying the money but, if news of it leaked out, it would seriously injure his reputation, he said.

While there, they visited their mother's old home Ballinafad, which had been taken over by one of the religious orders; it had been presented to them by Llewellyn Blake, Joe Blake's brother and heir.

When he finally returned to Ely Place towards the end of 1910, it was to tidy up in preparation for a final return to England. He enlisted the help of Lennox Robinson, the Cork playwright who had just come to Dublin to join the Abbey Theatre, and left a copy of *Esther Waters* for Robinson to dramatise. He also left a scenario for another play, *The Apostle*, based on his ideas about a meeting between Christ and St Paul, twenty or thirty years after the Crucifixion, with a Dublin publisher for immediate publication because he wanted to forestall Frank Harris who, he had heard, was working on a book along the same lines.

A farewell party was given for Moore in Dublin by W. E. Bailey of the Land Commission and among those present, according to Hone, were Susan Mitchell, John Healy, the editor of the *Irish Times*, and John Eglinton of the National Library – not a very glittering gathering. He left on a misty February morning in 1911.

Here is his description of his final departure from Ireland: 'On a grey, windless morning in February the train took me to Kingstown, and I had always looked forward to leaving Ireland in May, seeking the words of a last farewell or murmuring the words of Catullus, when he journeyed over land and sea to burn the body of his brother, fitting them to my circumstance by the change of a single word: ATQUE IN PERPETUUM, MATER, AVE ATQUE VALE.

'But our dreams and circumstances are often in conflict, and never were they in greater opposition than the day that took me from Westland Row past a long, barren tract of sand: a grey sky hanging low over the sea far away in the offing without a ripple upon it. If the evening had been a golden evening, my heart might have overflowed with fine sentiments; for it is on golden evenings that fine sentiments overflow the heart! The heart is then like crystal that the least touch will break; but on a cold, bleak, February morning the prophet is as uninspired as his humblest fellow, and a very humble fellow, forgetful of Ireland, forgetful of Catholicism, forgetful of literature, went below to think of the friends he had left behind – AE and the rest.'

# NINETEEN

# More Quarrels and Arguments

When he returned to London in February 1911, Moore stayed for a time at the Burlington Hotel, before moving into 121, Ebury Street, in the district where Chelsea and Belgravia overlap. He never liked the place. Shortly after he settled in, he was writing to his French friend Dujardin to tell him that the first volume of *Hail and Farewell* would appear in September, adding, 'I am in London and am renting this house, or rather this little hole in which to carry out my authorship.' He described Ebury Street to Nancy Cunard as being completely 'lacklustre'. Later, he was to come to dislike it even more. 'Ebury Street is not worthy of my death,' he announced, when he first succumbed to the disorder from which he was eventually to die. In fact, 121, Ebury Street was about the same size and similar in many ways to his house in Ely Place, Dublin, though he no longer had an orchard in which to walk, and he missed it sadly. He refused to have a telephone but could be contacted, in any emergency, via the apothecary opposite.

He used the dining room, which ran from the front to the back of the house, as a writing room, though his writing now took the form of recasting and remoulding and revising typed pages of copy which he had dictated the previous day. He had a bow window put in to give him more light, and there was a small study at the back of the house where he spent the mornings dictating.

Three landscapes by his painter friend, Mark Fisher, hung on

the walls of his dining room along with two portraits, one by
Couture and one by David, and the Aubusson carpet, its bright
colours which had so upset AE a decade earlier now considerably
muted and dimmed by general wear and tear, covered the floor.
Other pictures in his collection included portraits of himself by
(Miss) S. C. Harrison and William (later Sir William) Orpen; a
Constable; two Manets, a Monet, two Berthe Morisots, drawings
by Ingres and Degas, and a water-colour by Ford Madox Brown.

During the year, he worked on the text of his scenario for *The
Apostle* which was published by Maunsel & Co in Dublin in May
1911, and he completed the dramatisation of *Esther Waters* on
which he had been working in Dublin with Lennox Robinson,
who was later to remark, in a letter to Hone: 'Moore used to come
around to my rooms every afternoon to see how I was getting on;
he was very agreeable and complimentary, and became more and
more interested. Then one day he took the manuscript from me,
and I did not give the matter a thought until years later, when I
read the book of the play and found something very familiar in the
dialogue of the second act.'

To Moore's considerable gratification, George Bernard Shaw
recommended the adaptation of the novel to the Stage Society
and it was produced at the Apollo Theatre in December 1911,
with Miss Lucy Williams as Esther Waters. It was only moderately
well received, probably because, apart from the second act, which
had been partly rewritten by Robinson, Moore left most of the
dialogue exactly as it had been in the novel, perhaps not realising,
in his fifty-ninth year, that theatre audiences of 1911 were not as
patient as readers had been in the early 1890s when the novel was
published.

The publication of his scenario, *The Apostle*, had, as Moore put
it in a letter to Dujardin, 'fallen a little flat', and he did not develop
it any further until 1930 when, revised and retitled *The Passing of
the Essenes*, it was produced at the Arts Theatre.

But it is more than likely that the novel *The Brook Kerith* also
grew out of this scenario. He wrote to Emily Lorenz Mayer: 'I am

now going to write *The Apostle*, and I shall devote a long time to it, several months. A great many new ideas have come to me and my Jesus at fifty-five will be quite different from Renan's young man, polite and charming.' He is referring here to Ernest Renan's *La Vie de Jésus* (1863), which he had read in Dublin.

Long before he left Ireland, Moore had entered into yet another of those extraordinary, intimate, sexy exchanges of letters with an American lady. In 1906, while he was still living in Ely Place, a lady from Boston called Hildegarde Hawthorne had written to him to say that she greatly admired his work, and in his second letter to her he wrote that he would like to come into her room, and talk to her: 'A windy night always sets my fancy flying: I hear things, I feel things and anything might happen. Perhaps I shall hear a step on the pavement, a hand on the door and you will walk in.'

Hildegarde Hawthorne was thirty-six when she first began to correspond with Moore, then in his middle-fifties, though she led him to believe that she was at least ten years younger, and he gave her the impression that he was still in his forties. She was a grand-daughter of Nathaniel Hawthorne, and at the time she began to correspond with Moore had written a guide to the Chicago World Fair of 1893, *The Fairest of the Fair*, and a novelette, *A Country Interlude* (1904).

She wrote to him in Dublin towards the end of 1906, and his reply, from the Hotel Continental in Paris, dated January 29, 1907, was fairly non-committal, though it did contain the phrase that the pleasure he had experienced on receiving her letter was a subtler one than 'flattered literary vanity' and he referred to 'the sudden touch of a friendly hand in the loneliness of life'. And he did send her a copy of his latest book, *The Lake*.

However, by March 1907, he was well into his stride. After going into some detail about one of his many fantasy love adventures, he concluded: '. . . And now I have written you a long and intimate letter and I hope it will call for as long and intimate a letter from you. Tell me about yourself, that is what I am interested in. You want a confidant, let me be yours. Confide in me, though the Atlantic divides us. Indulge your whim, sure that I shall understand everything . . .'

She seems to have been very quick to realise what it was that he was after, for his next letter thanks her for her description of herself swimming naked like, as he puts it, 'a fine nead [naiad]', and goes on: '. . . but why do you say you are tired of being a virgin, you see no way out of the difficulty, not being disposed to run the risk of having a child in your present circumstances. Surely you know that love is possible without incurring any risk whatever; if love were so restricted, how would I have managed all these years? . . . A girl can even indulge herself and her lover a great deal without ceasing to be a virgin.'

And in another epistle: 'I read with interest how the lovely Hungarian came down to your tent every night, how you kissed him for his courtesy, allowing him finally to lie with you in your fragrant bed of balsam, and how in your holy intercourse of kisses he discovered you to be a virgin. It seems a pity that your intercourse should have been broken off at this point. I cannot understand how it is that natural instincts did not tell either of you that kisses need not be confined to the mouth and that kisses placed within the nest of love are more intimate and exciting than the act of love . . . It would be a sad thing indeed if love were limited to the mere act which grocers and their mates perform at midnight in the middle of a four poster.'

In yet another letter he told her: 'You will find me a middle-aged man, with a career behind me sufficiently brilliant to be able to talk about many things interestingly; and I am not an unkindly soul, I believe.'

And again: 'The photographs interested me and pleased me . . . for they revealed your long and beautiful legs . . . The black shadows completely conceal the breasts and that is a pity; get your friend to take some more snapshots in the house where the shadows are not so black, for it gives me a great deal of pleasure to see you.'

By March 1912, he was writing to Emily Lorenz to say that the second volume of his trilogy, *Salve*, was ready to be revised before going off to the printers and would be published in August or at the beginning of September; and to Werner Laurie about a preface he was composing for a new edition of *Spring Days*, which was due to be published in May 1912.

For a large part of the year, he was involved in a tedious correspondence with his brother Maurice, both about the affairs of the Moore Hall estate, and the attempts then being made by the Congested Districts Board to force landlords to relinquish more and more of their lands for distribution to landless peasants, as well as on the subject of a book that Maurice Moore was writing about their father, George Henry Moore the Politician. He was also deeply involved in long and bitter arguments with his various publishers about paper, typography and binding. In a letter to Werner Laurie, dated April 1912, he wrote: 'What I object to is ugly books and cheap books . . . When Fisher Unwin showed me a specimen copy of his cheap edition of *Evelyn Innes* I begged him not to publish it; I went to see him half a dozen times on the subject . . . I may be right or wrong, but I am resolved to do all in my power to resist cheap and ugly books; on every other point you will find me quite amenable.'

In another letter to Werner Laurie, dated November 26, 1912, he wrote: 'I am still waiting for the page proofs of *Impressions and Opinions* . . . I hope the printing will be straight on the page this time, and not crooked as in *Spring Days*. It may be of some interest to you to hear that when Mr Gosse [later Sir Edmund Gosse] pointed out to Mr Heinemann that the new edition of [his] *Father and Son* had been very badly printed, Heinemann at once said, "The whole edition must be destroyed." Nothing does a publisher so much harm as ill-printed books. There may be a law suit on this point, however!'

By now Moore had Margaret Gough working with him as a secretary on a regular basis; she took dictation from ten o'clock until lunch-time, and then went home and typed out the morning's work to have it ready for him to revise the next day. When in 1912 she left him to get married, she was succeeded by Ethel Palmer.

By now, too, Maurice Moore had decided that he had had enough of Moore Hall and of his brother's constant complaints about the cost of repairs and maintenance, and left Ireland to live in Brussels. Before he went away, he closed up Moore Hall, and it was never to be reopened. On his way to Brussels, the Colonel called on his brother in Ebury Street; they were both fascinated by all the material Maurice had managed to discover while research-ing the life of their father, and they parted on better terms than they had been on for several years. In the early autumn of 1912, George Moore spent a fortnight in Brussels with his brother, discussing the book.

Moore also came to an agreement with the Congested Districts Board under which, having repaid all outstanding mortgages, he realised about £30,000 (about £1,500,000 today) on the sale of the bulk of his land to his tenants, leaving him with only his 'dreaming house' and some five hundred acres of demesne land surrounding it.

Towards the end of the year, while visiting Ebury Street, Maurice picked up a copy of *Salve*, which had not yet been published, but was lying on Moore's writing table, and chanced upon a passage about himself. Understandably enough, he took the gravest exception to his brother's description of him as having 'a faded, empty look', 'vague, inconclusive eyes' and 'an untidy mind' and to learn that he slouched along, 'hands dangling out of his cuffs'.

Subsequently, Maurice wrote to his brother, asking why he had not shown him the offending paragraphs before publication and concluding: 'You have tried to represent me as mentally contemp-tible and physically ridiculous so as to contrast with your own extreme cleverness. It will not make matters any better to write any more, so I will drop the subject . . .'

Moore replied: '. . . You ask me why I did not show you those parts of the book. Because if I had, heaven only knows what you might not have asked me to change – in half an hour my book would have been a wreck, and if I had shown it to Magee he would have wished many things altered, and AE would have revised the book from his point of view . . . I have caricatured, yes – but I did not think anybody minded that. Max [Beerbohm] and others have caricatured me out of all human resemblance, but I never objected . . .'

To Maurice Moore's charge that his brother had always given him the worst lines in their reported arguments about religion, Moore replied: 'Of course you get the worst of the argument, but that is inevitable – whatever may be the ultimate truth, the believer has the worst of the argument all the time.'

Towards the end of 1912, George Moore was working on a new Werner Laurie edition of *Impressions and Opinions*, a collection of magazine articles and other short pieces originally published by David Nutt in 1891.

Early in 1913, he agreed to write a preface to his brother's book about their father, but soon they were quarrelling again; when Moore was going through the illustrations that Maurice proposed to use in the book, in the offices of Werner Laurie, he came across the photograph Maurice had selected for the frontispiece. Immediately he wrote: 'Among them I found a terrifying portrait of you – you in all your youth and beauty, the darling of the garrison hacks. So now we know the light in which you wish people to see you! Lord have mercy upon us sinners! It will make you and the book look rather silly.'

Early in 1913 he had written to Hildegarde Hawthorne sending her a copy of *Impressions*, and he heard from her by return; she was coming to Europe that year but not to London. He wrote again, thanking her for a review of *Salve* she had written for the *New York*

*Times Book Review* and assuring her that, if she could not get to London, he would go to Paris and meet her. They did meet and apparently were mutually disappointed in the reality because thereafter their correspondence waned both in warmth and frequency, though they remained in touch with each other until well after the war.

In a letter he wrote to her in the late summer of 1913, he said: '. . . Our meeting in Paris is not a matter that I can allude to in a letter and you will forgive me if I don't speak of it. Goodbye. It does not seem to me that I ever said goodbye before . . .'

*Elizabeth Cooper*, the revised version of the play he had been working on with Pearl Craigie when they quarrelled, was produced by Clifford Brooke at the Haymarket Theatre in London in June 1913, under Moore's name only; and Moore was working on his preface for his brother's biography of their father, now called *An Irish Gentleman*, which led to a further estrangement. The first hint of it came in a letter from Moore to his brother Maurice containing the phrase 'I have struck out the sentence that I am glad that our father died without the help of [the] sacraments', but it is clear that he had also tried to suggest in the preface that their father had died, like an ancient Roman, by his own hand, a harmless, attractive conceit so far as Moore was concerned, but anathema to Maurice.

Moore resolutely refused to omit altogether the reference to his father having committed suicide, though he agreed to change it to that *he would like to think* that the circumstances of his father's death pointed to this conclusion. Maurice sought the advice of relatives and friends in Galway who were absolutely adamant that all reference to any question of suicide should be removed. By now, it was too late to do this, but Maurice had a slip inserted in the book at the frontispiece which made it clear that the words in the preface about the suicide theory represented the prefacer's wishes, and not the facts.

When Moore came across the slip in the first copy of the book he opened, he accused his brother of trying to start a family row for the sake of the publicity it would generate for the book. He did not believe this – indeed he knew, better than anybody else, that it was totally against Maurice's nature to try to stir up a family row, for the sake of publicity, but where Moore was concerned no holds were barred when it came to generating a family row. And, after an exchange of letters that grew more and more bitter, the breach between the brothers was almost complete. They rarely spoke again, and, towards the end of their lives, would pass each other in the street and on the stairs of public buildings without any hint of recognition.

Moore was now working on *Vale*, the final volume in his trilogy. One section of *Vale*, written as far back as 1909, was omitted at the request of the Irish poet Seamus O'Sullivan (James Starkey), who said he had enjoyed what Moore had written about him, but was afraid it might upset his family. In this one case, Moore acceded to Starkey's request, but in general he seems to have been incapable of understanding why people should mind being caricatured if it was for the sake of art (his art). 'A man can have only one sort of conscience,' he frequently used to say, 'and mine is a literary one.' Carried to its logical conclusion, this meant that he was prepared to sacrifice anything (truth, accuracy, the embarrassment of his friends) for what he regarded as the requirements of his art, his literature.

In her book about George Moore – which, incidentally, is dedicated to AE and John Eglinton 'who alone were treated mercifully by the author of *Ave*, *Salve*, and *Vale*, and who are therefore not likely to be indignant of the association of their names with this study of George Moore' – Susan Mitchell makes the point that Moore never had any private life himself and regarded as total eccentricity the objections of his friends to the private lives he invented for them. He did not want to get to know people too well, because too close an acquaintanceship would only interfere with the fiction he was planning to weave around them. And she goes on to give an excellent example of his attitude. After he had been entertained to a very good lunch by Sir Horace

Plunkett (whom he had lambasted in *Hail and Farewell* in a caricature pastiche), he remarked to Susan Mitchell: 'Why, Plunkett is a most intelligent man, he has a real intellect. I never understood AE's belief in him. AE was right, he is never wrong. But why does Plunkett treat me like this after the way I wrote about him? He must be a very good man.'

Then, she goes on, his first generous impulse spent, he reverts to the only subject that really matters to him, his own writing, and with a sly smile he adds: 'How fortunate it was that I wrote my book before I met him.'

> There was something pathetic in Mr Moore's return to his native land [she writes]. Her son, who had made himself famous in France and England, returning to build up her fortune with his fame and to swagger a little in his benevolence. And Dublin – Dublin who cares for none of Ireland's sons, famous or infamous, except those who stand her drinks – killed no fatted calf for the prodigal, nor even knew of his return; worse still, never even knew he had been away . . .
>
> Ten years of Ireland couldn't fetter Moore . . . Neither the Gaelic League, the Nationalists, the Catholics nor the Protestants could detain this slippery customer, and he left Ireland with a gibe for them all, sparing only those among his friends whose own independence of mind and indifference to his opinion protected them – AE, John Eglinton, and Dr Oliver St John Gogarty.
>
> Mr Moore's contributions to literature since his return to London have been lamentable. Casual articles in newspapers on such subjects as whistling for taxicabs, politics and barking dogs . . . Mr Moore came to Ireland in search of a Messiah, and though having tried to fit the part to each of his friends here, and finding that they failed him in some essential characteristic, he cast himself for it, [but] he cannot have been satisfied with his own presentation of the part, for in *The Brook Kerith*, he starts the quest anew.

With *Hail and Farewell* out of the way, Moore was looking for a new subject. He had kept the scenario of *The Apostle* by him, still fascinated at the idea of a meeting between St Paul and Jesus Christ. And, towards the end of 1913, he surprised his friends by announcing that he was about to set out for the Dead Sea in order to do some research.

'I leave Marseilles by the *Macedonia* for Port Said, bound for the land of camels and concubines,' he wrote to Dujardin on February 16, 1914. 'I have ordered 50 of the first and 500 of the others.'

# TWENTY

# The Fifth Gospel

Whatever one may feel about George Moore's peculiar sexual proclivities, or the degree of bad taste he exhibited in writing, at his age, and in the way he did, to various young women, in America, in Germany, and elsewhere, it is impossible not to admire his energy, his determination and indeed, as his contemporaries called it, his infernal cheek, in setting out, alone, and in indifferent health, at the age of sixty-two, and at a time when most of the western world realised that a major war was about to break out, in order to retrace the footsteps of Jesus of Nazareth and his disciples. He wanted to sample for himself the feel of the Holy Land and to find a remote Essene monastery somewhere in the Jordan valley which might serve for the setting for a fifth gospel, which he was planning to write himself, a gospel which would involve a total re-telling of the New Testament with a different ending, an ending which ruled out the resurrection, and resulted in a meeting between Jesus and Paul, twenty years after the event, or non-event, as the case may be.

Moore made his pilgrimage to the Holy Land early in 1914, and before he left England he gave a press conference. In her *Memories of GM* Nancy Cunard relates Moore's comments on his reasons for making the trip, as quoted in one newspaper interview: 'I feel I cannot describe a country I have never seen, if I don't know whether this place is on a hill or that in a plain, whether there is a river in sight or not. The smallest doubt of this kind stops the pen; it bothers you. You can't idealise when you don't know how far it is from the monastery to the Jordan. The monastery is in the wilderness. Is there a river there? If there is, I should like to see the river, and spend a morning by its banks. There is sure to be a spring or well; if so, what sort of a spring? Can you see the Dead Sea or can't you? These are the questions I must get answered before I begin writing, and so I am going to the Holy Land.

'What I should like to describe is the contrast between the two characters: between an ironical mystic – that is Jesus – and Paul, a man in the full tide of belief. This is what I am going to try to write – mind you, I don't say that I shall succeed – and I think I shall write it first as a story. That will enable me to become familiar with the subject, to get into it. The play will follow later.'

He was not keen on making the journey alone and he tried to persuade several people, including his eventual biographer, Joseph Hone, a frequent visitor to Ebury Street, to accompany him. He recalled, shortly before he left, that a member of his family had once predicted that he would end his days as a monk and he commented that it was true to the extent that his later writings show the attraction of religion drawing him ever closer and closer.

At Marseilles, according to Susan Mitchell, Moore embarked on the bluest of blue seas, thinking: 'I am afloat for the first time on the Mediterranean, that sea around whose shores all the old stories sprang up like flowers.

'Moore was so enchanted by antique names and classical memories that he raved around the ship to callous fellow-passengers. Here was Sicily, where the naughtiest idylls of Theocritus evoked memories he would willingly have discussed with his shrinking companions. In the lands about this inland sea were born the old gods, and especially the goddesses, Venus foam-bright, rising from the waves and floating shorewards in her shell, Europa and the Bull, Proserpine gathering daffodils on the plains of Enna – on all these legends he dilated. But, alas, his intoxication with classical myth fell flat on companions who desired intoxication with whiskey and soda, and were more interested in a volcano in eruption than George Moore in eruption. Only one fellow-passenger, a silent, pleasant, middle-aged man, seemed to listen to Moore with interest. Who he was, Mr Moore did not know or care. He was a listener, and the art of picturesque conversation did not rust for want of practice. At Port Said, Mr Moore had to ship for Joppa, and here he became aware of a sudden increase in respect for himself.

'He desired a cabin to himself, for the thought of being polite to a fellow-passenger horrified him, but a cabin was a difficult thing to get; yet when he appeared with his silent companion, he was treated as if he were an Emperor. All difficulties were smoothed away.

'He was rowed ashore at Joppa in a great galley like a Roman barge, twelve-oared, two men to an oar, the rowers chanting their boat songs . . . here again the hotel melted into obsequiousness to George and his mysterious companion, and so it was all the way to Jerusalem . . .' Never before attended with such ready service, Moore commented on it to his companion. 'I do not know who you are,' he said, 'but they treat me as if I were a king.'

His mysterious companion replied that his name was Frank Cook and that he was a member of the famous family of Thomas Cook, the first travel agent, who was, as Susan Mitchell puts it, 'the adept who conjures tours out of the strange places of the earth, and whose presence caused all obstacles to melt'.

When Moore found at Damascus that it was a long way to Jerusalem, and that the only feasible way of getting there was on horseback, and that he would have to wait a week for a horse, he determined to ride anything he could get, and left the choice of horses to his dragoman.

Aside from some of the details relived in The Brook Kerith of the difficulties and discomforts of travelling and transportation in the Holy Land, Moore left several accounts of the problems he

encountered in letters he wrote to various people, notably in a
long letter to a Mrs St John Hutchinson, a recent friend:

On arriving in Jerusalem I went away on an Arab horse whose
pacing is different from anything I had [ever] experienced before,
and rode to Jericho about twenty miles from Jerusalem through
stony hills rising steeply out of, and descending into many valleys;
sometimes the hills fall asunder and reveal precipitous sides of
white clay, nearly chalk; and the colour of the wilderness is a dirty
white and a dirty green – the green of wild rosemary and thyme. A
little grass grows here and there and the flock guided by wild
shepherds nibble it as it passes. A country as naked and savage as
the psalms. A Roman road winds to the right and left along the
sides of precipices, several hundred feet deep – a very unpleasant
country for horse-riding. At last the fair green of Jericho appeared
between the hills and it was then that I learned the beauty of green,
and it brought home to me the sensations of home and friends.
Why the Romans ever came to this fearful place I have been
thinking ever since we passed the ruins of a Roman outpost on the
borders of the plain. But it was a desert till within a mile of the
town, and so tired was I that the beautiful hills of Moab could not
rouse me and I failed to admire that evening the long wavering
rose-coloured line that the vapours rising always from the Dead Sea
veil, making the scene more beautiful – no sea is as blue as the Dead
Sea – a poisonous, chemical blue.

It was almost impossible for me to dismount; I threw myself from
the horse and tottered into the house asking for a hot bath and a
bottle of vinegar. And these two remedies enabled me to pursue the
journey the next day. We crossed the Jordan, a muddy stream, and
rode through some cultivated hills till we came to a village. Ten
miles was my start that day. Jackals howled all night and the insects
in the carpet and the insects afloat in what I suppose I must call the
air, made the night one that I shall not forget easily . . .

We had to spend a couple of nights in Jericho and as soon as the
horses were fit for travel we rode along the coast of the Dead Sea – a
long day's journey; we were in the saddle for twelve hours and our
horses were very tired when we arrived at our desolate destination.
A town had once been there and this sulphuric spot is mentioned
by Josephus as being the principal settlement of the Essenes . . . I
think that I rode on in a dream, and on arriving in Jericho I felt that
I should never be rested again. A century of a sleep in a feather bed
would not be enough . . . A sort of chimney in which there were
broken steps and passages took us to stony hills and stony valleys

through which I remembered that Jesus once led his flocks, and tired beyond all words I lay among the lilies of the field and said: 'It was here that Jesus conversed with the shepherd.'

And to Eliza Aria, another American lady, he wrote from the P&O liner *Macedonia* on the return journey: 'I rode day after day before finding the monastery passing it [the desert] by again and again, but a wonderful monastery I found, perched between a cliff and a cliff in the Brook of the Chariots, a chasm a thousand feet deep. A path three feet wide winds round the abrupt cliffs under overhanging rocks and down ragged loose places where a horse slips along the edge of the precipice. I spent two days in this monastery, one leg hanging over the ledge, teaching my eyes to remember the ledges, fissures, caverns and projecting rocks which they would never see again.'

And to Hildegarde Hawthorne: 'I have just returned from Palestine whither I went to search the desert for a monastery suitable to the story I have had in mind this long time – Jesus does not die on the cross but retires to his monastery in the desert of Judea and twenty years after the crucifixion, Paul, before he goes to Rome, takes refuge in this monastery and discovers, *so far as his temperament allows him to discover*, that the Resurrection never happened at all. The underlined phrase is the root of the story. My story is perfect and complete but I don't know if I shall succeed in writing the fifth gospel; I shall know in about three months.'

*The Brook Kerith* is the story of Jesus of Nazareth, a shepherd belonging to a brotherhood of Essenes living in a great settlement along the eastern bank of the Jordan, who leaves to preach in Jerusalem. At the end of his mission, his seemingly dead body is removed from the Cross by his friend, Joseph of Arimathea, who puts it in a tomb he had prepared for his own mortal remains. In Moore's version of the gospel story, Jesus is not dead, but merely in a coma, and is restored to health by Esora, a member of Joseph's household. When he is fully recovered, Jesus is taken back to the Essene Monastery known as the Brook Kerith, the place where the story began, and where Jesus now resumes his boring task of looking after the sheep, putting all thoughts of what might or might not have happened in Jerusalem out of his head.

Twenty years later, Paul takes refuge in this monastery which is so remote and cut off from the world that it is quite conceivable that the monks there had never heard about the Crucifixion of Jesus, and finds him there, alive and well.

Nancy Cunard sympathetically tells the remainder of the story: 'That night it comes about that Jesus, now fifty-three years of age, must tell his story to the monks, in front of Paul, of the two lost years that led to the crucifixion. When he reaches the point that he held himself to be divine and the Son of God, Paul, unwilling to believe that this shepherd-Jesus of today can ever have been Jesus of Nazareth who was crucified, died on the cross and was resurrected, is sorely troubled. And when Jesus has said a little more, Paul, to whom Jesus-the-Son-of-God spoke out of a cloud, bidding him to carry the Christian faith to all, rushes out shouting, "A madman!", and disappears into the night.

'It had been promised that Jesus, who knew all the mountain paths, should set Paul on his road the next day to Caesarea, and this, on finding Paul again in the wilderness, Jesus now does. They walk together, at first avoiding all mention of the extraordinary and troubling meeting; so Jesus himself at this moment is helping Paul, by setting him on his way, to spread a great untruth; while Paul, who rushed out in a frenzy and thus could not hear how Jesus remembered how he had come back to life, continued to wonder if the shepherd-Jesus be demented. Little by little they talk, the dilemma now spreading like a sea around Paul: if Jesus is really alive and actually speaking to him, what shall become of Christianity without the miracle of the resurrection? All the work done so far, in vain; work that will have to cease if . . . Jesus questions his conscience again: should he not go to Jerusalem to show himself, a living man? The priests will welcome this, for it will mean the downfall of Paul, their enemy. Or will they turn him away, scornfully saying the poor shepherd from the hills is out of his mind? In the end, neither prevails over the other, and when Jesus leaves Paul, this meeting with him is almost as if it had never been, for Paul's decision to continue spreading the faith is unaltered. Jesus has told him that the voice that spoke from the cloud was that of a Jesus of Paul's own imagination, the true Son of God – after a long and at times bitter haze of argument they part, Jesus to wander and perhaps to join some monks that have come from India rather than return to the Essenes, Paul faring forward on a great wave of vigour towards Rome and later Spain, making new converts to Christianity everywhere for many years.'

The real genius of *The Brook Kerith* was missed by almost all of the reviewers of the day – possibly because they were primarily concerned with whether the New Testament story was a suitable one for a writer with a reputation like George Moore to explore, and could not look at it in a sufficiently detached way to see that Moore might be jesting yet again – and by most of the people who have written about it since. The important point is that it is written in vernacular: Moore uses a sort of Sussex (or sometimes Irish) accent for people like Peter and the other fisherfolk, a very sharp Jewish – Yiddish, almost – dialogue for Joseph of Arimathea, and his father, Dan, and various, carefully chosen accents for all the other characters in the book. When some reviewers suspected that they detected an Irish accent throughout the work, Moore denied it and said that every phrase in the book had been used in Shakespeare and the Bible, and he was probably right; but Moore had such an uncanny ear for dialogue that he could easily have written it for the disciples in Irish or Sussex dialect, or a mixture of both, without even realising it.

So, the essential thing with *The Brook Kerith* is to read it in dialect. If you do, it all becomes quaintly and quietly hilarious, though you can easily see how this aspect of it could have been missed in England in 1916. St Peter's wife does not object to him following Jesus to Jerusalem, but adds: 'But let's us have a little bit more fishing, and a lot less miracles.' Or try an Irish accent: 'Was it to Peter, the publican, he was to give his boats? One who was never on the water in his life until I took him out for a sail a week come Tuesday? A fine use that'd be but to drown himself. A puff of wind, and not knowing how to take in a reef, the boats would be over and the nets lost. Now who would be the better for the loss of my nets? Answer me that. And I'd like to be told when my boats and nets were at the bottom of the lake to whom the Son of Man would turn up for a corner in which to lay his head, or a bite or a sup of wine?'

And a little bit later (this from Peter's extremely sensible, down-to-earth wife, in a Sussex accent): 'Now, Simon Peter, answer me, art thou going into Syria to bid the blind to see, the lame to walk, and the palsied to shake no more, or art thou going about thy trade? For in the house, there be four little children, myself, their mother, and thy mother-in-law. I say nothing against the journey if it bring thee good money, or if it bring the Kingdom, but if it bring naught but miracles, there'll be little enough in the house to eat by the time of thy return.'

And now listen to Dan, father of Joseph of Arimathea, and try to imagine him talking in a New York Yiddish accent: 'Give to the poor, he says. That is what I always hear . . . but if we gave all to the poor we would be as poor as the very poorest; and where, then, would the money come from, with which we may now help the poor?'

Here is Peter talking about what has happened; and, again, try to think of it said with a Sussex accent: 'But sayest thou, master, that we've been wrong in leaving our wives and children to fish for ourselves? It seemed hard at first, and thou wast weak, Master, and stayed with thy father; but after all, he has money and could pay for attendance, whereas our wives and little ones have none; ourselves will be in straits to get our living if the Kingdom be delayed in its coming, for what good are fishermen except along the sea-coast, or where there is a lake or a river, and here there isn't enough water for a minnow to swim in . . .'

How are they all going to get back to Galilee, Peter wonders.

'For Jesus seems to have forgotten us and everything else but his father's will, and we cannot make him understand that we shall want money, that money will be wanting to get us back to Galilee . . . and we would like a word from him as to when we may expect the Kingdom; and a word, too, as to what it will be like; whether there'll be rivers and lakes, well stocked with fish in it, and where our chairs shall be set; Peter on the Master's right hand to be sure . . .' Peter began to raise his voice and, straightening his shoulders, he declared that his brother Andrew must sit on Jesus's left. 'Thou rememberest, Master?'

'I remember,' Joseph interrupted, 'that the Master answered you all, saying that every chair had been made and caned and cushioned before the world was. Thou can'st not have forgotten, Peter, this saying: that everyone would find a chair according to his measure?'

'Yes, Master, he did say something like that. I'm far from saying we'd all sit equally easy in the same chairs, and if the chairs were before the world was, all I can say is that there seems to have been a lack of foresight, for how could God himself know what our backsides would be like, years upon years before they came into being?'

This is mockery of a very high order; and it is impossible not to rejoice in Moore's arrogant and highly human blasphemy, if it is possible, for someone as cynical and faithless as Moore was, to blaspheme; it is only blasphemy, after all, if you believe.

*The Brook Kerith* is a long book, which seems even longer because Moore sometimes allows his paragraphs to stray over eight or nine pages; but it did not take him more than fourteen months to write it, a very considerable achievement. And, while he was writing it, he brought out a revised edition of his novel about the Galway girls, now simply entitled *Muslin*, and a new edition of *The Untilled Field* with the preface in which he parodies Synge-Song.

Moore had mixed feelings about *The Brook Kerith*. 'I think on the whole I have done better with Jesus than with Paul,' he wrote to Dujardin, 'Paul is an historical, Jesus a legendary character. Paul painted his own portrait and did it so thoroughly that he left very little to add.'

Nancy Cunard recalls 'coming out' during the 1914 season and remembers renewing her acquaintance with George Moore: 'Nancy, you were a funny child,' he remarked to her. 'Do you remember what you said to me in the churchyard at Holt? You bade me to come with you and we sat on one of the beautiful old gravestones, you and I. Then you said to me, – I often come here alone. And I often wonder where we go when we are dead. Don't you remember, Nancy?

'But I did not remember,' she adds and goes on: 'I remember nothing definite about GM during that London season of 1914, my first *and last*, I swore to myself as one ball succeeded another until there were three or four a week and the faces of the revolving guardsmen seemed as silly as their vapid conversation among the hydrangeas at supper . . .'

One of the most peculiar things about this most peculiar man was that World War One, which probably changed the world Moore had known more than any other single factor or event, hardly impinged upon him at all. In a flush of bogus patriotism he wrote to *The Times* and denounced his former friendship with Kuno Meyer, the German expert on Celtic myths and legends, but soon regretted it and recanted. He regarded the war largely as a nuisance, which prevented him for a period from visiting his Paris friends, and he seemed to be totally unaware of the massive haemorrhage that was going on in Flanders, of the blue-uniformed walking wounded who crowded the London streets at this period, of the art and music and poetry that the war had unearthed. If his reaction seems strange, it is only fair to add that George Bernard Shaw was almost equally unmoved both by the first and second world wars; during the course of the second Shaw's only concern seemed to be that he should receive his royalties from America in the form of coal, jam, biscuits and tinned fruit, so that he would not have to pay any income tax. It could be that they were both Irish to the core, and did not regard England's wars as any of their affair.

William Heinemann, Moore's new publisher, wanted nothing to do with *The Brook Kerith*; he did not think that George Moore was a suitable author to attempt a rewrite of the New Testament; and consequently the book was published by Moore's former publishers, Werner Laurie. While the book was being printed, Moore visited his agent Tom Ruttledge at Westport, stopping in Dublin en route to meet AE, Richard Best, Eglinton and Gogarty, the only people in Dublin who were still speaking to him. Yeats had already clearly indicated that he had no wish to meet Moore again, after the way Moore had described him in *Hail and Farewell*: 'Yeats, standing lost in meditation before a congregation of white swans assembled on the lake, looking himself in his old cloak like a huge umbrella left behind by some picnic party.'

The book was published on August 23, 1916, and the edition included 250 signed copies; publication had been delayed again and again by wartime shortages of type and paper, by last-minute alterations made by Moore and by a printers' strike in the spring of 1916. Orders came in so rapidly that the publisher was obliged to increase the print order even before publication. The reviews were mixed and revealed the confusion many of the reviewers felt when faced with what must have appeared to them as a piece of undisguised blasphemy.

The *Saturday Review* said that 'the first part of the book, which deals with the youth and manhood of Joseph of Arimathea, is a fine piece of writing' and added: 'Mr Moore is singularly indifferent to public opinion. He writes to please himself.' The *Times Literary Supplement* took the easy way out by concentrating on the sub-title: *A Syrian Story*. There was no question, the reviewer said, of making any comparison between *The Brook Kerith* and all the other 'lives' of Jesus, whether written by believers or unbelievers. The reader might, if he wished, give different names to all the characters in Moore's book, but Moore, in using the biblical names, was guiltless of offence against tact and good manners, 'since his Jesus was meant to personify an ideal of moral beauty, and gave no impression of a satire upon belief.' John Freeman, the poet, made the cautious comment: 'It is a tribute to the eternal freshness of the life of Jesus Christ that this restatement in mere human terms should contain so much of beauty and so much of truth.'

In the day-by-day controversy that followed the publication of the book, Moore made no effort to disguise the fact that he regarded the book as an imaginative reconstruction of the origins of Christianity and would not agree that his shepherd mystic was incompatible with the Jesus of the gospels. A Major-General Hardy wrote a letter to the *Daily Express* calling for the prosecution of the book for religious reasons, but it came to nothing, though the controversy over the book rumbled on well into the next year, 1917.

George Bernard Shaw was as bored with the controversy as he was with the book. 'I read about thirty pages of *The Brook Kerith*. It then began to dawn on me that there was no mortal reason why Moore should not keep going on like that for fifty thousand pages, or fifty million for that matter.'

# TWENTY-ONE

# Trials and Tribulations

Shortly before *The Brook Kerith* was published in August 1916, Moore had paid another visit to his agent, Tom Ruttledge, at Westport, and had stopped off in Dublin for a few days on the way to view the ruins of the GPO and other buildings damaged or destroyed during the Easter Rising of that year. Unlike his father, he had never taken any great interest in the Irish struggle for Home Rule, any more than he took any interest in the Great War, though he had his own ideas about the Irish fight for freedom, conveyed in a couple of stray letters; he remarked in one of them that, unless five of the 'loyallest' Ulster counties could be excluded, Home Rule would never work in Ireland. In a letter to Ernest Boyd of Texas, he wrote: 'Patriotism is the refuge of those who cannot express themselves in the arts.'

Hone says that, nevertheless, the troubles in Ireland preyed on Moore's mind, and that he had nightmares about Moore Hall going up in flames, which eventually it did, during the Civil War in 1923, when his brother Maurice, who was widely believed, quite wrongly, to own the place, had become a Free State Senator opposed to the Republican break-away section of Sinn Fein. In August 1916, George Moore wrote to Miss Viola Rodgers: 'A dream woke me up suddenly; the light shining on the brass of the bedstead deceived me and thinking the bed-clothes were on fire I threw myself forward to extinguish an imaginary flame and fell headlong from the bed across the hearthrug, sustaining a pretty severe shock and breaking my wrist very badly.' He wrote several descriptive pieces of Dublin in ruins for the *Evening News* which he later included in a new book, *A Story-Teller's Holiday*, which he started on his return from Ireland.

He knew that Susan Mitchell was writing a book about him and he had told her that she must feel completely free to say about him exactly what she pleased, taking any liberties she chose: 'Well, I am part of life, like Yeats and Lady Gregory,' he had said to her. 'And you have as much right to sketch me as I had to sketch them, and if your book have any value, its value will depend upon how much of yourself you put into it.'

However, when the book appeared in September 1916, he was not at all pleased. It was the first book written about him during his lifetime and what he particularly disliked about it was the way she dismissed his Protestant pretensions. She had started by saying that Moore might have cried, with Walt Whitman: 'Do I contradict myself? Very well, I contradict myself. I contain multitudes.'

And she went on: 'He has paraded before us unabashed, in a multitudinous personality; ashamed of only one George Moore, the little Catholic boy of that name who went to confession. Yet why should he, whose whole life has been spent in making confessions, object to confession? Perhaps it was the privacy of the confessional that affronted him, that so much good copy should be wasted, poured into the ears of unliterary priests, whose lips were sealed and unable to retail all that valuable material. Of course as a literary man he would deny the Catholic George Moore, and, as I do not desire to wound him, I will not refer any more to this child who was so likely a father to the man we know; no need to, when we have Moore the pagan, Moore the Protestant, Moore the artist, Moore the realist, Moore the stylist, Moore the patriot, Moore the anti-Irishman, Moore the dramatist: all personalities which he himself has revealed to us in the most enchanting fiction. I will come to each of these personalities in turn, but I shall begin with the only one of which he is not the creator, the George Moore, minted in Mayo, stamped somewhere towards the middle of the last century with an unmistakable Irish birthright which he has never been able to obliterate.'

Moore later referred to it in letters as 'an absurd little book' and 'a string of facetious observations'. In a letter to Ernest Boyd of Texas, who was himself contemplating a book about Moore, he wrote: 'Miss Mitchell's book has fallen about as flat as a book can fall. She thinks I am angry with her, whereas I am merely disappointed that I should have inspired such a complete ineptitude.'

If Moore's output seemed to fall off sharply once he had completed *Hail and Farewell*, one reason could be that he was suffering from a lack of what he called 'regilding' since, because of the war, he was no longer able to escape from time to time to sharpen his wits – and his sensibilities – in Paris and Bayreuth. But the new book was slowly coming along. *A Story-Teller's Holiday* is, like *Hail and Farewell*, part fiction and part autobiographical. It begins with Moore setting out for Ireland, just as he had done, spending some time in Dublin with his friends, where he views the damage done during the Easter Rising, and then going on to the West of Ireland where he meets Alec Trusselby, a (fictitious) fern-gatherer who is also a *seanchie*, and they vie with each other in exchanging the short stories that make up the remainder of the book, some of them based on old Celtic myths and legends.

But, before settling down to work on it seriously, Moore did a complete rewrite of his first novel, *A Modern Lover*, changing its title to *Lewis Seymour and Some Women*. He did almost all of the revision in the Shelbourne Hotel, sending the corrected copy to his new secretary, Ethel Palmer, for transcription. It was published by Brentano in New York on January 26, 1917 and by Heinemann in March 1917; Brentano published an eleven-volume uniform edition of Moore's work between 1912 and 1917.

Around this period Moore was contemplating a lecture tour of the United States but always seemed curiously reluctant to go, when it came to the moment. Some of his best friends, particularly his women friends, were American, and there were, he admits in a letter, no people he liked better than Americans, yet Americans whose opinions he respected had assured him that America was the most detestable place in the world. The plain truth is probably that, although he was constantly dashing backwards and forwards between England and France and between Ireland and England, Moore hated travelling, and particularly long train journeys; that is the explanation why, for all his great love for the ancient, pagan, classical world, he never once went to Italy or Greece.

He remained in constant touch with people in Ireland throughout 1917, while he was writing *A Story-Teller's Holiday*: with Richard Best, the librarian and historian, to check historical details; with James Stephens, the Irish poet, whom he asked 'to sprinkle the idiom' through the stories, one of them loosely based on Kuno Meyer's translation of the seventh-century love story of Liadin and Cuirthir; and another based on an account in the Irish Texts Society of *The Madness of Suibhne Geilt*, which told how a tenth-century Irish king called Sweeney (*Suibhne* in Gaelic) went mad from the horrors of battle.

By July, he was back in Ireland, at the top of his form again, staying with the Ruttledges in Westport, where, according to Hone: '. . . one hot day, he joined in a game of tennis, playing not at all badly, said the critical girls, and wonderfully for a man in his sixty-sixth year – in a fine suit of tussore silk pyjamas. At any hour of the day, he was apt to stroll into one of the girls' rooms, wearing a puzzled look; he had, he explained, lost his way downstairs.'

It was during this visit to Ireland that George Moore and his brother came face to face for the last time; they passed each other on the stairs up to AE's office, without a word.

Both of the Colonel's sons, Peter (nicknamed Ulick) and Maurice (nicknamed Rory) were away at the war; Ulick, who had been wounded in Flanders, called at Ebury Street while Moore was away in Ireland; on his return to London, Moore heard about his visit and wrote to his nephew, reminding him that he was not on speaking terms with his father, 'and never shall be again'. And, unable to resist a reference to their differences on the religious question, went on: 'You may say that if we were to meet it would not be to discuss the religious question . . . but the fact remains that I despise Roman Catholics and one cannot change oneself. But Protestant or Roman Catholic, whichever you may be, you are certainly a brave fellow who has done the right thing . . . So you are going out again, your wound being healed. Bravo.'

Moore also used to write to Peter Moore, Augustus's only son, who had had a flat in Paris just before the war, and when he returned to London on the outbreak of war sought Moore's help – arranged with the assistance of his friend, Lord Howard de Walden – to get him a commission in the army.

Maurice's other son, Rory, called on Moore in London shortly after the Armistice, and spent a night with him before returning to Dublin, where his mother and father were now living. When Rory had left, Moore wrote to his sister-in-law, Evelyn – who he did not consider was in any way involved in his feud with his brother, since she was a Protestant – to tell her how much he had liked his nephew: 'I cannot call to mind a finer young man,' though he still could not resist adding: '. . . I did not ask him what his religious beliefs were but in telling me about the superstitions of the North American Indians he revealed his truly Catholic soul . . . His father would never allow me to see him when he was a child; now it is too late to save him and I am writing to tell you that I have suffered too much from Catholicism to wish to meet Catholics . . .'

During the war, Moore had been involved in two lawsuits, the unsuccessful attempt to suppress *The Brook Kerith*, and an extraordinary libel action taken by a man called Louis N. Seymour, who claimed that Moore's description of the unprincipled central character in *A Modern Lover*, originally published twenty-four years earlier, and now rewritten and republished as *Lewis Seymour and Some Women*, had damaged his reputation.

Moore immediately wrote to the Society of Authors: 'You will see that if Louis N. Seymour wins his action, the writing of fiction will have to be discontinued and all the past will be jeopardised, for if a man can bring an action and win it against the publishing of a book bearing his name, thirty-four years after publication [when, as he pointed out, the plaintiff was four years old], a man can bring an action against a publisher for re-printing an eighteenth century book. All the Tom Joneses can [now] issue writs.

'I need hardly labour the point that this is a matter in which your Society is concerned – you should stand in with me and get the benefit of the advertisement.'

And in a letter to his counsel, Sir William Jowitt, he commented: '. . . there are two or three Lewis Seymours in the London Directory. Are these, too, to bring an action against Heinemanns? . . . In the days when the book was written there was no Lady Helen Trevor. Today there is . . . the present suit is an indictment against nearly all literature – only prayer books will escape . . . any man called Abraham can bring an action against the publishers of the revised edition . . .'

Moore won the case – it was reported in *The Times* on November 23, 1917 – but had to pay his own costs. 'The times are strenuous and difficult,' he wrote to St John Hutchinson. 'Our paths are interrupted at every moment by new obstacles. There was the Seymour v Heinemann case, and Heinemann says that the clause in the agreement makes me liable for costs . . . I have also just heard that my tenantry have started cattle-driving in my domain. Liberal government has turned Ireland into a new Russia.'

Towards the end of July he was in Dublin again and, in order to place on record – not that anybody in Ireland cared – his own views of the Sinn Fein movement, he made his way to Phoenix Park, to pay a formal visit on the Viceregal Lodge; when he discovered that the Viceroy was away in Belfast, he insisted on inscribing his name in the visitors' book. 'His Excellency is in Belfast,' he wrote to Mrs Hunter, 'and probably won't see it. All the same, I am glad I did it, for [to] do so is to confirm my sanity in a country where there are so many madmen.'

During 1918, a new edition of his second novel, *A Mummer's Wife*, appeared; once again, he had completely reworked it, removing many clichés and phrases that he considered immature and clumsy and bringing it more into line with his recent style of writing. All through his life, Moore was aware that there were times when he wrote clumsily.

'Some of his early drafts could be very bad,' wrote Charles Morgan in his *Epitaph on George Moore*, 'bad with a virulent badness, with a pretentiousness, a snobbery, a sentimentality, a seemingly hopeless incompetence which, if one had not known that the genius of Moore was waiting to redeem them, would have tempted one to say that they and their writer were beyond redemption . . .

'The astonishing and significant thing is the persistence of this unregenerate Moore. To the very end of that long life, he had to be tutored and whipped and expurgated. He was forever popping up, seizing the pen and writing nonsense. In every book he wrote, George Moore went through the whole process of self-renewal; he went back to the beginning and taught himself to write all over again.'

Moore himself believed this bad writing to be the work of a *doppelgänger* whom he christened Amico Moorini. 'All these books,' he wrote to Morgan (and the list included *Mike Fletcher, Vain Fortune, Parnell and His Island*, the plays *Martin Luther, The Strike at Arlingford* and *The Bending of the Bough*, as well as the two volumes of verse), 'if they are ever reprinted again, should be issued as the work of a disciple – Amico Moorini I put forward as a suggestion.'

Morgan comments: 'Amico Moorini, then, shall be his name, but he was very far from being George Moore's disciple or his friend. He was his enemy who, though beaten down a thousand

times, always rose up from under his feet; and it was this struggle
which gave to Moore's character the stress of extreme complexity.'

Morgan, who was one of a new circle of London friends, which
now included Edmund Gosse and Sir William Geary, believed
that Moore remained an adolescent even in his old age, but adds:
'In his devotion to his art, and his readiness to sacrifice all else to it,
he was a saint or a devil, according to your prejudice. Self-creation
was the end, self-discipline the means, and the cost to him was the
joy, the ease, the warmth, the natural humanity of living. He was
always on his guard; he had to be, because Amico Moorini was
always at his elbow, trying to get at his work.'

Moore finished A Story-Teller's Holiday – without much
interference from Amico Moorini – with a 'voyage to childhood'
in which he addresses his agent, Ruttledge, who had called his
attention to the woods around Moore Hall, warning him that they
might be in danger, in view of the scarcity of fuel during the war,
and it is clear from this extract that he sees himself as one of the
Andreyevs in Tchekov's The Cherry Orchard: 'But even if you
succeed in preserving Moore Hall unchanged for a few years . . .
[it] will certainly fall into ruin. As soon as you have gone, the trees
will be felled and the lead taken from the roof . . . time overtakes
the most enduring monuments, but men continue to build . . . The
past tells us whence we have come and what we are, and it was well
that I refused to allow the trees to be felled, for sitting by my
fireside in Ebury Street I should hear the strokes of the axe in my
imagination as plainly as if I were living in Moore Hall, and the
ghosts of the felled trees would gather about my armchair in Ebury
Street.'

By now Moore had reached the conclusion that his days as a
popular novelist were over; indeed, as far back as June 1914, he
had written to the American publisher, Alfred Knopf, to say: 'It is
a great pleasure to hear that you like Vale as well as the other
volumes; for you see I write for a very small circle and if I fail to
please them, I should have no readers at all.'

He finally decided in 1918 that in future he would publish all his books in limited but beautifully printed editions, subscribed in advance of publication, and arranged to have *A Story-Teller's Holiday* published privately under the imprint of a non-existent Society of Irish Folklore (*Cumann Seaneolais na h'Eireann*). Hone, who knew him well at this period of his life, seemed surprised at the change in Moore's lifestyle: '. . . he came to demand the same conscience in the type-founding, type-setting, and paper-making of a book as he himself showed in the writing. The dignified privacy of publication harmonised well with the aristocratical pose, as of some survivor of the eighteenth century, which he now adopted in life, not indeed among old friends but to newcomers in his acquaintance, and so successfully that upon his death one of the obituarists referred to his possession of beautiful manners.'

In the year that *A Story-Teller's Holiday* appeared, Moore wrote to James Stephens: 'I am fairly tired out with composition and am determined not to write any more, if ever.' And he often remarked, both in conversation and in letters to his friends, that writers have twenty to twenty-five books in them at the most; by now, he had himself passed the thirty point.

But *Avowals* was still unfinished, and he was in the middle of yet another row, this time with Edmund Gosse. Moore had proposed to open the book with a discussion between himself and Gosse on the deficiencies of English prose narrative, and wrote to Gosse to tell him so. In what reads very like a repetition of one of Maurice Moore's letters, Gosse replied: 'You [intend to] present me as a *journalist*, come to interview you for some newspaper!! This I absolutely refuse to allow you to do. You must not start by giving yourself *le beau rôle* and making me venal and ridiculous . . . How DARE you propose that I should "apologise for interrupting your work"? Damn your infernal cheek.' But Gosse relented, because he both liked and admired Moore and the dialogue was completed; and, before Christmas 1918, Moore was writing to Werner Laurie about the type face in which *Avowals* was to be set. In another letter to the publisher, earlier in the same year, he had said: 'Millions of cheap books, by dead and living authors, have been published in the last ten years; short, thick, bulky volumes, like dictionaries, the sight of which makes a room look vulgar, and that the public has wearied of these ugly books is the best reason we can find for the rapid filling-up of the subscription list for *A Story-Teller's Holiday*; a well-printed and well-bound book is an ornament, so our ancestors thought and so it would seem we moderns are beginning to think.'

And despite all his protestations to James Stephens that he was determined not to write any more, if ever, he had already suggested two new projects to Werner Laurie; a retelling, in the style he had evolved in *The Lake*, and had perfected in *The Brook Kerith* and *A Story-Teller's Holiday*, of the ancient legend of Daphnis and Chloe and the mediaeval tragedy of Héloise and Abélard.

# TWENTY-TWO

# Rigmarole
# from Ebury Street

George Moore, having reinvented himself half a dozen times in his first sixty-seven years, now devised a totally new approach to writing. Instead of dictating for three hours every morning, revising the resultant typescript the following afternoon, and then re-dictating his revisions and reshapings and remouldings over and over again until he had got the flow of his prose to his full satisfaction, he conceived a system which enabled him to let his imagination run full rein. He started to dictate entire books straight out of his head, without even glancing at any notes nor at any of the daily rations of dictation, which he referred to as 'the rigmarole'. He described his new method of writing in a letter to Mrs Audrey Williamson, daughter of his old friend, Mrs Mary Hunter, the lady who had presented him with the Bible which had been the inspiration for his investigation of the scriptures which had led him to *The Brook Kerith*: 'My life passes by in loneliness and composition. I see hardly anybody, nobody for long but my secretary . . . *Héloise and Abélard* is the theme of my dictations; and these are continued without interruptions and are locked away as soon as transcribed, for my plan is to proceed with scarcely more knowledge of the furrow behind me than the ox. I am told that the dictations read very pleasantly, lapsing occasionally into rigmarole which is inevitable; I am not credulous but the story seems to shape itself easily and well.'

He was already writing to Nia Crawford to ask her to do some research for him on the number of rooms there might have been in Canon Fulbert's house in the Rue des Chantres in Le Pallet, near Nantes in Brittany, where Abélard promised to marry Héloise, and soon he was petulantly complaining: 'I am afraid you are treating me with very little consideration. I asked you to help me with a work of art and I find to my great regret that almost anything is accepted as more important. I asked you to give me some help and mentioned that it would be paid for, and literary work such as I asked for demands some concentration. You said you would give the week to it, but of course, a Catholic girl had to come down for the weekend. Do you think you are treating your old friend quite fairly? I am sure you do not . . .'

Nancy Cunard remembered rows with other people, even one with his dear friend, Mary Hunter. 'Mrs Hunter was,' she says, 'inexplicably, a great friend of the American writer [Henry James] whom Moore had described as "vain and pompous"; she had been very angry indeed with GM; no more visits to Hill Hall, once, for a very long time!' And Nancy herself was cross with him for running down his old friend, Arthur Symons, reminding him of how he used to praise Symons in the days of his 'cock-loft' in the Temple. 'Oh, *then*,' he said: 'Symons was a very good writer, he was indeed, earlier on. But now he seems ineffectual; his time is over – a ghost!'

In July 1919, he went on a protracted tour of Brittany and Touraine to retrace the footsteps of the mediaeval lovers and to 'put some geography' into what he had learned about their lives from Walter Pater's *Two Early French Stories* published as part of his *The Renaissance*; from the letters of Abélard and Héloise; from Charles Rémusat's *Abélard* (1845), and from Eugène Emmanuel Viollet-le-Duc's *Dictionnaire raisoné de l'architecture Française du XIme au XVIme siècle* (1858–68).

Moore wrote to Nia Crawford from Tours: 'I walked around the old fortress of Le Pallet with Monsieur Le Curé who knows all about Héloise and Abélard. The Musée de Beaux Arts would have delighted you – the sculpture of the 12, 13 and 14 centuries – *la sérenité triste de la vierge d'Amiens et la tristesse mondiale du roi Salomon* . . . I return to London in nine or ten days, my memory stored with memories of the Loire, and a more precise image of Abélard before me. I lie in bed in the morning and lose myself in dreams, seeing Abélard and Héloise and hearing them talking and suddenly I fall to wondering if I shall get all this dreaming down on paper . . .'

There were endless rows during the printing of *Avowals*, and when eventually he received a finished copy in September 1919 he told Werner Laurie that it might best be described 'as a hideous mass of typographical error[s] . . . All these mistakes might be corrected in an ordinary book, but there is to be no second edition of *Avowals*, so these terrifying mistakes remain during my natural life'. Nevertheless, his friend Magee, writing as John Eglinton in the *Irish Statesman*, described it as 'the most delightful of Moore's books'.

And there were further tedious rows with Laurie about the quality of the paper and the precise proof-reader to be employed in connection with a new limited edition of *Modern Painting* he was planning to bring out. By December he was writing to the publisher to say that he was already dictating the last chapter of *Héloise and Abélard* (in rigmarole form), and asking for the sheets of *Modern Painting* to be sent to him, so that he could revise and edit it, before beginning the actual writing of *Héloise and Abélard*. The dictation, he reported, had gone very rapidly, and the book would be about as long as *The Brook Kerith*.

He spent most of 1920 turning the rigmarole into polished prose in his new style, though during the year he managed to find time to bring out a revised limited edition of *Esther Waters*, with a new dedication to his Dublin friend, T. W. Rolleston, and a limited edition in book form of the play *Elizabeth Cooper*, both titles under the imprint of the Society of Irish Folklore.

By March 1920, he had written enough of *Héloise and Abélard* in its final form to be able to offer some chapters to the *Fortnightly Review*, which published extracts from it in September and October 1920; and by October 13 he had sent off the last batch of copy to Laurie. It was published by Werner Laurie on February 17, 1921, and by Boni and Liveright in New York on May 12, 1921. It was well, if not widely reviewed; as his books were now issued in privately published, limited editions, they were not automatically reviewed by the newspapers in the ordinary way, though several general articles on his expensive hand-set books appeared from time to time, notably Lewis Rose MacLeon's piece on 'The Two-Guinea Novel' in the *Daily Mail* in February 1921; two guineas, the average price of Moore's books at this period, would be equivalent to a price of about £100 today.

Charles Morgan, who was at this period being considered by Moore as a potential biographer, was later to comment, in *Epitaph on George Moore*, that in writing *Héloise* Moore's aim had been to construct a type of prose free from any kind of colloquialism, any conscious trick of phrase, any contemporary allusion that might make it obscure or tedious in time to come. He rejected, as far as possible, the use of the word 'you', preferring the 'thee', 'thou' and 'thine' form which, he felt, had the double merit of freshness at the time when the books appeared, and of carrying the unshakable authority of the Bible. 'But to think of his style as if it consisted only in a faultless control of phrase and cadence, is to deny him his place in literature,' Morgan argued. 'Good English, however good it may be, will gain no man immortality, and we shall arrive at the significance of Moore only by recognising the validity of his claim to be a master of anecdote and by concluding that Moore desired, above all else, to evolve a new method of story-telling . . . and went back to the directness of a story that is told orally, a good tale invented by the bedside, or a fable passed down by word of mouth.'

And he selected this quotation from *Héloise and Abélard*, as a sample of the style at its best: 'But the summer is not yet come, Abélard, she said: I am but the month of April. Call me not the month of March, for this is a cold month, and I am not cold. A fair month indeed, he answered, is the month of April, one not to be despised, though the month of May is a better month, and the month of June is – Well, June is a month for the Gods. But thy June, Héloise, is many months distant, and waiting for it shall be my joy. Wilt grow tired of waiting? she asked. Tired of waiting? How little thou knowest yet about love. A true love never tires or wanes, Héloise, but is with us always, like our blood, like our breath.'

Charles Morgan was only one of a group of writers Moore was considering as a possible biographer. The suggestion of having his biography written came, it is only fair to add, in the first instance from Werner Laurie, and among the candidates short-listed for this honour were his friend Magee (John Eglinton); Arthur Symons; Joseph Hone; Max Beerbohm; Jean Aubry; D. H. Lawrence; G. K. Chesterton, and John Freeman. Of these, only Symons and Freeman were ever very seriously considered by Moore, though he did remark that he thought the money might come in very useful to D. H. Lawrence, then still a struggling author with *Sons and Lovers* and *Women in Love* behind him, but with success and *Lady Chatterley's Lover* still in the future.

Moore scornfully dismissed Laurie's suggestion of G. K. Chesterton with a typical and highly entertaining diatribe against a man who was 'a firm believer in the power of the priests to turn God into biscuits and wine every morning, to eat him, to shut him up, and distribute him . . .'

The absurdity of what he usually referred to as the 'Roman' Catholic religion was, of course, still a subject very dear to his heart. In her study of Lady Cunard and her daughter, *Emerald and*

*Nancy*, Daphne Fielding remembers occasions at Nevill Holt when the host frowned at the head of the table 'as George Moore, ignoring the possible presence of Catholic guests, would launch into an attack on popery: "You can't change God into a *biscuit*!" he would fulminate. "And what are they going to do in America when they bring in prohibition? Will they use coloured mineral-water for communion wine, as the mummers do on the stage?" Then he would be up and off on another of his hobby-horses, poking fun at "the obscene state of marriage" or telling a risqué story to an apprehensive audience.' By now, Lady Cunard had left her husband and was living in Carlton Terrace in London; and, though Sir Bache had died in 1925, his widow never married again.

John Freeman, who had written an article on Moore in the *London Mercury* in July 1920, was a firm favourite for the task of official biographer, but when his *A Portrait of George Moore in a Study of his Work* appeared in 1922 Moore was very upset that the first chapter was 'too burdened with facts' and contained allusions to his family's Catholicism.

Eventually Moore settled on Charles Morgan, author of *The Flashing Stream*. When he invited Morgan to be his official biographer – and appointed him as such in his will – he said that the biography should not be a 'tombstone in two volumes', but a story of his life based, as far as humanly possible, upon a novelist's complete knowledge and intuitive understanding of his subject, 'and told with that indifference to all but aesthetic consequence by which a story-teller is fortified'. To write such a book, it would be necessary, Moore said, for his biographer to see him as he saw himself at different periods during his life, and in order to achieve this his biographer would need access to a series of letters addressed by him to one single correspondent. Although Morgan does not say so, Moore was obviously referring to his own letters, written to Lady Cunard, over the years.

'Your story is of a man who made himself because he imagined himself, and you must discover when his imagination went with his nature and when against it; for it is that which, in the end, determines a narrative's shape. The man you will tell of imagined himself as an artist; but when he imagined himself as a painter, the imagination was sterile, like a man mated with the wrong woman, and it was not until he threw away his brushes that his imagination paired with his nature.'

It would not be necessary to publish these letters, Moore argued; but, without some knowledge of their content, it would not be possible for the biographer to have a complete knowledge of his subject. Morgan says that Moore explained this to the person he discreetly calls 'this correspondent' and requested that Morgan be given access to the letters. However, for some reason which she never explained to anybody, Lady Cunard refused to allow Morgan access to the letters, and, in her will, bequeathed them to Sacheverell Sitwell; Nancy Cunard's first poems had appeared in an anthology, *Wheels*, published by the Sitwells.

When Lady Cunard refused to let him have the letters, Morgan offered to resign the task of writing the biography, but Moore would not allow this. If only Morgan would be patient, Moore would make sure, in his will, that the letters would be made available to Morgan. After Moore's death, Morgan renewed his request, and was again refused the letters, and had to abandon his biography, as another life of George Moore was being written by Joseph Hone, with the consent of Moore's literary executor, and presumably with the connivance of Maurice Moore, who had always been more friendly with Hone than Moore himself was, and who had managed to obtain a few of Moore's letters to Lady Cunard.

Morgan was saddened, but not embittered, at having to drop the biography: 'Private letters are private letters even though they be written by great men,' he commented, 'as long as they are not destroyed against posterity, their owner's right to withhold them is not, I think, to be questioned.'

*

In 1921 a Moore Hall edition of *Memoirs of My Dead Life* was published by Heinemann, and Moore was well pleased with Philip Teldon's work in rearranging and re-drawing an old engraving of the house on Lough Carra for the title page. His play *Elizabeth Cooper*, rewritten yet again under the title of *The Coming of Gabrielle*, was scheduled for production in the autumn of 1921, and by the end of the year he was working on a tale about a mediaeval lover, Hugh Montfert, who is about to marry his best friend's sister, when he suddenly realises that he was attracted to Beatrice, not for herself, but because of her resemblance to her brother; it was similar to a theme he had tackled in his second book of *Pagan Poems*, and it carried echoes of *A Mere Accident* and featured the same character, John Norton, from *Celibates*; all three were based on the character of Edward Martyn, recreated far away from his Irish background. 'We never come to the end of dear Edward,' Moore used to say, though he did, and Dear Edward certainly came to the end of Moore, commenting, in an unpublished manuscript, quoted by Denis Gwynn in his *Edward Martyn and the Irish Revival*: 'Mr George Augustus Moore by constituting himself my Boswell has obtained a certain notoriety of mean vanity like his prototype.' By this time, Martyn was very ill; when he died, in 1923, he bequeathed his two long-forgotten plays, *The Heather Field* and *Maeve* – possibly ironically – to Moore, and left instructions that his body was to be given to medical students for dissection, and the remains buried in a pauper's grave, along with the unclaimed Dublin workhouse dead.

Most of the year 1922 was spent in revising, reshuffling and in various other ways recreating Moore's published works for the Carra edition of his collected works, to be published in the United States by Boni and Liveright. With Werner Laurie he was now on much better terms; and he was particularly pleased with the fifth impression of *The Brook Kerith*.

Most years, he now once again spent several weeks in France, where he still had a circle of friends which included Dujardin, Miss

Viola Rodgers, Paul Valéry, and the young Jean Aubry, whom he had met in London during the war, and who now suggested a French translation of the Moore Hall edition of *Memoirs*; Moore, as usual, did not like the original translation and had two of his Paris friends, Daniel Halévy and Edmond Jaloux, attempt to correct it to his satisfaction. It was published first in one of Halévy's *Cahiers Verts*, with a woodcut illustration of Moore Hall, as seen from the lake; and then by Bernard Grasset, though without 'The Lovers of Orelay'.

Although Moore felt in a way that he had discovered Paris in the 1870s, he never reached as large a body of French readers as many of his contemporaries did, nor did his works ever appear in France in a collected edition. Worst of all perhaps was what Hone refers to as 'the discomfort of watching the conquest of intellectual Paris by *Ulysses* and *Lady Chatterley's Lover*'.

He kept talking about returning to Paris, and at one stage was very anxious to be accepted as a lodger by his pen-friend, Viola Rodgers, the American journalist formerly working for *Cosmopolitan*, whom he had met in Dublin; she was now living in Paris, in an apartment overlooking the gardens of the Palais Royal, the only place in Paris, Moore reckoned, where it was possible for him to get a good night's sleep. But, for all her fondness for Moore, she, in common with almost all of his other friends, now fought shy of having this argumentative and cantankerous old man staying with her on any sort of a permanent basis.

By 1922, he had even started to quarrel with one of his oldest French friends, Dujardin. A visit to the Val Changis in 1922 ended with Moore saying that he would never return. 'It is too wearisome. Dujardin seems to go out of his way to meet the disagreeable things which I spend my life trying to avoid.'

Before going to Paris in 1922, Moore had finished his book of short stories (very largely a rewrite of *Celibates*) which appeared under the title, *In Single Strictness*, in a limited edition published by William Heinemann later that year.

\*

Moore's brother Maurice, the Colonel, had been living in Ireland since leaving Brussels just before the war, and had played some part in the formation and training of the Irish Volunteers who had been principally responsible for the Easter 1916 Rising and the success of Sinn Fein in its struggle against the forces of law and order in Ireland in the years between 1919 and 1923, the years during which the Irish Free State was born. When the Sinn Fein party split over the Treaty in 1922, Maurice supported Collins and Griffith in the Civil War and, after the defeat of de Valera's break-away Republicans, became a Free State Senator.

On the night of February 1, 1923, the steward at Moore Hall was roused by a party of Irregulars, as they were called, and told to make himself scarce while they set fire to the house. They took some church vestments – which had originally been brought from Spain by George Moore the Wine Merchant – out of the house and left them in the carriage-way for safety; everything else was destroyed. In the morning, only the smoking outer walls remained.

The steward, Reilly, sent his employer such an excellent account of the outrage that, according to Hone, Moore published it in the *Morning Post* under his own name with only one word altered, and sent Reilly a cheque for twelve guineas.

Between June and December 1923, Moore published a couple of articles in the *Fortnightly*, both of them extracts from a new book he was working on, *Conversations in Ebury Street* and *Sunt Lacrimae Rerum*, a reverie of childhood. He also saw Athene Seyler play in his *The Coming of Gabrielle* at the St James's Theatre, and wrote to Mrs St John Hutchinson: 'I saw it yesterday and it seemed to me one of the prettiest comedies ever written. I cannot imagine anything better. The press seemed to think differently but journalists will not quench so pretty a comedy and *The Coming of Gabrielle* will add one more to their long list of mistakes . . .'

But it was Moore who was mistaken; *The Coming of Gabrielle* played for three nights only and has never been revived.

# TWENTY-THREE

# Return to Mayo

Although he never wrote a really successful play, Moore continued to be attracted to the theatre, and in 1923 published a
dramatisation of *The Brook Kerith*, under the title of *The Apostle*,
his only publication that year. In the following year, he prepared
three books for publication: *Ulick and Soracha, Conversations in
Ebury Street*, and *The Pastoral Loves of Daphnis and Chloe*.

*Ulick and Soracha* was a historical romance set in mediaeval
Ireland, during the period following the arrival of Robert Bruce in
1315, in an unsuccessful effort to unite the Scottish and Irish Celts
against the Anglo-Normans, and Moore was attracted to the
subject because he remembered that Castle Carra and the other
island strongholds on Lough Carra in County Mayo had legendary
associations with the 1315 invasion of Ireland.

*Conversations in Ebury Street* is exactly that: a collection of
remembered, or invented, or enhanced conversations with various
interlocutors, including an American writer and Moore fan, who
was formerly a miner, and who is introduced only as Mr Husband;
John Freeman, the poet; Desmond (later Sir Desmond) MacCarthy, the writer and critic; Walter De La Mare, the poet; Henry
Tonks and Wilson Steer, his London artist friends; and the book
inevitably also contains some direct communications from Moore
to his readers, all designed to allow him to unburden himself of his

vivid views on life, literature and art, interspersed with random memories and recollections.

A sample (from his conversation with Mr Husband on the way the world appeared to him to be going at that particular period): 'The mediaeval world was hardly larger than the ancient world, I replied, only portions of the planet being known to men. But today we are without Gods, and in a world no bigger than a band-box, with every man looking over the next man's shoulder: A portrait painted in Christiana is indistinguishable from a portrait painted in Lima. The circumstances of the antique world and the modern were, till a hundred years ago, practically the same. We lived till eighteen hundred and fifty in isolated communities; every town had a society, customs and a dialect of its own. Till eighteen hundred and fifty, many languages were spoken in these islands. I remember the humming of looms in the village street, housewives spinning at cottage doors; and at the end of a passage in my house in Mayo stands a grandfather-clock which came from Castlebar at the end of the eighteenth century; the precise date I cannot vouch for, but it is certain that a grandfather-clock has not been made in Castlebar since eighteen hundred and fifty. It was about that time that beer ceased to be made at Moore Hall; the brew-house still existed in my childhood, but we got our beer from Ballinrobe; now the beer comes to Ballinrobe from Dublin.'

*The Pastoral Loves of Daphnis and Chloe* was Moore's retelling, in the style he had perfected in *The Brook Kerith*, of the ancient Greek legend, which he described in a letter to Lord Howard de Walden as 'the beautifullest story in the world'. On the title page of the book it says 'Done into English by George Moore'; and he always referred to it as a translation, and was not at all averse from people assuming that this was meant to indicate that it was a translation from the original Greek, though most people who knew him also knew that he had never studied Greek. In fact, it was very largely a translation from the old French text of Paul Louis Courier (1772–1825), though he also referred, according to Hone, to an equally old English translation by George Thornley;

but, to give verisimilitude to the widespread notion that it was actually a translation from the ancient Greek, he made vague and sometimes obscure references in letters to arguments he was having with Greek scholars. To Miss Mary Somerville of Oxford, who had helped him with some of his books, he wrote: 'I am more in love than ever with my translation. It seems to me to be the only thing worth doing that I have been able to do. I have redeemed the loveliest of stories from bad Greek and bad English.'

It is the story of two young foundlings, one reared by a sheep and one by a goat, though Moore refers to them as a she-goat and a yoe, his own preferred, bucolic version of the word ewe. They are brought up by Greek shepherds on the Isle of Lesbos, and given the names Daphnis and Chloe, and, in the fullness of time, fall in love. Daphnis appears to share some of the problems Moore himself experienced in his dead life, in carrying his relationship with Chloe much further than the purely platonic, or at any rate beyond the kissing stage, until he encounters Lycoenium, the young city wife, 'dainty and blooming', of a wasted old farmer living near by. Lycoenium has been watching Daphnis and Chloe and has realised what the problem is; and, since she has taken a great fancy to young Daphnis herself, she decides to solve their problem while at the same time ameliorating her own, by teaching Daphnis how to go about it.

'And Lycoenium, seeing him even more simple and natural than she had imagined, began to instruct him and in this manner. She ordered him to sit close to her and to kiss her as he and Chloe were accustomed to kiss each other, and whilst kissing her to embrace her and to lie on the ground beside her. And as he was sitting by her, kissing her, and lying beside her, she, finding him ready, raised him up, slipped beneath him, and put him in the way that he had long sought; and then nature coming to his aid, the natural was accomplished. No more was done; so finished the amorous lesson. Daphnis, as innocent as before, was [for] running to Chloe to teach her what he had learnt as if he was afraid he should forget it, but Lycoenium detained him. Thou must know,

Daphnis, that being a grown woman, thou hast not hurt me; for another man a long while back taught me what I have taught thee, and, for his pains, he had my maidenhead. But Chloe, when she will struggle with thee, will cry out and will weep, and will bleed as if she had been killed. But do not be afraid. And when she would give herself to thee, bring her hither, so that if she cries out nobody will hear, and if she weeps, nobody will see, and if she bleeds, she can wash herself at the spring. But never forget that it was I, and not Chloe, that made thee a man.'

But, the gentle reader may well be wondering, did it work? Here is Moore's version of how the tale ends, on their wedding night, Chloe still as intact as ever: 'Meanwhile Daphnis and Chloe lay naked in bed, where they exchanged kisses and embraces without closing an eye all night, wakeful as night-jars, Daphnis practising with Chloe all that Lycoenium had taught him, and Chloe coming to understand that all they had done hitherto in the woods was but the play of children.'

Pretty tame stuff, coming out a couple of years after Molly Bloom's hair-raising reminiscences as she lay in bed in Dublin. It is not surprising that Moore was no longer hitting the headlines.

He was, however, just as busy as ever. In 1924, in addition to the books mentioned above, he also published a short story *Peronnik the Fool* and an anthology of poems called *Pure Poetry*. *Peronnik the Fool* was a pendant to *Héloise and Abélard*; it is a tale told to their son, Astrolabe, and initially it was only published in New York, by Boni and Liveright. The original English edition, interestingly, was the first book hand-set by Nancy Cunard herself, and printed on a century-old hand-press which she had installed in a house she had bought in Normandy; she called her publishing venture the Hours Press, and *Peronnik the Fool*, revised by Moore from the American sheets, was published in 1928 as a slim volume of ninety-nine pages.

Towards the end of his life, George Moore was probably closer to Nancy Cunard than anybody else, including her mother, to whom she always referred either as 'Her Ladyship' or as 'a polished termagant'; she certainly understood him and sympathised with him in all his moods. In 1913, when she was seventeen, she was at a fashionable finishing school in Paris, run by the Mesdemoiselles Ozanne, and George Moore frequently called on her there and took her out to lunch, or afternoon tea.

After coming out in 1914 (the Prince of Wales, the future Edward VIII, was a guest at her own coming-out party and danced with her several times) she was briefly married to a young officer called Evan Morgan during the war, but they parted company after twenty months or so. She saw George Moore only once during the time she was married, but started to see him again as soon as the marriage broke up. 'You have come into your own,' Moore told her when he met her just after her divorce in 1925.

One thing that they had in common was a love of France; Nancy had been living there since 1921, first in the village of Saint-Martin-Eglise, four miles inland from Dieppe, where Moore spent five or six days with her, slightly put out at the fact that she also had a young man staying with her. 'A young man, alone with me, for two days!' she wrote in GM: *Memories of George Moore*. 'A very cultured young man, of course, he was bound to admit, who could not be more deferential and so on, but a-lone! People would talk . . .'

He stayed with her again when she moved to Sanary, in the Var, near Toulon, and was a frequent visitor to her ground-floor flat at No 2, Rue le Regrattier, an eighteenth-century building on the Ile de la Cité in Paris; indeed, in 1925, Moore suggested that he and Nancy should exchange homes for six months of every year, though that notion came to nothing. Nancy had many happy memories of Moore in Paris when he was in his late sixties and seventies, and she was about thirty, including one evening when he sat at a restaurant between two beautiful girls, Marie Beerbohm, niece of Max, and Dolly Wilde, niece of Oscar. He always referred to himself as her 'first friend' and was, she says, forever asking her to tell him all about her lovers, and telling her what a 'dab hand' he had been, in his youth, at making love. Almost alone of all his close friends, she believed him.

She also recalled chance remarks of his. When they were discussing *Du Coté de chez Swann*, he said to her that Proust wrote like a man 'trying to plough a field with a pair of knitting needles'. And, about Joyce, he said: 'Joyce has invented a language that only Joyce can understand.' They did not always agree; she was interested in modern movements in paintings which he made no effort to understand; about Cubism, he remarked: 'The Pons Asinorum of Euclid done in scarlet and blue paper lozenges has never been a pleasure to me.' And on his use of dialect in his books: 'Living speech is to literature what the wheel is to the wheel-barrow.'

In 1924, when his anthology, *Pure Poetry*, was published, he wrote to her in Paris: 'When you were a little girl I used to talk to you about an anthology of pure poetry but you were too young to understand objective poetry, and now the anthology is completed. Would that we had searched out the lovely flowers together but we cannot go searching for poems whilst a sea is between us . . .'

In 1925, Tom Ruttledge died; he had been negotiating with the Irish Government for compensation for the destruction of Moore Hall during the Civil War, and shortly after his death the Government agreed to pay Moore £7,000 (worth £140,000 today). Moore was well pleased because, as Hone remarks, he knew very well that he could not have sold the house, before the arson attack, for anything like that.

*Ulick and Soracha* was ready in the summer of 1926; it had been delayed by the preparation of an illustrated edition of *The Brook Kerith* with engravings by Stephen Gooden, a former Slade student of Tonks's. At this stage, too, Moore met the only man who could out-talk him, G. Leverton Harris, MP, a man who discovered, when well past the age of fifty, that he had a talent for painting and became a student at the Slade; it was Tonks who introduced him to Moore. Tonks's Saturday evenings at the Vale in Chelsea now became as important a part of Moore's social life as his own Saturday evenings in Ely Place in Dublin had been twenty years earlier. There is a marvellous reconstruction of one of these evenings in the Tate Gallery, painted by Henry Tonks; it shows Moore reading something – almost certainly something composed by himself, and almost certainly aloud – with St John Hutchinson behind Moore, Steer fast asleep, on his left, Henry Tonks himself, propped up against the mantelpiece, and Mrs St John Hutchinson listening raptly to what The Sage is reading.

In 1926, Lady Cunard wrote to him from Switzerland and signed the letter Maud Emerald. He wrote back by return of post: 'Your lover of other days is mystified and chagrined today. At the end of a graceful and charming letter came a new signature: "Maud Emerald." I took your letter to Tonks and his words were "Is she married?" I answered, "I can put no other meaning on it." After considering carefully, he said that he did not know of anybody called Emerald, and after searching in the telephone book, he declared the name to be mere whimsy, no more serious than a new plume in a hat. But I don't feel sure, far from it, that he is right and I beg you to send me a telegram. A yes or no will be enough. You cannot fail to understand that it is unfair to leave a man who has loved you dearly for more than thirty years in doubt.'

The following day he had heard nothing, and he sent her a telegram: 'Who is Emerald? Are you married?'

He received a reply that evening: 'Emerald is not a surname but the jewels I wear are emeralds and since I am nicknamed The Emerald Queen I have adopted it as my Christian name.'

At the time of this flirtatious exchange, Emerald, as she was now known, was fifty-four and Moore seventy-four. Moore wrote to her again on March 3, 1927: 'Dearest Maud, This letter is to tell you before I have the delight of seeing you that I long to see your face and hear your voice. Since you left London I have worked hard, but work is not enough and I have felt constantly how much I need you and for good reason – you are the only real thing I have met in life, real to me. And better kill a man than deprive him of the woman he needs. With much love, George Moore.'

In 1927, Moore's extraordinarily robust health began to fail him. He had for years been having some slight difficulty in micturating, but had neglected to take any medical advice, possibly afraid that he might discover that he was suffering from something far more serious, such as cancer. And, by the time he sought medical advice, it was almost too late, since in those days, long before keyhole surgery, treatment for prostate trouble usually involved a major operation, which, at seventy-five, he was too old to withstand.

His specialist, Sir John Thomson-Walker, one of the most distinguished surgeons involved in that particular field of medicine, did all in his power to make life a bit less uncomfortable for Moore, and became a great friend; Moore dedicated his last finished work, *Aphrodite in Aulis*, to him.

*Aphrodite in Aulis* grew out of an imagined incident. Two girls are swimming across a strait somewhere in Greece and then admiring their bodies on the bank, observed by a sculptor who finds in the sight the inspiration for a statue of Aphrodite. Moore set it in the fifth century BC, and, in his usual fashion, started to write to various authorities for details of the state of the tide in the particular area he had chosen, suitable names for his characters, and so on.

While he was engaged in this research, a revised version of his book of short stories, *In Single Strictness*, appeared under the title of *Celibate Lives*; it was largely neglected by the reviewers but he was far too busy on his Greek story even to notice.

By November 1927, he had most of *Aphrodite* on paper and was preparing *Hail and Farewell* and *Memoirs of My Dead Life* for publication in the uniform edition of his works.

In February 1928, he was in a luxurious nursing home, complaining that it was 'like trying to sleep between the rails in Waterloo Station at the height of the holiday season', and writing to Lady Cunard to say that, if he should die before her, most of his property would go to her, and enjoining her to keep his books in print, properly advertised, and advising her that he was leaving her £500 for that task. Later in the year he had recovered sufficiently to go to Paris, where he saw Dujardin, the Halévys and Madame Duclaux, as well as Nancy Cunard, who was bringing out the first English edition of *Peronnik* on her hand-press in Normandy; in September 1928, he wrote to her: 'It seems a pity that I should not have been all this while living in your lovely house, which I long to see almost as much as I long to see you. I shall not be happy till I am there, walking around the little domain with you and hearing about the printing. But when will this be, Nancy? You cannot help me and I cannot help myself . . .'

Nancy Cunard has left us this recollection of a fragment of his conversation during a visit to Ebury Street around this time. He had quoted to her the passage from *Memoirs* which ends: 'Whosoever he may be, proof is not wanting that the world can do very well without his work.' And he went on: 'This, ah this, is what an artist takes on, and the sooner he comes to terms with it, the better for him. For of course, he would say, an artist, a writer has to go on: What should I do, Nancy, if I had not to write? I cannot stop. Sameness and change, both of them without purpose, yet we go on – go on we must. Oh, pull the blind, do, and light the lamp – turn on the light, I mean . . .'

The completion of the Greek story was delayed by renewed efforts to dramatise the second part of *The Brook Kerith* for the Arts Theatre, under the title *The Passing of the Essenes*. It was finally produced in October 1930, with plainchant for the Essenes written by Gustav Holst, but Moore was not there to see it; he had accepted an invitation to Viola Rodgers's manor house at Lardy, outside Paris, where there was a footman to attend to all his needs, and a doctor near by. On the night of the London performance, according to Hone, he read the script of *The Passing of the Essenes* aloud to Viola Rodgers and a few of her friends.

On his return to London, he saw the play, but was far from

pleased. 'It will be many days before I recover from the odious memory,' he wrote to Viola Rodgers. 'The poor play did not come out as it should have come out, and what pleasure is it to me that other people liked it? I wanted to like it and didn't. The uninspired actors were between me and it all the time.'

Gosse had already reported to him that the Prince of Wales had been seen coming out of a bookshop with a couple of copies of books by George Moore under his arm; now, in 1930, Moore was summoned to an audience with the Prince. He set out from Ebury Street in high spirits but a persistent nosebleed forced him to return home and telephone Lady Cunard, who had been instrumental in arranging the invitation, to ask her to apologise on his behalf.

The invitation was renewed and he reached Marlborough House safely with a presentation copy of *The Brook Kerith* under his arm. All went well until he arrived back in Ebury Street and suddenly remembered that King George V had just recovered from a long and serious illness during the course of which his loyal subjects had been fervently praying for his recovery. What demon could have caused him to choose *The Brook Kerith*, he wondered. To leave with his son a book which denied the divinity of Jesus! Surely I have lost my O.M., he thought.

On his eightieth birthday he received from his friends the tribute printed in *The Times* on February 24, 1932, and later in the year Tonks did the last portrait of him, a study in pastels of an old man in a red dressing-gown seated in an armchair by the fire; it is now, as he knew it would be, in the National Portrait Gallery.

His last will and testament had been made more than two years earlier, on October 31, 1930, bequeathing all the rights in his books to his London solicitor, C. D. Medley; his furniture and most of his pictures to Lady Cunard, though he bequeathed his grandfather's portrait to the National Gallery in Dublin, and left one of his favourite pictures, a Manet sketch, to Nancy Cunard. Charles Morgan was to write his official biography. Moore left £5,000 (£100,000 today) to be divided among Tom Ruttledge's

He was cremated at Golder's Green cemetery after a service attended by, among others, Ramsay MacDonald and Augustus John. Canon Douglas, an Anglican clergyman who officiated, offered prayers for the dead man's soul, but out of respect for Moore's views omitted all references to specifically Christian dogmas such as 'the sure and certain hope of immortality'.

After the bizarre ceremony, during which Moore's ashes were placed in a hollow in the rocks on Castle Island in Lough Carra, opposite the ruins of Moore Hall, his friend, Richard Best from the National Library, read some words written by AE, to be spoken over the urn.

Moore and AE had had something of a tiff when Susan Mitchell's book about Moore first appeared. Moore had believed, probably wrongly, that AE was behind it, though it is likely that he provided some of the material inadvertently, in conversations with Susan Mitchell. Moore retaliated by inserting in *Vale*, the final volume of his trilogy, the accusation that AE was being unfaithful to his wife, but when AE heard about this and threatened legal action, Moore softened it to a suggestion that he was neglecting her and irritating her with his lack of interest in money and food.

AE was so relieved when nothing more scurrilous appeared in the book that he again became friendly with Moore, and called on him in London. However, about the time of Moore's death, when AE was himself an ill man, racked by cancer, he made a vicious attack on what he considered to be the novelist's 'leering sensuality' in a book called *The Atavars*. This was actually being printed at the time when Colonel Maurice Moore asked AE to recite a eulogy over Moore's ashes. In the circumstances, AE had to refuse, but wrote a slyly ironic tribute, fully aware that if Moore had been alive, he would immediately have seen what AE was getting at. He is reported as having admitted that the oration was a masterpiece of double-meaning which Moore would have greatly admired.

The eulogy, as read by Best, went as follows:

'If his ashes have any sentience, they will feel at home here, for the colours of Carra Lake remained in his memory when many of his other affections had passed. It is possible that an artist's love of earth, rock, water and sky is an act of worship. It is possible that faithfulness to art is an acceptable service. That worship, that service, were his. If any would condem him for a creed of theirs he had assailed, let them be certain first that they laboured for their ideals as faithfully as he did for his.'

It is not difficult to picture the scene. On the island, the workmen are closing the hollow in the rock where the urn has been placed, and raising a rough cairn above it. On the lake shore, as Hone described the scene, the dreaming house stands gaunt and still, open to the grey sky. The small group of mourners move quietly towards the boats, almost as if in slow motion, taking time to pause and look yet again at the dull sparkle on the surface of the lake, at the blue ridge of mountains behind the shell of the house, at the tall woods standing unchanged around Moore Hall, now gone along with the way of life that went with it.

I like to think of the shade of Moore, sourly surveying that joyless scene, hardly from the bar of the Christian heaven, perhaps, in view of his inability to accept the resurrection of Jesus of Nazareth, but among a small, select group of classic immortals maybe, in some fashionable Graeco-Roman paradisal resort. He would be furious initially at the frugal austerity of the ceremony he was witnessing – no Bacchanal, no bonfire, no satyrs, no dancing girls, but would then recall with a faint smile, that it did not really matter. When he had first conceived the notion of a vast funeral pyre, on the shores of the lake, at the time of his own mother's burial, it had occurred to him that it would all come to pass again, millions and millions of years hence. And maybe they would get it right next time.

# A Note
# about Sources

As I have explained in the text, my principal source of material has been George Moore's own work, particularly his semi-biographical books, *Confessions of a Young Man* (1888); *Memoirs of My Dead Life* (1906); *Hail and Farewell: Ave* (1911); *Hail and Farewell: Salve* (1912); *Hail and Farewell: Vale* (1914); *Conversations in Ebury Street* (1924); and *A Communication to My Friends* (1933), as well as some of his newspaper and magazines articles, published under the title *Impressions and Opinions* in 1891. I have also relied to a considerable extent on Joseph Hone's excellent biography, *The Life of George Moore* (London, Victor Gollancz, 1936), and his equally invaluable *The Moores of Moore Hall* (London, Jonathan Cape, 1939); and found some useful material in Susan Mitchell's *George Moore* (Dublin, The Talbot Press, 1916), the only book about Moore published during his lifetime, and in Charles Morgan's *Epitaph on George Moore* (London, Macmillan 1935).

Colonel Maurice Moore's book about his father, George Henry Moore the Politician, *An Irish Gentleman* (London, T. Werner Laurie, 1913) contained some illuminating details of life at Moore Hall.

For material about Lady Cunard and her daughter, Nancy Cunard's *GM: Memories of George Moore* (London; Rupert Hart-Davies, 1956) is extremely well written; other helpful books are Daphne Fielding's *Emerald and Nancy* (London, Eyre and Spottiswoode, 1968) and *George Moore: Letters to Lady Cunard, 1895–1933* (London, Rupert Hart-Davis, 1957), which has an excellent introduction by Rupert Hart-Davis. Helmut E. Gerber's commentary on two published collections of letters from Moore to his publishers, secretaries, researchers and many friends – as well as the letters themselves – proved invaluable; the collections were called *George Moore in Transition: 1849–1910* (Detroit, Wayne State University Press, 1968) and *George Moore on Parnassus: 1900–1933* (London, Associated Universities Press, 1988). Richard Cave's introduction and very extensive annotations to the first one-volume, paperback edition of *Hail and Farewell* (Colin Smyth; and Washington DC, Catholic University of America Press, 1985) proved very helpful, as did A. Norman Jeffares' introduction to the 1981 edition of *A Drama in Muslin*. And, of course, the book that first interested me in George Moore the man – Oliver St John Gogarty's *As I Was Going Down Sackville Street* (Penguin Books, 1954) – remains the most colourful account of Moore's sojourn in Dublin, apart, of course, from Moore's own account of those years.

# Acknowledgements

I have to begin this list of Acknowledgements by making it clear that among the chief sources of a great deal of the straightforward background material have been the two books about Moore and his family written by Joseph Hone, *The Life of George Moore* (London, Victor Gollancz, 1936), and *The Moores of Moore Hall* (London, Jonathan Cape, 1939).

Hone's biography of Moore is the only complete one in existence until now and it was obviously written with the help and connivance of Colonel Maurice Moore, George Moore's brother, who also clearly supplied many of the letters and family photographs.

Ever since I started work on this book two or three years ago, I have been greatly encouraged and assisted by my friend and fellow-author, Joseph Hone, grandson of Moore's biographer, and I would like to take this opportunity to thank him, and other members of the Hone family, including his uncle, David Hone, who currently holds the copyright of the Hone books, for allowing me to use a few direct quotations from the two books mentioned above, as well as the background material. I feel sure that the publication of this book will lead to a general revival of interest in Moore's work, and, I hope, in Joseph Hone's book about Moore and his family in particular.

I must also express my gratitude to the late Nancy Cunard's literary executor, Anthony Hobson of The Glebe House, Whitsbury, Fordingbridge, Hampshire, for permission to use extracts from Nancy Cunard's GM: *Memories of George Moore* (London, Rupert Hart-Davis, 1947); to Mr Rivers Scott of Scott Ferris Associates, 15 Gledhow Gardens, London for permission to use a couple of extracts from Charles Morgan's

*Epitaph on George Moore* (London, Macmillan, 1935); and to Dr Richard Cave for permission to use some comments from his introduction and footnotes to the first one-volume paperback edition of *Hail and Farewell* (Gerrard's Cross, Buckinghamshire, Colin Smythe, 1976).

# The Works of George Moore:
# A Short Bibliography

This list includes Moore's works in English, published in England and the United States during his lifetime.

1874(?)  *Worldliness*: A Comedy in Three Acts. (London:?)

1878  *Flowers of Passion*: Poems. (London: Provost & Co.)

1879  *Martin Luther*: A Tragedy in Five Acts. (London: Remington & Co.)

1881  *Pagan Poems*. (London: Newman & Co.)

1883  *A Modern Lover*: Novel. (London: Tinsley Brothers.)

1885  *A Mummer's Wife*: Novel. (London: Vizetelly & Co.)

1885  *Literature at Nurse*: Pamphlet. (London: Vizetelly & Co.)

1886  *A Drama in Muslin*: Novel. (London: Vizetelly & Co.)

1887  *A Mere Accident*: Novel. (London: Vizetelly & Co.)

1887  *Parnell and His Island*: Sketches. (London: Swan Sonnenschein.)

1888  *Confessions of a Young Man*: Autobiography. (London: Swan Sonnenschein.)

1888  *Spring Days*: Novel. (London: Vizetelly & Co.)

1889  *Mike Fletcher*: Novel. (London: Ward & Downey.)

1891  *Impressions and Opinions*: Essays. (London: David Nutt.)

1892  *Vain Fortune*: Novel. (London: Henry & Co.)

1893  *Modern Painting*: Essays. (London: Walter Scott.)

1893  *The Strike at Arlingford*: A Play in Three Acts. (London: Walter Scott.)

1894  *Esther Waters*: Novel. (London: Walter Scott.)

1895  *Celibates*: Three Short Stories. (London: Walter Scott.)

1895 *The Royal Academy 1895*: Criticism. (London: *New Budget* Office.)

1898 *Evelyn Innes*: Novel. (London: T. Fisher Unwin.)

1900 *The Bending of the Bough*: A Comedy in Five Acts. (London: T. Fisher Unwin.)

1901 *Sister Teresa*: Novel. (London: T. Fisher Unwin.)

1903 *The Untilled field*: Short Stories. (London: T. Fisher Unwin.) Published in Irish by Sealy, Bryers & Walker, Dublin, in 1902

1905 *The Lake*: Novel. (London: Heinemann.)

1906 *Reminiscences of the Impressionist Painters*. (Dublin: Maunsel & Co.)

1906 *Memoirs of My Dead Life*: Autobiography. (London: Heinemann.)

1911 *Hail and Farewell: Ave*: Autobiography. (London: Heinemann.)

1911 *The Apostle*: A Drama in Three Acts. (Dublin: Maunsel & Co.)

1912 *Hail and Farewell: Salve*: Autobiography. (London: Heinemann.)

1913 *Esther Waters*: A Play in Five Acts. (London: Heinemann.)

1913 *Elizabeth Cooper*: A Comedy in Three Acts. (Dublin and London: Maunsel & Co.)

1914 *Hail and Farewell: Vale*: Autobiography. (London: Heinemann.)

1915 *Musin*: Novel. Revision of *A Drama in Muslin*. (London: Heinemann.)

1916 *The Brook Kerith*: A Syrian Story. (London: T. Werner Laurie.)

1917 *Lewis Seymour and Some Women*: Novel. Revision of *A Modern Lover*. (London: Heinemann.)

1918 *A Story-Teller's Holiday*. Limited Edition. (London: Society for Irish Folk-lore.)

1919 *Avowals*: Criticism. Limited Edition. (London: Society for Irish Folk-lore.)

1920 *Esther Waters*: Revision of the Novel. Limited Edition. (London: Society for Irish Folk-lore.)

1920 *The Coming of Gabrielle*: A Comedy in Three Acts. Limited Edition. (London: Society for Irish Folk-lore.)

1921 *Héloise and Abélard*: Novel. Limited Edition. (London: Society for Irish Folk-lore.)

1921 *Fragments from Héloise and Abélard*: Additions and Corrections. Limited Edition. (London: Society for Irish Folk-lore.)

1921    *Memoirs of My Dead Life*: 'Moore Hall' Edition. (London: Heinemann.)

1921    *The Lake*: Revised Edition. (London: Heinemann.)

1922    *In Single Strictness*: Short Stories. Limited Edition. (London: Heinemann.)

1923    *The Apostle*: Revision of the Drama. Limited Edition. (London: Heinemann.)

1924    *Avowals*. Uniform Edition. (London: Heinemann.)

1924    *Conversations in Ebury Street*: Criticism. Limited Edition. (London: Heinemann.)

1924    *Pure Poetry*: An Anthology. Limited Edition. (London: Nonesuch Press.)

1924    *Peronnik the Fool*: Short Story. (New York: Boni & Liveright.)

1924    *The Pastoral Loves of Daphnis and Chloe*: Translation. Limited Edition. (London: Heinemann.)

1925    *Héloise and Abélard*. Uniform Edition. (London: Heinemann.)

1925    *Hail and Farewell*. Limited Edition in Two Volumes. (London: Heinemann.)

1926    *Confessions of a Young Man*: Revised Edition. (London: Heinemann.)

1926    *Peronnik the Fool*. New Limited Edition. (New York: W. E. Rudge.)

1926    *Ulick and Soracha*: Novel. Limited Edition. (London: Nonesuch Press.)

1926    *The Untilled Field*: Revised Edition. (London: Heinemann.)

1927    *The Making of an Immortal*: A Comedy in One Act. (New York: Bowling Green Press.)

1927    *Celibate Lives*: Revised from *In Single Strictness* for the Uniform Edition. (London: Heinemann.)

1927    *The Brook Kerith*: Revised for the Uniform Edition. (London: Heinemann.)

1928    *Memoirs of My Dead Life*: Revised for the Uniform Edition. (London: Heinemann.)

1928    *A Story-Teller's Holiday*: Revised Edition in Two Volumes, including *Ulick and Soracha*. Uniform Edition. (London: Heinemann.)

1928    *Peronnik the Fool*: Revised Limited Edition. (Eure, France: The Hours Press.)

1929    *Letters from George Moore to Édouard Dujardin*, 1886–1922. Translated by John Eglinton. (New York: Crosby Gaige.)

1929    *The Brook Kerith*: Limited Edition, with engravings by Stephen Gooden. (London: Heinemann.)

1930    *Conversations in Ebury Street*. Uniform Edition. (London: Heinemann.)

1930    *A Flood*: Short Story. (New York: The Harbor Press.)

1930    *The Passing of the Essenes*: A Drama in Three Acts. Limited Edition of a further Revision of *The Apostle*. (London: Heinemann.)

1930    *Aphrodite in Aulis*: Novel. Limited Edition. (London: Heinemann.)

1931    *The Passing of the Essenes*. Uniform Edition. (London: Heinemann.)

1931    *Aphrodite in Aulis*: Revised for the Uniform Edition. (London: Heinemann.)

1932    *Muslin*. Uniform Edition. (London: Heinemann.)

1932    *Esther Walters*. Uniform Edition. (London: Heinemann.)

1932    *The Untilled Field*. Uniform Edition. (London: Heinemann.)

1932    *The Lake*. Uniform Edition. (London: Heinemann.)

1933    *Peronnik the Fool*. With engravings by Stephen Gooden. (London: Harrap & Co.)

1933    *A Communication to My Friends*: Autobiography. Limited Edition. (London: Nonesuch Press.)

1933    *Confessions of a Young Man*. Uniform Edition. (London: Heinemann.)

1933    *Hail and Farewell: Ave*. Uniform Edition. (London: Heinemann.)

1933    *Hail and Farewell: Salve*. Uniform Edition. (London: Heinemann.)

1933    *Hail and Farewell: Vale*. Uniform Edition. (London: Heinemann.)

1933    *The Pastoral Loves of Daphnis and Chloe and Peronnik the Fool*. Uniform Edition. (London: Heinemann.)

1933    *A Mummer's Wife and a Communication to My Friends*. Uniform Edition. (London: Heinemann.)

# Index